Advance praise for
The Unfinished Project

"This brilliant new work critically addresses and comparatively evaluates the implications of modernism and postmodernism on multiculturalism. Neither emerge unscathed, but Simpson takes the positive contributions of each to develop a postmetaphysical humanism, one that acknowledges that individuals can never wholly transcend their culture and history—their identity, in other words—but that also rejects the permanence of absolute difference or incomprehension across cultural divides. Humanity, Simpson urges, will be forged rather than found, and as such, is the unfinished project yet to be accomplished."
                      Linda Martín Alcoff, Professor of Philosophy, Syracuse University

"Responding to the philosophical situation of our time in which the voices of postmodernism—declaring the death of humanism and the bankruptcy of reason—wage war against the Enlightenment concepts of a common humanity and a rational social order, Lorenzo Simpson deftly splits the difference as he wends his way towards a new perspective on rationality and a viable humanism for the new millennium. This skillfully crafted volume should become required reading for all those who have worries about the future of philosophy."
                      Calvin O. Schrag, George Ade Distinguished Professor of Philosophy,
                      Purdue Unversity, and author of *The Self After Postmodernity*
                      and *The Resources of Rationality*

"If there is a philosopher who manages to be both vigorous and gentle, both circumspect and courageous, it is Lorenzo Simpson, and in this book he leaves us with an appropriately encouraging conviction—we all can learn to live together honestly and with mutual understanding."
                      Albert Borgmann, Regents Professor of Philosophy,
                      University of Montana, and author of *Holding On to Reality*

"Simpson's defense of humanism as a 'situated cosmopolitanism' displays tremendous range. Few philosophers have mastered the nuances of music theory, cultural criticism, postmodernism, hermeneutics, and critical theory to the same degree; and those who have seldom write with such clarity."
                      David Ingram, Professor of Philsophy, Loyola University of Chicago,
                      and author of *Group Rights: Reconciling Equality and Difference*

THE UNFINISHED PROJECT

Toward a
Postmetaphysical Humanism

LORENZO C. SIMPSON

ROUTLEDGE
New York and London

Published in 2001 by
Routledge
29 West 35th Street
New York, New York 10001

Published in Great Britain by
Routledge
11 New Fetter Lane
London EC4P 4EE

Routledge is an imprint of the Taylor & Francis Group.

Copyright © 2001 by Routledge

All rights reserved. No part of this book may be reprinted or reproduced or utilized in any form or by any electronic, mechanical, or other means, now known or hereafter invented, including photocopying and recording, or in any information storage or retrieval system, without permission in writing from the publishers.

Library of Congress Cataloging-in-Publication Data

Simpson, Lorenzo Charles.
The unfinished project; toward a postmetaphysical humanism / Lorenzo C. Simpson.
    p. cm.
    Includes bibliographical references and index.
    ISBN 0–415–91637–2 — ISBN 0–415–91638–0 (pbk.)
    1. Humanism. 2. Postmodernism. I. Title.

B 821.S546   2001
144—dc21

00–068389

For Sean and Eva,
may they further the unfinished project
and benefit from its pursuit.
And to the memory of Armstead L. Robinson,
a true situated cosmopolitan.

Contents

Preface and Acknowledgments   ix

Introduction: Humanism, Postmodernism, and Irony   1

I. HISTORICAL CONSIDERATIONS   17

1. On Arnold and Herder: The Idea of Culture and the Idea of Difference   19

2. Musical Interlude: Adorno on Jazz, or How Not to Fuse Horizons   42

II. THE UNFINISHED PROJECT   61

3. Critical Theory and the Politics of Recognition   63

4. Situated Cosmopolitanism   78

5. "Postmodern" Rejoinders   99

Epilogue: Toward a Humanistic Multiculturalism   127

Notes   143

Bibliography   165

Index   175

Preface and Acknowledgments

This argument represents an extension of my project—begun in my last book, *Technology, Time, and the Conversations of Modernity* (1995)—to develop a critical pluralism, a nonrelativistic but hermeneutic version of critical rationality. I do so here by revisiting the question of humanism. One of the genuine difficulties facing multicultural societies is how to negotiate judiciously the criteria of worth or value that will guide us in deciding what should command our recognition as "consumers" of culture and as participants in political communities. The dilemma lies in discerning how to pursue such a negotiation in a way that does not beg questions against the yet-to-be included or against what is taken to have established worth. Forging a language for such a negotiation seems to me one of the central challenges facing the humanities and, indeed, our society now, and I hope in this book to make a contribution to that project. By revisiting humanism in the way that I propose here, I hope also to say something useful about ongoing debates about multiculturalism, which, I believe, has not yet received adequate philosophical attention.

My earliest sustained work on this study was supported by a year-long fellowship in 1996–97 granted by the Woodrow Wilson International Center for Scholars in Washington, D.C., a haven for scholarship in the midst of our political capital and an ideal place for surveying broad intellectual trends across a number of disciplines. I would like to express my appreciation to that institution and to its gracious director of fellowships, Ann Sheffield, for research support, a collegial setting, and a challenging environment. I also acknowledge with gratitude my former institution, the University of Richmond, for granting me a sabbatical and two Summer Research Fellowships to pursue this project as well as a year of leave in order to take advantage of the Wilson Center fellowship.

The collegial, cross-disciplinary interaction at the Wilson Center was unusually stimulating, and a reading group in which I participated there on "ethics and political culture," organized by Dorothy Ross, was particularly useful to me as I worked on this book. My conversations with, among others, historians Temma Kaplan, Steven Pincus, and Dorothy

Ross; religious scholars Anne Feldhaus and Ernest Wallwork; legal philosopher David Luban; novelist Peter Schneider; anthropologists Dale Eickelman and Henry Munson; and social theorist Shmuel Eisenstadt proved immensely valuable to this undertaking.

I have read versions of chapter 4, the core of my argument, at several places, beginning in 1995 at Amherst College, where I was invited by Robert Gooding-Williams to participate in a lecture series on "Contemporary Currents in Continental Philosophy." Subsequent versions were presented at the Woodrow Wilson International Center for Scholars, the Society for Phenomenology and Existential Philosophy, and at my current institutional home, the Department of Philosophy of the State University of New York at Stony Brook. I extend my thanks to all of these institutions for providing me the opportunity to present my work and to the respective audiences for helpful discussion.

Though we have not communicated directly about its contents, Iris Marion Young was instrumental in inspiring this study. In informal conversation after I had delivered a commentary on her presentation at a conference entitled "Democracy and Difference"—organized by Seyla Benhabib and sponsored by Yale University's Program in Social Thought and Ethics—Iris asked me, "Why is community so important to you?" In part, this essay in a sense is an extended response to that question. A number of individuals have generously and graciously offered sage advice at various stages of this project, and I have greatly benefitted from comments, suggestions, and criticisms made on earlier drafts of various chapters by Robert Gooding-Williams, Lydia Goehr, Gary Shapiro, Hugh West, and by my current colleagues, Edward Casey, Robert Crease, and Krin Gabbard. Additionally, I found the comments on the penultimate version of this study by Routledge's anonymous reviewers to be especially helpful. I am truly indebted to all of these individuals. Needless to say, I bear full responsibility for the final content.

I wish also to thank the members of my first graduate seminar at the State University of New York at Stony Brook, entitled "Humanism, Multiculturalism and Difference," where I tried out some of the ideas that appear here, and especially to acknowledge the contributions of two members of that seminar, Robb Eason and Daniel Thiel, who assisted in the final preparation of this manuscript in a variety of ways. In addition to providing general research assistance, they assisted with proofreading, prepared the index, and—building on what Peter Krek, my research assistant at the Wilson Center compiled—completed the bibliography. I am also grateful for the assistance provided me by Regina Davis and Michael

Preface and Acknowledgments

Feola at the University of Richmond and by Michael Moore and Paul Humphrey at Stony Brook. In addition I would like to acknowledge the staff and editors at Routledge; it has been a pleasure to work with them.

I would like to express my gratitude to my children, to little Eva for her patience with her daddy's inability to play with her as much as she would like, and to Sean for his good-natured response to being pressed into service as a proofreader. Lastly, I thank my wife, Marsha, who—in addition to reading portions of the book and offering helpful suggestions to repair stylistic infelicities—shouldered far more than her share of the domestic responsibilities over the course of its production. I hope I can make it up to her.

Earlier versions of portions of this book have appeared elsewhere. I would like to thank the publishers for permission to make use of the following:

"On Habermas and Difference: Critical Theory and the 'Politics of Recognition,'" in Lewis E. Hahn, ed. *Perspectives on Habermas* (Chicago, IL: Open Court, 2000), revised as chapter 3.

"Communication and the Politics of Difference: Reading Iris Young," *Constellations* 7 (2000): 430–42, for a portion of chapter 5.

Introduction
Humanism, Postmodernism, and Irony

I

At the dawn of the millennium, the forces of globalization, electronically mediated communication, and postcolonial migration have increasingly transformed modern societies into sites of cultural confrontation and difference. As the anthropologist Clifford Geertz put it in a recent interview, "the deprovincialization of the world [means] we're going to be in each other's faces more."[1] The geographical scope of "struggles for recognition" widens almost daily to include places that formerly were remarkable only for their relative homogeneity and provincial character. With the permeability of borders and the economic vitality ushered in by membership in the European Union, many European nations such as Ireland—finding itself losing its status as "a small, white place of emigrants"—have become destinations to newcomers, many of whom are refugees from places like Nigeria, Kosovo, and Chechnya, and whom the locals profess not to understand and, consequently, fear.[2] Not traditionally known as "melting pots," European countries agonize increasingly over their becoming multicultural societies.[3] And, of course, struggles for social and racial justice and for cultural recognition are far from won here in the United States. Central among the concerns of democratic and democratizing societies the world over is the challenge to find principled ways to acknowledge the claims of the distinct cultural groups comprising them. Such societies will therefore increasingly become laboratories, microcosmic sites where experiments to forge global humanity will succeed or fail.

Given the growing salience of matters of difference on the world stage, what are we to make of the legacy of humanism, with its insistence on universal aspirations valid for the species as a whole? The traditional conception of humanism allowed us to speak ingenuously of progress; it enabled social criticism in terms of a notion of common humanity; it provided a basis for the presumption of humanity, of the dignity of the individual; and it provided a rationale for the pursuit of humanistic learning, for the humanities.[4] Increasingly, however, the humanist banner has been regarded either as a cloak for an at best unwitting ethnocentrism, or as a flag heralding empty platitudes. What are we to make of these features of humanism traditionally conceived once we can no longer speak of the idea of an unambiguous progress toward freedom and reason without a knowing wink, once we admit that traditional ideas of a common humanity are on the one hand ethnocentric or racist, or on the other, essentially vacuous, and that humanistic learning needs to acknowledge globally dispersed traditions of thought?

What exactly is being challenged by these worldwide encounters with difference? What *is* the traditional conception of humanism? Perhaps in its most generic sense, the term refers to the anthropocentric intellectual orientation—prominent since the Renaissance—that holds that the study of humanity provides the foundation for all else. However, one need not delve into the literature very far to realize that *humanism* is somewhat of a floating signifier, is an overdetermined term. In what follows, I seek to highlight briefly its salient semantic strands, emphasizing those that are most significant for my discussion.

Though first employed in German usage in the nineteenth century, the term *humanism* is derived from the Latin *humanus*. In Classical Latin, *humanus* had three families of meaning: "whatever is characteristic or *proper* to humankind"; "benevolent"; and "learned."[5] Its first signification, "that which is proper to humankind," is retained in modern derivatives, as is the second. The third meaning, "learned," had most resonance during classical times and during the Italian Renaissance. In its derivation from the Italian *umanisti*, reflecting the classical Latin mean-

Introduction: Humanism, Postmodernism, and Irony

ing of "learned," the term *humanist* was in use before *humanism* itself. In this, its third sense, *humanism* came to refer to what the fifteenth-century Italian humanists, or *umanisti*—students and scholars of classical literature who designated their field of learning *studia humanitatis* (the course of classical studies consisting of grammar, rhetoric, poetry, history, and, later, moral philosophy)—were engaged in.[6] In this way *humanism* retrieved its third, scholarly, sense that had all but been lost during the Middle Ages. *Humanism* as *Humanismus*, meaning "classical learning," appeared first in early-nineteenth-century Germany and from there spread throughout Europe.[7] It reached the United States via the New Humanism movement in literary criticism inspired by the nineteenth-century English critic Matthew Arnold. Through today, *humanism* and the related term *humanities* are used in a sense that reflects an equivocation between the first and third senses of *humanus*.

Renaissance humanism had also a normative dimension, namely, its tendency to see classical antiquity as providing the model or standard in terms of which all cultural activities were to be judged.[8] There was also a characteristic emphasis upon the distinctiveness of humanity, upon its dignity and place in the universe. The Renaissance humanists strove to redirect the reflective gaze from religious preoccupations per se to focus on highlighting, exploring, and promoting humanity's distinctive creative capacities. Among those distinctive capacities is freedom. The humanist Giovanni Pico della Mirandola, in his influential *Oratio de hominis dignitate* (Oration on the dignity of Man), spoke of human freedom in terms surprisingly close to those used by Jean-Paul Sartre to express his existentialist humanism: what is distinctive about humanity is that it is free to determine its own destiny.[9] The Renaissance zeitgeist emphasized the importance of aiming at a harmonious development of these faculties or powers, with each power cultivated in due measure, without onesidedness or overemphasis—echoes of the Greek ideal that inspired J. G. von Herder, J. J. Winckelmann, J. W. von Goethe, Friedrich Schiller, and others.[10] The connection between the literary humanistic concerns of the Italian humanists and these implicitly philosophical concerns was the humanists' belief that the classical disciplines provided the education requisite for the effective exercise of our distinctive powers and capacities. However, the Renaissance's philosophy of humanity remained latent. For a full appreciation of humanism as a "philosophy of man" we need to return to the first sense of *humanus*.

Humanism as a philosophical term apparently appeared in France at roughly the same time that its literary sibling appeared in Germany, and itself soon gained currency in Germany.[11] In the wake also of Marxism, and mediated by the Enlightenment—Denis Diderot's *Encyclopédie*, in its belief that human history is a record of civilization's progress made possible by the potential inherent in human reason, was strongly humanistic in tone—humanism came to be understood as a systematically articulated account of what is proper to humanity, of what human fulfillment consists in, and of what counts as ultimate moral progress.[12] Although he concluded that humanism is a deeply vexed concept, it was Martin Heidegger who helped stage the retrieval of humanism in this philosophical sense and to shape its reception as a term referring to the essence of humanity.[13]

II

Humanism, under siege for at least the last thirty years, has been all but left for dead. Few academic disciplines, including some of the so-called hard sciences, have escaped. Based in part upon a particular reading of Heidegger's work—especially of his famous *"Brief über den Humanismus"* ("Letter on Humanism") of 1946—antihumanist strains have arisen in much of postmodernist and/or poststructuralist thought. Influenced by the pragmatist tradition and by the later Ludwig Wittgenstein, many influential Anglo-American philosophers such as Richard Rorty also evince little patience with the concept of the "essentially human" or of "humanity as such."[14] What unites these two sets of positions—both the Continental European and the Anglo-American—is a rejection of the claim that there is some *interesting* shared feature or metaphysical essence that embraces and connects us all.

At issue is a particular conception of humanism, traceable to Heidegger's "Letter." The "Letter," written in response to a young French philosopher named Jean Beaufret who asked about the significance of the idea of humanism in the wake of the Second World War's devastation, took to task a particular conception of humanism, namely, that of humanism as a kind of metaphysics. By "metaphysics" Heidegger refers to the Western philosophical tradition spanning from Plato to Friedrich Nietzsche which, no matter how various its manifestations, has in the main been consistent in its failure to acknowledge Being. This means roughly that each of the great philosophical traditions took itself to have articulated once and for all the nature of reality without having understood itself as merely *a* framework for such an articulation. In other words, each of those traditions was an interpretation that failed to recognize itself *as* an interpretation. Each, in Heidegger's view, had taken its

Introduction: Humanism, Postmodernism, and Irony

central vocabulary—for example, Plato's Ideas, the medieval conception of God, René Descartes's *cogito*, Nietzsche's will—to be the one that reality itself would use to announce itself, and, in taking its vocabulary to mirror nature's own, has viewed that vocabulary to be, in Richard Rorty's terms, final. But, Heidegger avers, each is only a provisional interpretation of Being or, like a Kuhnian paradigm, a provisional system of intelligibility from which are drawn descriptions of what there is. Therefore, these philosophical traditions do not mirror "reality there bare,"[15] but rather reality under a description, one which has its purchase only within a particular and provisional framework of intelligibility. In losing sight of this, each metaphysical tradition has been oblivious to its status as an historical product or, in Heidegger's words, to its status as a "dispensation of Being." Metaphysics must be overcome because truth most fundamentally has not to do with the correspondence between statements within a framework and a self-announcing reality nor with inferential relationships between statements within such a framework, but with the opening up or disclosure that is the framing itself.

So to say, as Heidegger does, that every historically important humanism has either been a metaphysics or been complicit with metaphysics is to say that each has lost sight of Being and its history by taking a specific characterization of reality and, in particular, of human reality to be its essence, by believing itself to have captured what it is to be human in a transhistorical and transcultural fashion. Humanist discourse then betrays a desire for a commensurating grid or final vocabulary that is adequate to do justice to everything that is properly human. Such discourse is accordingly oblivious to its own implication in a dialectic of blindness and insight.

Even the relatively unphilosophical humanism of the Renaissance fails to escape Heidegger's censure. By strategically blurring the line between the first and third senses of *humanus*, Heidegger is able to present Renaissance or "historical" humanism, too, as a "philosophy of man" that expresses a metaphysics. For it expresses the Greek ideal of humanity, as it was refined and codified in the Hellenistic era.[16] The immediate target of Heidegger's letter, Sartre's existential humanism, its rejection of an objectively definable human nature that precedes our free choices and of transhistorical notions of a human essence notwithstanding, also remains metaphysical in Heidegger's view. For in taking the freedom of the human subject to be the basis of humanism, Sartre remains mired in Cartesian metaphysics, remains in thrall to a framework that takes the opposition of a thinking subject to an objective world to be fundamental and irreducible. This framework founded upon the idea of the solitary *cogito*, the "I think," the subject as the isolated seat of thinking and choosing, is what Heidegger dubs the modern "metaphysics of subjectivity."

Heidegger counters that an "authentic" humanism is one that recognizes our being claimed by Being and not by a particular framework for talking and thinking about beings. Beings are objects of reference; they are what statements framed in the terms of the various "final" vocabularies are about. Humanity's proper status is to be the site or clearing where the so-called ontological difference between Being and beings is revealed. By the latter he means first to invoke the difference between a language game, on the one hand, and, on the other hand, the particular facts represented by true statements made within that game. (Or, to use another idiom, he invokes the distinction between what the early Wittgenstein called a logical space or dimension of experience, on one hand, and a position within that space, on the other.) Heidegger holds further that each such language game or rule-governed prescription for "carving up" reality is a disclosure of Being, a framing that simultaneously reveals and conceals—that is to say, is a perspective.

III

Some have suggested that Heidegger's understanding of different Western metaphysical traditions as different historical manifestations of Being, a history culminating in the calculative, technological reason of our present epoch, provides a framework for calling our times into question *and* at the same time enables an opening to *other* cultures not constituted by technical reason.[17] With this all too brief intimation of the relevance of Heidegger's thought to discussions of difference, I want now to turn to the idea of postmodernism, highlighting what I take to be its most salient facets for the concerns of this book. To do so is to enter deeply and still hotly contested terrain. What I wish to do here is present an "ideal type" of postmodernism, an outline of this topos that will prove useful in pursuing the discussion of humanism.[18]

We might say that modernity marks the stage in the history of the West at which totalizing worldviews rooted in religion and tradition lost their power to command widespread credulity. Seized by an anxiety born of the fragmentation left by this loss, there nevertheless remained for some the conviction that some other sort of whole or totality (reason for some, human autonomy for others) could repair this spiritual wound, and could

Introduction: Humanism, Postmodernism, and Irony

do so in a way that would not require an impossible return to an earlier innocence. Hegel's great modernist project, to integrate rationally the various shapes of European consciousness into the metanarrative of Spirit's coming to a full understanding of itself, stands as testimony to that conviction. What gets called *postmodernity*, on the other hand, is the stage at which those who live modernity's fragmentary existence have given up the belief that *any* whole can soothe what ails us. All totalizing schemes and narratives have lost credibility, and there is no longer even any *sense* of where to look to repair the lack.

Today, it can be argued, this issues in a pervasive normlessness and rootlessness that underwrite a reluctance, if not refusal, to take anything seriously for fear of being "taken in." The postmodern attitude is one of ironic, if not cynical, detachment, a detachment characterizing our relationship to the world, to structures of meaning and to canons of rationality. The postmodern ironist is one whose sensibilities are fashioned by the characteristics just rehearsed, one who observes from a rather detached perspective the passing show mounted by diverse forms of life—as if they constituted a *musée imaginaire*—without being able to muster an allegiance to any of them, including her own, except through what she would understand as a sheerly *arbitrary* act of the will. Those earnest souls who participate ingenuously and seriously in such a form of life are regarded with bemusement as being quite naive. To paraphrase Paul de Man rather loosely, irony is constituted by the relationship between a self that is engaged in taken-for-granted but ultimately arbitrary and unjustifiable practices and a self that exists only in the form of the *knowledge* of this condition, of this ungrounded engagement. I would add that the self-duplicating self of the ironist lives in the knowledge that its coincidence with itself is merely a projection that exists only as a product of its nostalgia for an impossible foundation. Irony, I would argue, is the unhappy consciousness of this impossible coincidence. Richard Rorty, who has made irony rather fashionable of late, summarizes the ironist's attitude as follows: the ironist is one who has radical and continuing doubts about all final vocabularies, including her own, and realizes that there are no neutral, universal, non-question-begging metavocabularies for resolving those doubts.[19]

For the postmodern ironist, then, the spirit of seriousness gives way to a spirit of play, where the aim is to dance lightly over the surface of things and of life, being distrustful of the deep and the heavy. This cynicism, irreverence, and distrust, linked to an aesthetic spirit of play, lead to a fascination with surfaces. The world loses its weight, and within the ambit of this unbearable lightness of Being, any representation of the self, the other, or the world is taken to be just another interpretation.

This ironic attitude extends to the idea of referentiality in all of its forms, leading, in general, to a rejection of depth hermeneutics, a rejection that assumes four characteristic aspects: a rejection of the essence/appearance distinction; of the latent/manifest distinction; of the authenticity/inauthenticity distinction; and of that between the signified and the signifier—that is, between something meant and various ways of expressing it.[20] This list includes the well-known doubles that, in *The Order of Things*, Michel Foucault took to be characteristic of humanism, and so, in this rejection postmodernism flaunts its antihumanism. In fact, it is Foucault who perhaps most starkly proclaimed the "death of man" thesis, though it was probably Louis Althusser who first used the term *antihumanism* in this context (and Althusser admits to the influence of Heidegger's "Letter on Humanism" on his antihumanism[21]). As Foucault famously announced at the end of *The Order of Things*, "man is in the process of perishing as the being of language continues to shine ever brighter upon our horizon," and with the passing of the modern episteme, "man would be erased, like a face drawn in sand at the edge of the sea."[22]

While postmodernism is not a style, sensibility, or worldview that Heidegger would embrace, his thought was essential to its consolidation. Indeed, Jacques Derrida and others have plausibly suggested that the radicalization of Heidegger's critique of humanism *constituted* French philosophy of the sixties.[23] As a critique of the totalitarianism of the East and of the bureaucratic, repressive, technological society of the West, Heidegger's thought occupied a position of increasing authority in French intellectual life from the 1960s on, as his thought, somewhat ironically one might say in light of his complicity with Nazism, filled the vacuum left for leftist thinkers by a discredited Marxism.[24] (One of my colleagues has referred in this context to Heidegger as Germany's revenge on the French.) And Derrida *still* takes humanism to be the arch culprit, as he raises the question, in *Of Spirit: Heidegger and the Question*, of whether Heidegger's involvement with the Nazis was any worse than Edmund Husserl's commitment to humanism and its concomitant ethnocentrism.[25]

The reading of Heidegger—and especially of his "Letter on Humanism"—that exercised influence in this setting has been called by one commentator a "structuralist" interpretation, a reading that can be linked directly to the so-called death of man thesis of postmodernism.[26] Central to that reading is the idea that human reality is a mere empty receptacle, that it is merely the place of Being's revelation,[27] that, other than this vocation, there is nothing that is characteristically ours. Language, which is for Heidegger the "house of Being," speaks "man." Human reality is then quickly conceived to be the decentered subject understood as a *site* where relations of force are expressed and where Being at the same time manifests and withdraws itself.[28]

This take on Heidegger helped consolidate an outlook that was opposed both to the idea of humanity as a given, something settled and unchanging, and at the same time to the metaphysics of subjectivity that informed Sartre's idea of the unsituated, decontextualized self as the seat of freedom. So the French radicalization of German philosophy issued in a rejection of any form of thought where humanity in its essence, or the essence of humanity, was the basis or *subject* of reality—be that reality historical, psychic, or cultural.[29] What remains is a human subject no longer understood to stand at an imperial distance from time and history and to remain self-identical through history, but rather a "subject" understood to be constituted by the play of forces, both historical and social, one absorbed into the play of *differences* characteristic of a given epoch, episteme, or power/knowledge regime.

IV

This emphasis on difference has, in the right hands, been salutary in many ways. We have become accustomed to only two ways of responding to difference in our public world. One is to ignore it, for what counts about humans is what we all share—for example, the capacity to reason, which is the basis of the dignity we accord to all persons. This makes differences between groups of people inessential to what really counts about them. The other is to construe difference and use it to mark a crucially important distinction among persons, one so fundamental that the search for commonalities or universal descriptions that bind persons together is seen as wrongheaded. (This latter view has, of course, both its benign postmodern variants and its malignant racist, sexist, and xenophobic versions.) Postmodernists, particularly feminist postmodernists, have taken the lead in conceptualizing difference in such a way that it does not refer to matters of rigid hierarchical distinctions to be oppressively deployed (most often to the detriment of people of color, the poor, and women), but rather to marks of a diversity to be celebrated. Nonetheless, I find postmodernists in general to be unable to give a satisfying account of that which perhaps we need more than ever—namely, community. Some, like Iris Marion Young, think that community is actually a bad idea. I regard the accidental versus essential dichotomy that has informed much discussion of difference to be a false one. As an alternative to Enlightenment universalist and postmodernist responses to matters of difference in our public life, I shall in the course of this book present a third response—the possibility of an always provisional mutual understanding effected through dialogical interaction on the part of participants who bring their differences with them to the negotiation—one that holds out the possibility of a moment of community that would not be assimilationist.

The concern that animates this book is to respond critically to the postmodernist assault on humanism while retaining postmodernism's sensitivity to issues of social and cultural difference. Can any such attempt to resuscitate humanism now be viewed as anything other than a rearguard action? And even if so, why bother? I think that there are two sorts of reason for a rescue attempt. At one level, one can point to a philosophical path not taken by those who would prosecute this war on humanism, a path that warrants our concerned attention. This is all the more true given another sort of reason, one that arises from the fact that this "postmodern consensus" regarding humanism has profound implications for our understanding of the nature and scope of practical deliberation. That is, it has profound consequences for our confidence in our ability to frame non-question-begging critical responses to the manifold cultural practices that populate our increasingly global society, and for our understanding of the scope of community given the salience of matters of "difference" in multicultural societies.

Much contemporary discussion about issues of community and multiculturalism turns upon what I consider to be a false, and unproductive, opposition between homogenizing versions of community on the one hand and heterogeneous, fragmented, and "decentered" constellations of "difference" on the other. As a consequence of this false choice, advocates of a sensitivity to matters of difference accuse advocates of community of some form of ethnocentrism or of false universalism; in turn, advocates of community accuse their opponents of balkanization, relativism, and worse. Now it is often true that when critically examined the idea of community or of common humanity that is actually advocated by its adherents turns out to be either invidiously ethnocentric or so thin as to be uninteresting. By uninteresting thinness, I mean a notion of common humanity that so abstracts from matters of difference that we reduce ourselves to deracinated, bloodless creatures somehow hovering over history and culture. On the other hand, it is also true that the *rejection* of a common grid wherein the points of difference can even be articulated, let alone reconciled, *does* expose us to the threat of relativism, social incoherence, and irreconcilable conflict.

One way to put the thesis of this book is to say that this is an avoidable impasse, that talk of community or humanism need not presuppose notions of community that are on the one hand monolithic, exclusivistic, or essentialist or on the other, contentless, and that appreciative talk of difference need not entail fragmentation and relativism. Accordingly, I offer an account that purports to give difference its due without abandoning critical standards, to acknowledge the false promises of freedom and reason without giving up on their true promises, and to provide a basis for distinguishing between humanistic learning and an indiscriminate relativism. I shall make my argument by developing the idea of what I call "humanity as an unfinished project," suggesting that humanity is to be understood in a postmetaphysical fashion, as *forged* rather than *found*. I develop this position in part to propose an alternative, in discussions of community and difference, to liberal appeals to an overlapping consensus (one that underwrites only a rather thin form of community); to the communitarian failure to do justice to difference (where only provincial or exclusivistic forms of community tend to be promoted); and to postmodern attempts to valorize fragmentation (where the very *idea* of community comes under suspicion). I thus hope to demonstrate the plausibility of appealing to humanity in the midst of diversity, of having both community *and* difference.

Existing attempts to articulate humanism while doing justice to diversity are inadequate. They either, like the seminal intervention of J. G. von Herder, tend to entail an objectionable relativism and essentialist notions of group difference that conspire to undermine the cogency of the idea of cross-cultural learning, or, like some important recent French projects— notably those of Luc Ferry and Alain Renaut—they ultimately appeal to ahistorical models of the self. Indeed, apart form the work of the latter, there is very little in the philosophical literature that addresses directly the possibilities for a humanism that is critically responsive to postmodernism. In their recent attempts to reconstruct humanism in the wake of the postmodernist critique of subjectivity, Ferry and Renaut's project is perhaps closest in concern to mine.[30] Like Jürgen Habermas, they are committed to an internal critique of modernity, rejecting Heidegger's antimodernism, Foucault's postmodernism, and Theodor Adorno's "negative dialectics."[31] However, in their tendency to suggest that the rejection or transcendence of conventions or social codes *by itself* gives sufficient content to humanism, they do not do justice to the way in which we are always already encoded, to the extent to which that encoding is an enabling as well as privative condition.[32] Thus their privileging of a Sartrean existentialist conception of the self—one that is abstracted from social, historical, and cultural contexts—does justice neither to the intersubjectively constituted nature of the self nor to the important role of language in that constitution. Though we have a second-order relationship to our own language that permits a critically reflective response to any claim formulated within it, we are nevertheless also products of our language. Accordingly, I regard their position as entailing a reversal *behind* Heidegger and postmodernism to return to the metaphysics of subjectivity of Immanuel Kant and Jean-Paul Sartre. My notion of humanity as an historical, conversational project represents an attempt to respond to postmodernism by moving *beyond* that metaphysical position.

V

I respond to postmodernist antihumanism by arguing for an historicized notion of humanity as a negotiated, unfinished project. I articulate this idea in terms of a model of critical, hermeneutic dialogue—that is, of a critical dialogue oriented to the achievement of mutual understanding. Based upon this model, I argue that humanity is as much made as found, though it is not made arbitrarily. Its making centrally involves practices of forging commensurable or mutually enriched vocabularies for identifying and discussing differences, vocabularies that enable, among persons differently situated, a mutually critical and respectful dialogue about matters of common concern.

In the first part of this book I assess three historically important writers—Matthew Arnold, Johann Gottfried von Herder, and Theodor Adorno—whose views on humanism and culture, by having set the terms for contemporary "culture wars," continue to inform current discussion. I discuss Arnold and Herder in chapter 1. To Arnold's defense of a humanism that is predicated upon the saving power of a *single* vital center occupied by "culture," famously conceived as embodying "the best that has been thought and said in the world," Herder provides a democratic counterpoint, arguing that the center is *multiple* and highly dispersed. Despite the difference in their conceptions of culture, I argue that both views are beset, though in different ways, by the problematics of the cen-

Introduction: Humanism, Postmodernism, and Irony

ter. In a sense, the view that I develop under the rubric of "humanity as an unfinished project" can be usefully regarded as a sublation, in the Hegelian sense, of the dialectical tension constituted by Arnold and Herder. In chapter 2, a "musical interlude" devoted to Adorno's treatment of jazz, I provide an illustration of a(n) (in)famous and instructive failure to seek a vocabulary that allows for a noninvidious representation of difference. I argue that Adorno's failure to come to terms with the set of concerns that motivate the production of jazz led him to commit certain kinds of "category error" in his analysis of it.

In the second part of this book I develop my idea of humanity as an unfinished project by way of a critical response to a number of contemporary thinkers from both sides of what the philosopher of technology Albert Borgmann calls the "postmodern divide." I develop my argument in two stages. First, in chapter 3, I consider Habermas's conception of discursive democracy—a clear source of inspiration for my model of critical, hermeneutic dialogue—and assess its capacity to accommodate matters of difference and to do justice to community. Consequently, though this is not an essay in political philosophy per se, current debates concerning the capacity of liberal democracy to accommodate cultural difference are clearly of relevance to it. I argue that, because of its failure to do full justice to the hermeneutic dimension of dialogue, Habermas's position does not offer a sufficiently distinct alternative to the liberal conception of an overlapping consensus. Accordingly, I maintain that his framework does not sufficiently exploit the transformative potential inherent in cultural material that lies beyond the borders of such a consensus.

In chapter 4, I develop the second stage of my argument by deploying a model of intercultural dialogue that repairs what I take to be the lacunae in Habermas's framework. I justify and render plausible this model (and this is the heart of my argument) by an analysis of what I call the "situated metalanguages"—the commensurable or mutually enriched vocabularies for negotiating differences—that can be forged from intercultural encounter. A cultural negotiation based upon the model of dialogue that I propose will be one in which all parties are *addressed* by difference in such a way that perspectives that had been taken for granted are risked and challenged in and through the process of intercultural translation. Dialogue based upon this model will be seen to entail the openness of all parties to redescriptions of themselves in terms of newly and mutually forged cultural vocabularies and then to assessments of those redescribed selves in light of their own respective criteria, criteria that can themselves be critically assessed in an iterated process. Such practices of redescription, I argue, broaden our sense of human possibilities without fatally threatening identities. For this reason, I refer to my project as a form of "situated cosmopolitanism." Humanity, in its terms, is then the unfinished project of learning to treat others as equals in our conversations without, on the one hand, losing ourselves or our identities or, on the other, retreating into a rigid conception of self that is impervious to change. Additionally in this chapter, by making use of the conception of what I call "second-order rationality," I demonstrate, pace Rorty for example, that non-question-begging critical perspectives on cultural formations need not entail an objectionable universalism or essentialism, just as an appreciation of matters of difference need not entail a simplistic relativism.

In chapter 5, I turn to some postmodern critics of the sort of position I develop in this essay, with the aim of using my responses to them as a means of developing my argument further. I consider some influential thinkers—two philosophers and a loosely affiliated group of cultural anthropologists—who are noted for their concern with the phenomenon of alterity and with the deeply problematic status of representations of the other. I discuss Iris Young's conception of communicative understanding, Robert Bernasconi's critique of hermeneutic understanding, and the "crisis of representation" in what has come to be called "postmodern anthropology." I challenge some of the central claims of Young's influential *Justice and the Politics of Difference*, in particular her rejection of the ideal of community and her claims to the effect that discursive democracy cannot do justice to matters of difference. I show that her analysis suffers from a flawed conception of communicative understanding and from a question-begging, communitarian conception of community. Further, after having pointed out how Hans-Georg Gadamer's conception of hermeneutics tends to occlude important aspects of intercultural translation, I argue that Bernasconi's notion of "radical alterity" fails to do justice to the transformative potential inherent in an adequately conceptualized account of hermeneutic dialogue. I extend the critique of Young's conception of understanding in a response to the skeptical and relativistic thrust of postmodern anthropology. I argue that both Young and postmodern ethnographers are vulnerable to an illusory "objectivist" ideal of representation, one informed by so implausible a criterion of authentic intersubjective knowledge that they are logically forced into the untenable position that mutual understanding, even among those who are *similarly* situated socially and culturally, is impossible.

Introduction: Humanism, Postmodernism, and Irony

I conclude with an epilogue on multiculturalism. Here I acknowledge that multiculturalism is an overdetermined phenomenon. To some degree it represents a "substitute program" for genuine racial equality; it is social justice "on the cheap." Moreover, particularly under cultural nationalist descriptions such as "Afrocentrism," it can to some extent be understood as a reaction to the repeated failure to deliver on the Enlightenment democratic promise of a color-blind society. That is, multiculturalism is firmly inscribed in the domain of racial politics. While not in any way wanting to deny this, I nevertheless suggest that thinking of multiculturalism from the standpoint of "humanity as an unfinished project" highlights what is salutary about the movement. I exploit here the analogy between the idea of promising research programs in the sciences and the idea of what I call democratically chosen "promising life programs." In addition, I spell out the consequences of a noncommunitarian conception of community for the idea of multiculturalism. In the end, I reject nationalist styles of multiculturalist theory and practice. Further, while I am sympathetic to arguments for multicultural recognition and education that are based upon *descriptive* claims about the hybrid character of the identity of *all* Americans, arguments such as Susan Wolf's in response to Charles Taylor's *Multiculturalism and "The Politics of Recognition,"* my project emphasizes the *critical*, reflective, and mutually transformative learning processes that can be initiated in cross-cultural encounters, processes that not only reveal who we already are but also who we might, and perhaps *should*, become.[33]

In sum, in this book I aim to contribute to the existing literature by reprieving from the postmodernist juggernaut a conception of humanism that is responsive to our postmodern situation; one that is robust enough to do humanism's traditional work of enabling social criticism, of underwriting a discourse of progress, and of providing a rationale for the pursuit of humanistic inquiry; and one that is systematically related to a critical multiculturalism.

(In order to keep interruptions to the narrative to a minimum, I have in a number of cases reserved qualifications, fuller elaborations, illustrations, and responses to anticipated objections for the notes that follow at the back of the book.)

I
HISTORICAL CONSIDERATIONS

1

On Arnold and Herder: The Idea of Culture and the Idea of Difference

An engagement with the work of Matthew Arnold, Victorian English poet and critic, and Johann Gottfried von Herder, late-eighteenth-century German critic, theologian, and philosopher, provides an important historical context for contemporary debates. Moreover, as I hope to show, their contributions are of more than purely historical interest. For whatever we think about the idea of humanism itself or of the closely allied concept of culture that is often implicated in arenas where humanism is on trial, Arnold and Herder can be seen to have initiated or consolidated important strands of our conversation and to have prefigured much of what we are struggling with in our current attempts to come to terms with the fate of "the human" in a global society. Herder inaugurated an anthropologically tinged, descriptive deployment of *culture* that underwrites much contemporary multiculturalist discourse, while Arnold introduced a prescriptive or "humanistic" use of *culture* that authorizes much of the current "traditionalist" and neoconservative assault on that discourse.[1]

Ultimately, I wish to negotiate between these two positions. Like Arnold, I want to retain the evaluative or normative dimension long associated with humanism while, like Herder, foregrounding an acknowledgment and embrace of diversity. Neither Arnold nor Herder was known for the systematic nature of his thought. Conflicting and contradictory tendencies abound in the work of each. My aim here is not primarily exegetical, but reconstructive. Without downplaying the ambiguities and tensions in their thought, my intention, to borrow an expression of Herder's, is to bring forward the "center of gravity" of their teaching, with the goals of exhibiting them as representative thinkers and of excavating the implications of their respective positions for the concerns that animate this project.

On Matthew Arnold and the Idea of Culture

> The sea is calm to-night.
> The tide is full, the moon lies fair
> Upon the straits;-on the French coast the light
> Gleams and is gone; the cliffs of England stand,
> Glimmering and vast, out in the tranquil bay.
> Come to the window, sweet is the night-air!
> Only, from the long line of spray
> Where the sea meets the moon-blanch'd land,
> Listen! you hear the grating roar
> Of pebbles which the waves draw back, and fling,
> At their return, up the high strand,
> Begin, and cease, and then again begin,
> With tremulous cadence slow, and bring
> The eternal note of sadness in.
>
> Sophocles long ago
> Heard it on the Aegean, and it brought
> Into his mind the turbid ebb and flow
> Of human misery; we
> Find also in the sound a thought,
> Hearing it by this distant northern sea.
>
> The Sea of Faith
> Was once, too, at the full, and round earth's shore
> Lay like the folds of a bright girdle furl'd.
> But now I only hear
> Its melancholy, long, withdrawing roar,
> Retreating, to the breath
> Of the night-wind, down the vast edges drear
> And naked shingles of the world.

> Ah, love, let us be true
> To one another! for the world, which seems
> To lie before us like a land of dreams,
> So various, so beautiful, so new,
> Hath really neither joy, nor love, nor light,
> Nor certitude, nor peace, nor help for pain;
> And we are here as on a darkling plain
> Swept with confused alarms of struggle and flight,
> Where ignorant armies clash by night.
>
> —Matthew Arnold, "Dover Beach"

Given the context within which this book is written and the concerns it addresses, it may seem somewhat odd, if not downright perverse, to turn to Matthew Arnold with anything but a censorious eye. Like E. D. Hirsh for literary theorists, Matthew Arnold has been a canonical foil for cultural theorists for some time now. In particular, the latter's *Culture and Anarchy*, widely regarded as a sort of *ur-text* for Anglo-American humanistic education, has long been a favorite target. In the poem that constitutes the epigraph for this section, Arnold gives voice to a peculiarly modern anxiety—the withdrawal and eclipse of certainty brought on by the ebbing of the "Sea of Faith," a withdrawal accompanied by a sense of the forlornness, isolation, and alienation of modern humanity. *Culture and Anarchy* is a response both to this existential vision and to the threat of political disorder. Published in 1869 and conceived at the time of both a working-class riot in London's Hyde Park and the tragic Morant Bay Rebellion, in which blacks in the then English colony of Jamaica struggled for civil and economic rights, the book stages an opposition between culture as "the study of perfection" and the feared "anarchy" of an unbridled democracy bereft of standards and a firm sense of direction. By seeking and discerning such perfection, by concerning itself exclusively with "the best which has been thought and said in the world," culture would reoccupy the place vacated by religion's withdrawal and allow a reason and reasonableness to prevail that would be a healing balm, mending a tattered social fabric and exorcizing the uncanniness of individual existence. And this redeeming culture was taken by Arnold to be the property not of any one class of society but, as embodied in the state, of the society as a whole.

This Arnoldian conception of culture has met with determined opposition. Not atypical are claims to the effect that Arnold defines the racialist culture of the nineteenth century as culture tout court,[2] or Edward Said's claim that culture as Arnold conceives of it is a system of exclusions backed up by the power of the state in such a way that culture's hegemony over society marginalizes, devalues, and ultimately silences the *other*.[3] While there is clearly much to be said for such assessments, and we would only at our peril lose sight of what is important in them, there are aspects of Arnold's account that are salutary for my project. So while the racial subtext of Arnold's work would no doubt belie his claim to "disinterest," my suggestion is to read *with* Arnold *against* Arnold—to use, in his terms, his own "best self" against him in order to extract what is useful about his work, not from what it actually is, but rather from what it purports to be. I want first to attend to what I find promising in his views and subsequently to indicate why our continued wariness of Arnold's conception of culture is warranted.

We might begin by noting that *Culture and Anarchy* constitutes an explicit attack on English smugness and provincialism.[4] Further, it was Arnold's belief that the marginalized, defined as those who lack a vital connection to an organic national culture, to an integrated way of life, were fated to remain undeveloped and provincial. He believed, as did Herder before him, that only integration into an organic national culture assured true flourishing. Culture, as embodied in the larger sustaining and embracing wholes of established national churches and universities, worked for Arnold to situate us within contexts that are broader and more inclusive than are acknowledged by the limited vision of "special interest groups." Culture, then, has as its aim to bring us out of ourselves. Limited only to itself for the critical resources that would guide its action, such a parochial interest group could achieve only a circular affirmation of its narrow outlook.[5] Such a group would also presumably find itself engaged in the ultimately arbitrary project of a Sartrean self-grounding, where the good is the good only insofar as one has chosen it. Arnold accordingly takes great pains to contrast the privation intrinsic to iconoclasm's privacy with the edification bestowed by "swimming with the tide of national culture."[6]

Not only was Arnold a critic of English provincialism, he also openly acknowledged the hybridity of the English character.[7] Just as the English social agent was for him a composite of the inclinations and sensibilities of the three main classes (the aristocracy, the bourgeoisie, and the working class), English culture was to be understood as a dialectic between Greek and Hebraic spiritual imperatives. As a consequence, Arnold's account of culture does not in principle require the expulsion of the other in order for a national culture to establish its identity.[8] So while he does take at face value nineteenth-century racial science's claim to have demonstrated salient racial differences, he is inclined to speak of such difference in a Herderian fashion, alluding to the peculiar "genius" of various peoples and of the affinities among them.[9] Of course, the range of peoples whose genius he thinks fitting for incorporation into English culture, or for that matter, *human* culture, is predictably narrow—only Indo-Europeans and Semites need apply—and in this sense, his acceptance of nineteenth-century racial biology is unarguably, seriously to understate the matter, unfortunate.[10]

In spite of this, what is perhaps most salutary in Arnold's account of culture is his emphasis upon adopting critical perspectives on received wisdom and the importance he attaches to pursuing an ever-enlarged point of view.[11] In his estimation, the spirit of the human race finds its ideal in making endless additions to itself, in the endless expansion of its powers and in endless growth in wisdom and beauty. Consequently, within the ambit of culture, which is the sine qua non of such growth, perfection consists not in a settled achievement, not in the "given" or in "being," but in "becoming."[12] He invokes the idea of the "best self" to capture the importance of the development and transformation of the given self, a best self that is the site of a "free play" and an "enlargement of consciousness" that constantly interrogates "fixed rules of action."[13]

Also to be found in his writing (though I do not wish to make more of it than his work warrants) are hints of an appreciative awareness of a process that I shall discuss in this book under the label 'fusion of horizons.' In his discussion of the roles of Hebraic moralism and Greek intellectualism in culture, Arnold speaks of the importance of these two inclinations reaching a "mutual understanding."[14] Though he does not offer anything approaching a theoretical analysis of such a process, his discussion does indicate a recognition of the value of what we might call a symmetrical learning process wherein both viewpoints are brought to an awareness of their respective limits and of what in the other can be profitably used to supplement itself.

Even as we acknowledge the value of these insights, if we pursue Arnold's thoughts on these matters more deeply it becomes clearer why his views have met with such stiff resistance. While he explicitly challenges the idea of a perfect and final expression of truth,[15] he apparently operates with what can be called a "convergence thesis" with regard to the destination and destiny of the best self's efforts. He is keen to impress upon us that the criterion for the constant interrogation of fixed rules of action is to be the "intelligible law of things," a nomological structure beheld by "right reason," the legitimate source of authority.[16] Culture is to shepherd us in this direction, toward the realization of a Platonically conceived apprehension of *a* firm, intelligible law of things, whose apprehension can serve to guide action. The best self, the self that heeds the sublime call of culture, "is not manifold, and vulgar, and unstable, and contentious, and ever-varying, but one, and noble, . . . *and the same for all mankind.*"[17] Or, as one commentator puts it, Arnold's conception of culture posits the idea of the universal formal identity of the human.[18] This assumption that both *physis* and *ethos* are one, stable and the same for all, that they are somehow self-announcing, naturally gives rise to postmodernist charges of naive, if not deluded, objectivism, of an invidiously universalistic and absolutistic conception of culture. And Arnold does indeed have a rather presumptuous sense of what "all the rest of mankind" does or should admire.[19]

In fact, Arnold's appeal to the "best self" is in many important respects similar to the invocation of the "true self" in various doctrines of "positive freedom,"[20] and to Hegel's appeal to "reason" in his political philosophy. In such cases, questions of autonomy or of self-determination are adjudicated, not with respect to the expressed wishes of the given empirical or "natural" self, but with respect to a putatively truer and higher rational self of which the given self may or may not fall short. Given the peculiar history of notions such as that of the best self and its cognates, we would do well to ask: What content is to be given to the notion, even as a developmental or regulative ideal, and what warrants the claim for that content? What insures the neutrality of that content vis à vis given class and cultural loci?[21] These questions are even more pressing in Arnold's case because he, like G. W. F. Hegel, understands the state as the organ of the collective best self and as the power representing the right reason of the nation.[22] It is this vision of the state's arrogating to itself the power to enforce culture's monolithically construed system of exclusions that must give us pause.

Arnold does acknowledge what might be called a pluralist or relativist challenge. But to this Weberian rejoinder he offers little in the way of an argument except to aver that now that the lower classes are in on the political act, the threat of anarchy makes the defense of the monolithic order of right reason and of the site of its ideal embodiment, the state, paramount. He *assumes* that right reason's presumptive neutrality vis-à-vis social distinctions will ultimately resolve conflict.[23] His single-minded insistence that human perfection is obtainable only within a stable social order blinded him, or made him insufficiently sensitive, to the social and moral consequences of his vision. Even a "bad" state presumably furnishes the prerequisite stability for human perfection. Arnold's belief that the avoidance of anarchy is more important than withdrawal of support from even what is acknowledged to be a flawed established order, indeed even one that supports the slave trade, gives credence to Said's charge of "reactionary political quietism."[24]

The state of culture and the culture of the state are, for Arnold, opposed equally to the barbarism of the aristocracy, to the philistinism of the bourgeoisie, and to the crudity of the working class. Accordingly, because they are aliens to class allegiance but not to the humane national culture that is to come, intellectuals are for Arnold the "insiders-outsiders" who, though supposedly the vehicles of the interrogatory and critical spirit of free play, stand impotent before the established state. On the state itself they have no critical leverage. It would appear that Arnold did not think through this apparent contradiction deeply enough. Perhaps his political imagination was too parochial to allow him to see that his vision of the connection between culture and the state was viable, even on his own terms, only within certain fairly well-described political boundary conditions. What about cases where the state, no matter how organically well-integrated, is explicitly antithetical to culture as he understands it, for example, as in the case of "socialist realism" or of fascist aesthetics? Though Arnold goes to great lengths to criticize the liberalism of his day, it is, ironically perhaps, only in a polity approaching the characteristics of a liberal democracy that a conception such as his could gain a foothold.

At any rate, Arnold's intellectuals, his seekers after and purveyors of "sweetness and light," are not to view culture as the private property of an elite. Rather, these cultural missionaries are charged with saving the souls of all, with making available to everybody, their social circumstances notwithstanding, the "best which has been thought and said."[25] He believes this to make him somewhat of a democrat, one of the "true apostles of equality." What a colleague aptly calls Arnold's "trickle down" version of culture is thus perhaps democratic in that all are to be admitted to, and indeed encouraged to enter, its sanctum, but decidedly undemocratic when it comes to deciding what is to *count* as culture.

Putting the point in this way delineates a space for the discussion of cultural democracy that is defined by two axes, a space spanned by a two-by-two matrix of possibilities with regard to access to and constitution of culture. Hence, one can be a horizontal democrat with respect to what is to count but not a vertical democrat with regard to who has access, as are some Afrocentric multiculturalists who want to balkanize access: only blacks should teach black literature, and preferably to black students. Arnold represents vertical democrats who eschew horizontal democracy, and, of course, one can be both to varying degrees or neither. In the chapters that follow, I shall argue for the fullest possible democracy consistent with critical reason along both axes.

Arnold operates in a space created by, on the one hand, an anxiety over the loss of certainties and, on the other, a suspicion of dogmatic adherence to tradition (in the guise of unreflective acceptance of stock truths and fixed rules of action). Both concerns—about having nothing in which to believe and about the pitfalls of a dogmatic embrace of belief—are sublated in his conception of culture, which, for that reason, hovers in an unstable balance between privileging authority—the original title of *Culture and Anarchy* was "Authority and Anarchy"—and championing self-critique, thinking against oneself, as would Arnold's cultured "aliens." The idea of the best self, understood as a regulative ideal, captures for him the idea of a presumptively indisputable standard in terms of which any existing self could be indicted. Unfortunately, for Arnold this unstable synthesis of credulousness and reflection subsists within the highly restricted ambit projected by a monologically conceived and homogenized notion of culture.

Culture in the sense of a particular content should not, I would argue, achieve hegemony over society, especially if the primary promoter or locus of culture is the state with its sanctions. In this sense, I share Said's worry concerning Arnold. On the other hand, culture in the sense of encouraging and nurturing the inclination and capacity to make discriminations between the edifying and the trite while remaining open to and on the look out for the new, the unusual, the marginalized, the forgotten, the repressed, and so on, is *precisely* what should achieve hegemony. This is the aspect, or moment, of Arnold's legacy that I would like to appropriate. And we should be encouraged to subject the "non-canonical" to the best, the most sympathetic, and the most widely informed critical intelligence (itself subject to revision) that we can muster. Such a conception of culture, aware of its own implication in dialectics of blindness and insight, a conception that embraces both the ideas of critical discrimination and of hermeneutic modesty, would be consistent with what I propose in this book.

On Herder and the Idea of Difference

> Weak and childish must our creative mother have been, had she constructed the sole and genuine destination of her children, that of

being happy, on the artificial wheels of some latterlings, and expected the end of creation from their hands. Ye men of all the quarters of the Globe, who have perished in the lapse of ages, ye have not lived and enriched the Earth with your ashes, that at the end of time your posterity should be made happy by European civilization: is not a proud thought of this kind treason against the majesty of Nature?

—Johann Gottfried von Herder,
Reflections on the Philosophy of the History of Mankind

With these words, penned in the latter quarter of the eighteenth century and from within the "belly of the beast," Johann Gottfried von Herder enacted a provocation that has profound consequences for the decentering of Europe. Well before postmodernist attacks on the universalist pretensions of the European Enlightenment, and before Theodor Adorno's influential critique of the "logic of identity," Herder offered a wide-ranging challenge to the idea that Europe, or any other civilization for that matter, had the inside track to fulfilling humanity's highest calling. Because of his sustained preoccupation with, and elaboration of, the idea that humanity comes in a variety of tone colors, Herder was one of the first significant theorists of "difference" and, indeed, served as an inspiration both for contemporary multiculturalism and for a variety of cultural nationalisms.[26] As such, his work offers a trenchant challenge to the Arnoldian conception of culture examined in the last section and, specifically, to the notion that the "best self" is the same for all humanity.

Here, I want to explore the significance of Herder's thought, of both its resources and its limitations, for a critical democratization of the Arnoldian conception of culture. I shall argue that despite his salutary appreciation of cultural difference, Herder's implicit conception of the nature of culture threatens to undermine the intelligibility of cross-cultural learning processes.

In my account of Herder's views, I shall adopt Isaiah Berlin's useful expository schema by focusing on what Berlin calls Herder's "expressionism," his "populism," and his "pluralism," respectively.[27] "Expressionism" refers to Herder's belief that human activity expresses the entire personality of a group and that such activity is intelligible only to the degree that it does so; "populism" asserts the value of belonging to a *particular* group or culture, as opposed to being a rootless cosmopolitan; and "pluralism" refers to the belief in the multiplicity, incommensurability, and equal validity of the values espoused by different cultures.[28]

Herder rather famously offered little in the way of a systematic account of what he meant by *culture*, so I shall attempt a reconstruction of the way in which it functions in his work based upon indications scattered throughout his writings, but centering upon his important *Reflections on the Philosophy of the History of Mankind*. For Herder, each thriving human culture represents a different harmonic variation on the theme of humanity; each, though aiming at humanity in its full sense, has a different conception of it.[29] The species as a whole realizes humanity through each of its constituent people's realizing their version of it, so that *humanity* in one important sense refers to the free exercise and development of the powers of each in its own distinctive way. Or, as one commentator puts it, "The way to humanity's universal moral and aesthetic aims is through close identification with a particular culture pursuing its fullest potential."[30]

At a rather general level, a distinct culture refers to the distinctive collective consciousness of a community or of a *Volk*, to a distinctive self-conscious adherence to roots (*Wurzeln*).[31] Organic forces (*Kräfte*) of social and political cohesion work to bind communities together via an inner consciousness of sharing a common cultural heritage consisting of a common set of national stories, customs, and rituals and, most important, a common language.[32] The communal bond of shared meanings and sentiments is forged, reproduced, demonstrated, and expressed through the common language. Herder, like his successor Wilhelm Dilthey, viewed the linguistically embodied systems of thought that characterize the various cultures as expressions of the way the natural, social, and moral worlds appear from the standpoint of a particular configuration of environment and cultural character.[33] It has been pointed out that Herder's conception of language can be characterized as a form of linguistic holism, wherein the meaning of a term is determined by its place in a language as a whole.[34] And each such linguistic totality marks out a differentially articulated field of concepts, projecting a shared world. Similarly, what Berlin calls Herder's expressionism can be understood as a form of *symbolic* holism in that each and every cultural product (both doings and sayings) has its meaning determined by the entire system of significations from which it emerges and to which it gives expression. So an adequate understanding of such a product requires that we enter the hermeneutic circle wherein a grasp of the whole is necessary for understanding the part. It seems that for Herder such systems of signification stand in a one-to-one correspondence with cultures, or *Völker*, so that a distinctive culture represents a distinctive "consensus of meaning" or a distinctive pattern of what Charles Taylor calls "intersubjective meanings."[35] Such systems of meaning, like languages, are anchored in social practices and forms of life. Language is rooted in social practices and projects because it codifies the distinctions that are both significant to and constitutive of those projects. And since such practices articulate the intelligibility of social action, a Volk can be characterized as a collection of people who are party to the same field of practices.[36] They too may share a common sense of the good.

A corollary of Herder's expressionism is that different *types* of activity within a given culture will have something, and indeed something salient, in common with each other that they will not share with activities of the same type in other cultures. Minimally, this would require their having in common a mutually reinforcing intelligibility; they would have to comprise a system of interexplicable practices. Were this not true it would be difficult to see how each cultural product could bear testimony to one and the same distinctive consensus of meaning. This common element is the expression of the distinctive character of a people.

In keeping with what has been called his "cultural holism," Herder deploys metaphors of organic harmony and health, where health is assessed in terms of how the various parts of a culture are integrated into a whole, as opposed to assessing a culture in terms of the external commensurating standards that more typically underwrite notions of progress. He places a premium on internal integration and coherence, speaking of the extent to which reason fashions ordered, symmetrical unities, the extent to which it forges wholes out of disorder and the variety of powers.[37] Indeed he suggests that what is meaningfully distinctive about an enduring culture is not its achievement along a particular dimension of human excellence, but the degree to which its diverse potentials and achievements are in equilibrium or balance (*Gleichgewicht*).[38] The degree of harmony among a culture's achievements, which are themselves to be assessed within the context of the culture's distinctive imperatives, is the measure of a culture's health. The more closely attuned to this aspiration a culture's action-orienting self-understanding—its "center of gravity" (*Schwerpunkt*)—is, the better.[39]

The gravitational metaphor betrays a conception of culture that tethers it to a central core of ideas and ideals that hold it together, a point of convergence where the diverse mutually illuminating and implicating features of a culture should harmonize in sympathetic attunement. This conception of a culture as centered in this way privileges convergence and internal coherence. This orientation also strongly implies that flourishing cultures exhibit a high degree of internal homogeneity, resting as it does on a communitarian conception of the self, wherein one and the same national character is, as it were, attached to the backs of individuals and manifested in their expressive individuality. This in turn leads Herder to prize cultural authenticity and to despise what are for him the alienating and septic effects of cultural mixtures, which threaten to oppose the gravitational pull of the center, which indeed threaten to *de*center. There is consequently a tendency in Herder to emphasize the salience of the contrast between the pure and the alloyed, or impure, and to see cultures as ideally and paradigmatically, though not necessarily actually, as relatively closed systems that develop, when left alone, in accordance with their own internal principles as did nature (*physis*) for Aristotle. Herder saw Europe as the repository of cultural achievement on a worldwide scale; but he believed that as long as Europe was content merely to imitate the products of this cosmopolitan heritage and failed to fashion its legacy around its own vital center, infusing it with its distinctive "organic powers," it could not flourish. In general, Herder lay emphasis upon the dangers of the centrifugal, ec-centric forms of foreign cultural products that are unassimilated to a given home culture's vital center.[40] In this way, by placing such stress on the importance of a people's being true to itself, to its sui generis way of being, Herder's thought provided the context for the powerful idea of cultural authenticity as an ideal.

He evinced little patience with the cosmopolitan ideal that, in his view, threatened to enervate Europe. When instead of taking one's compass from one's own cultural center of gravity one seeks rather to relate oneself to the species as a whole, one finds oneself bereft of the resources necessary to engage fully and meaningfully with life. For since one's rootedness provides the wherewithal for comporting oneself with regard to others, the abstract cosmopolitan, having no (rooted) self, and thus not being able to love himself in others, finds himself unable to really love or embrace others at all.[41] For such a cosmopolitan, there's no "here" here. So Herder's populism is an articulation of the claim that rootedness, finitude, and cultural belonging are enabling conditions of genuine human practices. In that human practices are essentially social in nature, it is a given that their very being is inextricably anchored in a consensus of meaning. Social recognition is an ineliminable component of any distinctively human practice. Since ex hypothesi for Herder such consensuses are irremediably local and peculiarly related to a given identity, any attempt to abstract from any particular agreement must be a self-defeating exercise. In contemporary terms we might say that though Herder does not reject the Enlightenment project tout court, he is at best a communitarian *Aufklärer*. As opposed to Immanuel Kant's, Herder's conception of the self holds it to be a relational product that realizes itself *within* a particular context of affiliations, not *against* such a context. So with Herder we arrive at a rather stark opposition of the cosmopolitan universal to the local and situated, of the transcendent to the immanent.[42] I shall presently, and indeed throughout the course of this study, question this opposition.

Through his emphasis upon the ideal of cultural authenticity, Herder makes a highly influential case for cultural pluralism. It is here that his importance as a theorist of difference lies. Though he retains an Enlightenment derived belief in progress, he adamantly refuses to countenance a conception of it that arrays all civilizations along the same scale. Each group has a standard of perfection internal to it; Europe has no monopoly on the ends of a truly human life.[43] The grand problem of humanity is solved in a variety of ways by various civilizations. The success of a civilization will always be measured in terms of the degree to which arrangements have been established that allow for the free exercise and enjoyment of its members' faculties.[44] But these arrangements will consist in institutional frameworks that enable *distinctive* styles of flourishing among the various civilizations. So the idea of progress for Herder is an acknowledgment that the culturally specific institutional arrangements for supporting distinctive styles of flourishing will be differentially successful. He is therefore very much a proponent of progressive development, but understands it to occur along culturally distinctive vectors.

Herder's consequent democratization of cultural development, his removal of the idea of cultural maturation from the strictures of a monolineal interpretation underwritten by a univocal telos, makes his a useful counterpoint to an Arnoldian conception of culture. For Herder, given that Providence has ordained such a wide variety of Volk configurations, the distinctive modes of representation and development that are characteristic of human cultures must all be seen as embodying value and commanding our respect.[45] If for Kant we are not to make of *ourselves* an exception, for Herder we are not to make of our *culture* an exception. I shall call this Herder's presumption of humanity.[46] He prefigures and shares the postmodernists' abhorrence both of the totalitarian effects of a consensus that portends to marginalize the local and of a conformity that stultifies life and threatens freedom.[47] Roughly speaking, in this respect Herder stood to the *philosophes* as Jean-François Lyotard (outspoken critic of the hegemonic metanarratives of modernity) stands to Jürgen

Habermas (equally outspoken advocate of modernity's emancipative potential). There are also important affinities between Herder's understanding of a Volk and Alasdair MacIntyre's conception of a tradition. Consonant with these positions, Herder espouses a conception of cultural pluralism within which there is a plurality of standards for assessing cultural value and for informing judgments of cultural development. Each such measure would enjoy only local validity. Since ex hypothesi for Herder there are no standards that enjoy transcultural legitimacy apart from such formal ones as coherence, balance, stability, and so on, the imposition of the ideal of one people on another can be understood only as the imposition of something alien. If ideals are expressive of the personalities of groups and groups differ as greatly from each other as Herder suggests, then such an imposition must be viewed as illegitimate.

Though Herder is a staunch advocate of cultural pluralism and of the idea that the appropriate standards for cultural evaluation are unique in themselves, he does not shy away altogether from the *critical* assessment of cultural practices. Indeed he is quite critical of political despotism and of mysogynistic and racist practices, for example. His critique of political domination continues strongly to resonate within contemporary nationalist movements. And, as the foregoing paragraph suggests, he would not view these critical positions as inconsistent with his views on human history and culture. Indeed, Herder indicted despotism and the slave trade on the basis of his commitments to pluralism and populism.

Moreover, we can find in Herder resources not only for such "external" critiques of relations between civilizations, but also for "internal" critiques of civilizations themselves. And this is closely related to my adumbration above of his conception of progress. If for Herder *humanity* is understood to name both a regulative ideal articulated as "reason and equity in all conditions, and in all occupations of men" and also a dynamic force (*Kraft*) embodied in socialized human beings which actively shapes and forms us in accordance with that ideal, then we are entitled to impute to Herder what I shall call a second presumption of humanity, the presumption that human cultures strive for the state in which reason fashions ordered wholes out of disorder and variety.[48] So humanity's self-constraint by the self-imposed ideals of rationality and justice is the motive force of human history. This second presumption of humanity would authorize our judging cultures in terms of the extent to which such an ideal state has been realized, with of course the caveat that this ideal will assume a variety of forms. It would underwrite our non-question-begging assumption that a culture judged to fall short of humanity is either unaware of its condition or unable to do anything about it; its members either fail to have the appropriate beliefs or they are unable to carry out the action that is called for by the appropriate beliefs and the presumed desire.[49]

When we inquire about how we are to *discern* such a shortfall, we move from the terrain of the merely conceptual to that of the epistemological. In this context, it should be noted that there are two hermeneutic problems that would beset such a critical enterprise. The world in which the critic is at home, her interpretive horizon, is always implicated. In shaping horizons of expectation, the hermeneutic situation of the critic can have the effect of occluding the nature of the practices being judged, of preventing the articulation of those practices in terms that would be acknowledged by the people whose practices they are. That is, the interpreter may misdescribe the complex of intentions in which the practices in question are situated by those whose practices they are and through which those practices are related to each other. This can lead to misplaced, and therefore unfair, judgments of discord. On the other hand, and for the same reasons, the critic's hermeneutic anticipation may render her blind to inequitable or discordant practices insofar as she understands them to be "natural." For example, with his almost Rousseauian celebration of the natural over the artificial, Herder would run the risk of being unable fully to thematize asymmetrical relations of power where they occur under the cloak of the "natural" relations between husband and wife, for instance.[50] Indeed, one often wonders whether Herder, his moral progressiveness notwithstanding, operates with a troublingly normative and unhistorical notion of the "natural."

More generally, proceeding with cross-cultural evaluations while acknowledging the caveat concerning the variety of forms humanity can take presumes sufficient hermeneutic access to the culture in question to be able to articulate in an unbiased way just what the practices are whose harmony is at issue. But are we entitled to make this presumption? Given Herder's keen and abiding acknowledgment of cultural difference and what has earlier been referred to as his doctrine of expressionism, questions of the mutual intelligibility of cultures to one another inevitably arise. Berlin suggests that for Herder cultures are not commensurable, though Berlin seems to mean by this not so much that they are mutually unintelligible but that they cannot be assessed on the same scale.[51] Yet when Herder claims that what is taken seriously and literally by an indigenous population is understood—if at all—ironically or derisively by outsiders, he suggests that *at best* a clash of semantic fields in cross-cultural understanding is likely to be inescapable.[52] He often writes as if category mistakes are endemic to cross-cultural understanding and that differing cultures are the bearers of competing understandings of the cosmos, a condition that leads one people to view the core claims of others, when intelligible at all, to be false or even ludicrous.

Generally speaking, there are at least three positions one can hold regarding the mutual intelligibility of different cultural frameworks, and Herder at different times seems to have held each. One may hold that different cultures can be unintelligible to each other, either upon initial encounter, or also, intractably, after sustained attempts at mutual understanding. To hold the latter is to espouse an incommensurability thesis, to hold that the central claims of differing cultures may in principle not be intertranslatable, that the central claims of one culture may not be expressible in the language of another; this position has of course been persuasively challenged by Donald Davidson.[53] Second, one might hold that such claims are expressible or intertranslatable, but that they are not *accessible* outside the framework of their home culture.[54] That is to say that even though the concepts that inform the "exotic" claims of the other may be expressible in our language, we may not be able to make coherent and systematic use of them in articulating the way the world seems to us. We understand their concepts; we just cannot get very far using them. We find ourselves "bumping" into items in our world that we can rather smoothly navigate with our own conceptual grid. In the idiom of the philosophy of language, one might say that in this case we could mention their concepts but not use them. However, if after sustained study and interaction we could not at least understand their basic concepts to be plausible ways for members of our species to organize the world, then there is good reason to wonder about the adequacy of the translation that in the first place permitted us to express their concepts. For a translation that renders the central claims of a target culture as false or risible is questionable on pragmatic and methodological grounds. Lastly, and most unproblematically, when confronted by a novel semantic field, we may find ourselves able to expand or enrich *our* vocabulary, to reconfigure intelligibly our semantic fields, in such a way that those concepts can be viewed as providing plausible windows onto a shared world. This last position on cross-cultural intelligibility or something closely akin to it clearly informed Herder's ethnohistoriographic *practice*, but he showed scant evidence of *theorizing* it, of thematizing it as a possibility alongside the other two. His in some ways unfortunate theory was at odds with his often salutary practice, I believe, because of his views on the holistic nature and the internal homogeneity of cultures. It is to this discussion that I now wish to return.

Is Herder's tendency to understand cultures as discrete, internally homogeneous units tenable? Purporting to express a settled consensus among contemporary students of culture, the anthropologist James Clifford refers to the obsolescence of the view of cultures as autonomous, separate, closed, fully coherent, and homogeneous phenomena and proposes that they be conceived instead as overlapping, open, interacting, and internally negotiated.[55] It is a consequence of this latter view that the experience of cultural difference is *internal* to cultures.[56] By contrast, Herder wrote at a time when peoples, nations, and cultures were conceived to be—and no doubt *were* to a greater extent than they are today though not completely—separate, bounded, and internally uniform; indeed his expressionism is in large measure an articulation of this view.[57] But this organic conception of culture is deeply problematic. A people may embody several relatively distinct cultural patterns. To press an evolutionary metaphor, those relatively distinct patterns may have resulted from *independent* selection processes, from isolatable and independently varying features of a people's social and physical environment, and hence may not form or add up to a neat, coherent, organically unified whole. In this case, one set of distinctive cultural patterns need not necessarily illuminate another, as Berlin suggests they do for Herder.[58] Cannot cultural collisions and inheritances occur on multiple fronts? Are not pristine purity and unity mere fictions?

It would seem that Herder could respond to these provocations only by positing an *essence* of the people who sustain the distinct sets of culturally meaningful patterns—a distinctive, pervasive, enduring, and cohesive template that gives unity to the multiplicity of distinct patterns, a unifying power that fashions that multiplicity into *a single* distinctive and coherent set of mutually implicating and mutually illuminating patterns. That is, *Herder's holism requires his essentialism*, an essentialist view of cultural membership, and a communitarian conception of the self wherein the self is conceived as a national type: "that which is German in the Germans—which all these diverse activities uniquely evince."[59] This notion of national character would play a problematic role here, however. If, as Berlin claims, it refers to an indefinable essence that can neither be abstracted from the activities through which it is manifest nor articulated independently of them, then we could not provide an independent account of it that would provide a demonstration of the coherence of what appear to be rather disparate activities. We have obviously entered a circle here. Perhaps Herder's conception of national languages as the master matrices of national cultures would make the circle hermeneutic rather than vicious, but clearly more needs to be said. One need not be a fan of "postmodern ethnography," with its emphasis upon cultural discontinuities and fractures, to wonder whether Herder's "cultural holism" can do justice to the fact that cultures are, and no doubt always have been, sites of contested interpretations. And one could acknowledge such contestation and such conflicts of interpretation without undermining the purchase of claims to cultural distinctiveness, though the articulation of such distinctiveness would undoubtedly be more complex. One might view the contested interpretations as interpretations of a common semantic field. Or, pushing further, the doubts I raise here would question Herder's inclination to conceive of systems of signification as standing in a one-to-one relationship to cultures. Is it the case that for each Volk there is a *single* system, or might there rather be a common and distinctive *set* of such semantic fields, wherein each member or element of the set captures something of importance to the group in question?

To illustrate my doubts here, I turn briefly to the work of a noted cultural theorist. In a way that acknowledges the dispersed centers from which the cultural practices of persons of African descent emanate, the cultural theorist Stuart Hall speaks of the loosely configured "repertoires" that span the space within which black popular culture is enacted. Among these items he mentions thematizing *style* as itself the matter of interest, as opposed to its being understood as merely superficial packaging; the metaphorical use of musical vocabulary signifying music's role in the "deep structure" of cultural life; and the use of the body as a canvas of representation.[60] But Hall emphatically does not understand these repertoires to constitute a set of necessary and sufficient conditions that could be used to *define* black culture, to stipulate its *essence*. He, too, speaks of the marks of difference *inside* forms of culture.[61] This set of resources for signification cannot be employed as an algorithm for the decidability of black culture. Conflicts could arise both over the interpretation and of the salience relative to others of a particular field of meaning or of a particular resource for signification, much as for Thomas S. Kuhn scientists sharing a common set of values could reasonably disagree over the ranking, weighting, and interpretation of those values.[62] Of course, even the idea of a single set of such fields, with its suggestion of closure, belies the actual situation of cultural porosity. And lest one think that the example I have chosen, the culture of the black diaspora, loads the dice because of its widely acknowledged status as a hybrid product of intercultural encounters, it should be noted that one does not have to look very deeply into the social life of any people to discern a "politics of representation" fueled by contestable accounts of who they are.[63]

Furthermore, Herder's rightly celebrated emphasis upon the central role of language as the bearer of cultural distinctiveness, as "the matrix of [a nation's] civilization,"[64] needs both a Bakhtinian and a Wittgensteinian emendation. Cultural linguistic life is always beset by a heteroglossia that tracks the lines of stratification, the various social fault lines, that are endemic to any society, and it is indeed the exceptional culture that is host to only a single language game.[65] All of these considerations point to the inadequacy of the organicist conception of culture as a unitary phenomenon. Though Herder is clearly the opponent of uniformity at the metacultural level, a uniformity that he viewed as the enemy of life and freedom, his opposition to uniformity *among* cultures seemed to carry as a corollary a projected uniformity *within* distinct cultures.

In truth, it is difficult to discern just how separate and uniform Herder really took cultures to be—that is, the extent to which he unambiguously embraced what I am calling the thesis of cultural holism (see note 55, above). However, whatever the outcome of such an exegetical inquiry, there is massive textual evidence that this view *is* accurately ascribed to Herder. In any event, my real interest is in calling attention to a certain tendency in cultural studies, a tendency that is certainly brought to the fore in Herder's writing. I shall refer to the thesis of cultural holism, then, as articulating what I shall denominate "the Herderian tendency" as a way of acknowledging that though it may not have been unambiguously embraced by him it was certainly a powerful and galvanizing force in his work.

I now want to suggest that this Herderian tendency renders the possibility of mutually edifying intercultural encounters conceptually problematic.[66] To put the point succinctly, the more seriously we take the idea of cultural holism, the more seriously threatened is our confidence that cultural concerns can be formulated in a way that allows sufficient intertranslatibility to render the idea of mutually intelligible learning processes plausible. In a sense, it is indeed the case that for Herder human history is an extended learning process, a process of which *humanity* is itself the subject, a process in which trial and error gradually transforms chaos into order.[67] Herder does of course also allude to the possibility of cross-cultural learning processes in which the subjects are actual individuals in culture, as opposed to the species in general, but this stands in tension with his conception of culture. Let us take but one example that brings to the fore the deep ambiguity in his thought. At one point in his *Reflections on the Philosophy of the History of Mankind* Herder writes, in a way that is reminiscent of Hannah Arendt's Kantian-influenced conception of "enlarged thinking," "The mind nobly expands, when it is able to emerge from the narrow circle, which climate and education have drawn round it, and learns from other nations at least what may be dispensed with by man. How much, that we have been accustomed to consider as absolutely necessary, do we find others live without, and consequently perceive to be by no means indispensable! Numberless ideas, which we have often admitted as the most general principles of the human understanding, disappear, in this place and that. . . . What one nation holds indispensable to the circle of its thoughts, has never entered into the mind of a second, and by a third has been deemed injurious."[68]

My horizons can be broadened, my parochialism overcome, and my maturation stimulated by encountering others whose practices highlight the dispensability of what I took to be indispensable. By being made aware in this way of other ways to be human, I have the pedagogically productive experience of learning to *relativize* my own assumptions, but not necessarily of learning to *criticize* them. For, assuming the thesis of cultural holism, in other cultural systems, in other cultural wholes our assumptions might be dispensable precisely because they do not "fit"; they might not be fitting responses to those, different, natural/cultural conditions. Moreover, the *lack* of such assumptions may not "fit" in *our* cultural configuration. A critical learning process requires either that (1) a single problem requiring solution can be identified on *both* sides of a cultural divide, or (2) resources from one cultural context are sufficiently "detachable" from their home setting that they can be meaningfully employed in a foreign context. The first alternative stands in tension with the claim of the distinctiveness of cultures (depending of course on how far down Herder understands that distinctiveness to go), while the second stands in tension with a robust notion of cultural holism. If cultural resources derive their meaning exclusively from their usefulness as means to the realization of unique standards of cultural perfection, then it is difficult to see how they can be sufficiently transferable to function on foreign soil.[69]

Berlin emphasizes that, for Herder, values and ends "live and die with the social wholes of which they form an intrinsic part," and I myself have elsewhere spoken of the internal relationship of values to contexts of meaning.[70] This implies that values lose their point, their claim on us, when abstracted from the contexts that give them purchase. And if the various social wholes have the sort of unique character that Herder appears to attribute to them, if their defining practices are as incomparable as he suggests, then again it is difficult to see how one culture can learn from the values espoused by another, for the local interpretations of the cultural necessities—the satisfaction of which is enabled by the projection of a given set of values—will not, by definition, be shared.

Strictly speaking, a strong claim of cultural uniqueness would have as a consequence that at best cultures lack the resources for noninvidious mutual translation of each other's cultural expressions; at worst they would lack the resources for such translation altogether. The values and goals that are distinctive of a people are for Herder conceptually connected with that people's center of gravity (*Mittelpunkt, Schwerpunkt*). So a genuine and distinctive achievement within a culture will only count *as such* an achievement insofar as it is aligned with that center of attraction. Hence, what would count as a distinctive achievement in one culture might well not in another and indeed might not even be *intelligible* as a cultural move in another culture. However, Herder's doctrine of empathy (*Einfühlen*) offers a way out of *this* thicket: said achievement could be intelligible as a cultural move within its home culture to a sufficiently enlightened hermeneut from an alien context (presumably like Herder himself), though properly carrying this out would be tantamount to acquiring a new "first language." We could discern the worth of other values only insofar as we could "feel" our way into the form of life that gives them their meaning. Indeed one might find that the fittingness of such an achievement, its exemplariness, could be so striking as to inspire such a hermeneut and others of like mind to enact such "fits" between their centers of gravity and their achievements on their own home ground, to realize the creative achievements enabled through attunement to one's center. However, this edification would take place at a metalevel in that it would not be so much the *actual achievement* of the culture of interest that was of value as it would the *example* provided by its perfection in context. So, thus restricted to a merely contextual appreciation of the other, the enlarged mentality that Herder envisions represents a self able, reflectively, to dispute the categorical nature of its informing assumptions, but not a self that, through the critical modification of its assumptions, has itself been transformed. Indeed, the idea of a transformed self sits uneasily with Herder's anticosmopolitan ideal of populist communitarianism.

So there is a deep, and indeed irreconcilable, tension between the motif of cultural holism that courses through Herder's writing and the vision of genuine edification and learning that in part animates his appreciation of cultural diversity. Insofar as we view cultures as essentially homogeneous and distinctive constellations of meaning, each with distinctive ways of determining what counts as a salient problem and with correspondingly distinctive criteria for evaluating the success of solutions to those distinctly construed problems, then it is difficult to see how the achievements of one culture can be useful to another—except, as I have suggested, as an inspiration to reach one's own particular good.

On the other hand, if—as I shall argue at length in the chapters that follow—we understand cultures to be spanned by an array of dimensions that they *share* (though they may be unequally successful along the various dimensions), then the idea of the fusion of the "native" and the "foreign," of genuine learning from others, need not be viewed, as is Herder's wont, as a compromising alloy that promises only debilitation or corruption.[71] A culture that is doing less well along a given dimension of cultural experience can learn from one with more success provided that there is mutual acknowledgment of problems and problem resolutions. While Herder does acknowledge the multidimensionality of cultures, this chord is resolved into the idea of a unique and single center of gravity.[72] So, in contrast to both Enlightenment universalism and the Herderian emphasis on discontinuous diversity, I shall argue for a metalinguistically enabled and context-specific possibility of cross-cultural conversation and learning.

Further, given the ways in which cultural holism is logically implicated in Herder's conception of populism, the discussion that follows will also have implications for his populist commitments. When Herder speaks despairingly of displaced or uprooted individuals, he betrays an inclination to feel that there is a unique cultural center of gravity to which individuals "naturally" belong. But what about individuals who seem able to adapt to new cultural loci or even to be nourished by several at once and yet retain their creative powers? Herder's populist thesis reasonably suggests that without orienting ourselves with respect to *some* consensus of meaning, to *some* set of ongoing social practices, there is no true creation and no true realization of human goals. That is, there must be standards and frameworks in place in terms of which achievements are intelligible *as* achievements at all, let alone as exemplary or creative achievements, and those standards are underwritten by particular social arrangements. But must the relevant social consensus be the one that I was born into or the one with which people who are perceived as being like me in socially relevant respects are typically associated? Failing to take one's compass from one's group of origin is not to fail to take one's orientation from *any* group. In this sense my center of gravity need not be thought to be mine by virtue of an assumed proprietary connection between it and my ascribed characteristics, but rather by virtue of its having been in some sense chosen by me as an enabling system of meaning.[73] In the chapters that follow, I pursue responses to these two aspects of what I have called the Herderian tendency (a tendency still very much alive in contemporary nationalism and in nationalist styles of contemporary multiculturalism, such as some versions of Afrocentrism)—that is, to the view that for each culture there is one and only one "living center" and that each individual "naturally" belongs to the center associated with "his" or "her" culture. I develop these two lines of response through an articulation of what I call "situated cosmopolitanism."

2
Musical Interlude: Adorno on Jazz, or How Not to Fuse Horizons

The aim of jazz is the mechanical reproduction of a regressive moment, a castration symbolism. "Give up your masculinity, let yourself be castrated," the eunuchlike sound of the jazz band both mocks and proclaims, "and you shall be rewarded, accepted into a fraternity which shares the mystery of impotence with you. . . ." Jazz is the false liquidation of art—instead of utopia becoming reality it disappears from the picture.

—Theodor Adorno, "Perennial Fashion—Jazz"

If Matthew Arnold was too smug about what "right reason" would reveal and was therefore insufficiently *self*-critical, then J. G. von Herder, by being so understandably keen to take at face value the merit of cultural practices not his own, could be charged with being insufficiently critical of such practices. Given its critique of closed systems of reason that are refractory to difference and heterogeneity on the one hand, and its simultaneous commitment to thoroughgoing and principled social and cultural critique on the other, we might naturally turn to the tradition of Critical Theory for a reflexively critical analysis of culture that avoids the lacunae of both

Arnold and Herder. We might naturally appeal to this tradition insofar as it purports to take reason, progress, and humanism seriously while being critical of the ethnocentric, ideological, and elitist ways in which those concepts have been applied. However, were we to take as a model the way in which Theodor Adorno's cultural criticism treats cultural difference, in particular its assessment of jazz, we would be disappointed. Adorno's engagement with jazz was an opportunity for Critical Theory to showcase its resources for discerning and articulating the new, the oppositional, and the aesthetically challenging and compelling according to reflectively humanistic standards. Instead, Adorno failed to take advantage of this opportunity, and if we are to avoid similar failures, it behooves us to understand why he did so. For all of his progressive commitments and credentials, Adorno apparently remained too much the German mandarin to learn the lessons Herder has to teach us. As a result, Adorno, at least in his jazz analysis, failed to provide an effective counterpoint to Arnold's cultural conservatism and thus failed to rescue humanism from its traditional charge of elitism. In this "musical interlude," I treat Adorno's jazz analysis as a case study of some of the problems laid out in the last chapter.

Adorno's writings on jazz, black America's major contribution to aesthetic modernism, represent Critical Theory's most extensive engagement to date with African-American artistic practice.[1] I shall argue here that Adorno's treatment of jazz is a signal example of the failure to seek a vocabulary that would enable a noninvidious representation of difference. Moreover, since his treatment of jazz is an extension and application of a theory of popular culture that has continuing relevance,[2] a renewed interrogation of Adorno on "the jazz question" has wide implications for contemporary cultural theory.

I. Critical Theory, Aesthetic Theory, and the Culture Industry

"Critical Theory" refers to a rather heterogeneous tradition of social theory that traces its origin to the Institute of Social Research, established in Frankfurt, Germany, in 1923. Its central figures are Max Horkheimer (1895–1973), Theodor Adorno (1903–1969), Herbert Marcuse (1898–1980), and Jürgen Habermas (1929–). It is generally acknowledged that Habermas's work represents a decisive recasting of the research program of such earlier "Frankfurt School" theorists as Adorno and Marcuse. Accordingly, his work, which will be addressed in the next chapter, represents a new departure. However, what arguably unites Critical Theorists is the ongoing attempt to forge intellectual syntheses that are productive for a critical analysis of late capitalist societies, an analysis that is undertaken with an eye to possibilities for human emancipation from historically contingent social and economic fetters. Key ingredients in their syntheses, though with inflections characteristic of the various thinkers comprising the tradition, are G. W. F. Hegel's historicist sensibility, Karl Marx's conception of the critique of ideology, Max Weber's analysis of modernity, and Sigmund Freud's psychoanalysis.[3]

The classic articulation of Critical Theory's position on the culture industry is contained in Adorno and Horkheimer's *Dialectic of Enlightenment*. They speak there of cultural institutions so seamlessly wed to the forces of capital that cultural products become commodities, pure and simple. In terms to be given perhaps greater currency by Marcuse's famous one-dimensional society thesis, Horkheimer and Adorno hold that under such conditions, aesthetic practices and the products that issue from them comprise a thoroughly uniform system, a cultural and aesthetic ether fully obedient to the iron laws of capitalism that neutralizes political opposition.[4] Individual desire is subverted and reconfigured in accordance with systems imperatives. For the culture industry constitutes a system in which the needs necessary to justify cultural production are themselves manufactured by the system, a circle in which those needs that might resist it are suppressed at the level of the individual consciousness.[5] As Adorno claims, "The liquidation of the individual is the real signature of the new musical situation."[6] In such a society, the high art/low art contrast takes on the fetishized form of pure distinction for distinction's sake. Well before the work of Pierre Bourdieu, Horkheimer and Adorno pointed out that aesthetic taste had become a matter of a distinction that is itself a salable commodity; for example, being able to purchase tickets for the symphony was the mark of a social difference that was itself the object of enjoyment, as opposed to the actual symphony concert.[7] And the culture industry reinforces and cynically capitalizes on this situation, ruthlessly commodifying social distinctions. Its hegemony transforms genuine aesthetic differences into simulacra and leaves no space for critical reflection, as it reproduces individuals who come to believe that their needs can be harmonized with the existing state of affairs. As a consequence, popular cultural forms, particularly those of movies and music, are most adequately understood as being essentially media of manipulation. Even the reception of "serious" art has fallen victim to the iron laws of commodification. As Adorno summarizes it in a more recent reconsideration of their analysis of the culture industry, "[T]he substitute gratification which it prepares for human beings cheats them out of the same happiness which it deceitfully projects. The total effect of the culture industry is one . . . in which . . . enlightenment . . . becomes mass deception and is turned into a means for fettering consciousness. It impedes the development of autonomous, independent individuals who judge and decide consciously for themselves."[8]

Adorno's critique of the culture industry can be given greater definition by a brief consideration of that to which it stands in contrast, namely, the associated practices of autonomous art. As I have suggested above, Adorno is highly critical of the high art/low art distinction as it is typically deployed in bourgeois-capitalist culture. What is useful in this distinction for him, and what he wants to retain, is captured by the contrast between autonomous art and commercial art, a contrast that is not for him isomorphic to the antidemocratic opposition of elite art to folk art. But, advanced capitalism (and were Adorno alive today he would no doubt include postmodernism as a coconspirator) has leveled this distinction in all of its substantive forms.

The autonomy of "genuine" art consists in its serving needs that are orthogonal to those that reinforce existing social relations. Art's autonomy, won through its gradual emancipation from magic, the court, and religion, secures for art its own inner logic of development and of evaluation.[9] Ringing a change on Kant's description of aesthetic phenomena as exhibiting a purposiveness without purpose, Adorno claims on behalf of autonomous art that "[i]f any social function can be ascribed to art at all, it is the function to have no function."[10]

While art's autonomy vis-à-vis society means that it has no *function* in any straightforward sense, such an independence does endow art with a distinctive social *significance* for Adorno. Because art's autonomy as a separate sphere of value was the outcome of a development within bourgeois society, art's independence is predicated upon arrangements within that very society. The institution of autonomous art is an institution of bourgeois society and thus is itself a bourgeois institution. Works of autonomous art, then, belong to a society in which the principle of exchange has achieved hegemony in regulating social relationships, and such works circulate in accordance with this principle.[11] Works of art, even autonomous works, are therefore commodity fetishes.[12] Autonomous works, then, are marked by a double character—their autonomy and their commodity form; but they are also fetishes that call into question the system of commodification and reification itself.

Accordingly, the "ideological" status of autonomous art is at the same time a *critical* status. Like so many of his philosophical predecessors, Plato being perhaps the notable exception, Adorno pins his hopes on the redemptive power of art, claiming that "[w]orks of art are plenipotentiaries of things beyond the mutilating sway of exchange, profit and false human needs."[13]

Autonomous art voices a "promise of happiness, a promise that is constantly being broken."[14] As such, it is ineluctably the "language of suffering," and in this lies its claim to truth.[15] Genuine art is expressive of the contradictions inherent in the society from which it emerges. The atonality of Arnold Schoenberg, for instance, is an acknowledgment of social alienation, of the problematic relationship of the individual to the community, in contrast to the less uneasy insertion of the individual into the social nexus expressed in the tonality of earlier classical forms. By refusing to "sugar coat" deprivations and by representing fulfillment as a broken promise, genuine works represent the negative *as* negative and prevent us from being seduced into prizing our chains. The culture industry claims to procure for us the object of desire and thus desublimates it, but it is a repressive desublimation that presents the object only as a simulacrum with no *real* relation to instinctual gratification.[16]

II. Adorno's Jazz Critique

Adorno's approach to music in general, and to jazz in particular, is shaped by the concerns of, and grounded in the theoretical context provided by, the *Dialectic of Enlightenment*.[17] His approach to jazz is a ramification of his attempt to understand what, to him, is a paradoxical musical form—in particular what he took to be its pseudodemocratic character—and the dialectical tendencies it represents. However, my interest lies not so much in what motivates Adorno's reception of jazz as it does in the quality of understanding that his approach permits. I shall argue that his is a critical approach that does not allow us to look at jazz properly, to see what it offers on its own terms.

For Adorno, writing in 1936, jazz was a kind of dance music that *presumed* to be modern, its presumed modernity grounded in its putatively oppositional stance, a stance that was articulated musically in terms of a characteristic sound and a distinctive rhythmic principle that feigned transgression in their mechanical soullessness and licentious decadence.[18] Adorno designates syncopation as the central rhythmic principle.

Musical Interlude

The terms of Adorno's jazz critique are interesting in that he criticizes jazz for *not really* being a product of immediacy, of the primitive, the archaic, the "raw," and for being only a commercialized ersatz of this. The very criteria that jazz presumably fails to satisfy are themselves the warp and woof of the primitivist myth of black creativity. In his claim that, because of its prior colonization by the culture industry, the jazz subject is *not* the vehicle for the presentation of unmediated sexuality, "original, untrammeled nature" and instinctual liberation, Adorno implicitly criticizes exoticism and the racializing fetishization of black performers by the white intelligentsia, both American and European. Representative of this reaction were Gertrude Stein's and Pablo Picasso's responses to their first encounter with Duke Ellington's orchestra in Paris, where they marveled at what they took to be Ellington's ability to access the instinctual and unconscious layers of the psyche.[19] But in Adorno's salutary critique of the primitivist reception of jazz, of the tendency to fetishize it as the plenipotentiary of the "jungle," the archaic and the natural, there are two problematic moments. First, black creativity is saved from being viewed as the purely instinctual, unreflective, and artless expression of undomesticated animality only at the cost of its being understood as the thoroughly domesticated and packaged product of the culture industry. Such a rescuing strategy implies that the possibilities for black creative expression are exhausted, one might say, by the "jingle and the jungle." I shall suggest presently that this predicament is indicative of a manifest hermeneutic inadequacy in Adorno's encounter with black aesthetic practice. Moreover, Adorno was greatly suspicious of the primitive per se, even as and perhaps especially as it is invoked in Western "art music," as his critical response to Igor Stravinsky's *Rite of Spring* clearly demonstrates. For Adorno, any such invocation is ahistorical and thus necessarily regressive. He thus constructs a box in which black creative expression has no place to turn.

Adorno criticizes jazz for being mechanical, static, repetitive music that only *feigns* democratic and individual self-expression, for being music that only *appears* to be reflective of the autonomy of instinctual liberation and psychic integration. Its merely illusory status in this regard leaves it fit only for the ideological job of providing an ersatz liberation and thus for beguiling an already mutilated public into feeling that prevailing social and economic arrangements are "delivering the goods." And it is an agent of that mutilation, part of the apparatus facilitating the introjection of the administered society and its controls, an introjection that fashions a brutalized subjectivity. As Adorno famously notes in his first extensive treatment of the subject in 1936, in an essay responding to

Walter Benjamin's "The Work of Art in the Age of Mechanical Reproduction," jazz "is not what it 'is': its aesthetic articulation is sparing and can be understood at a glance. Rather, *it is what it is used for.* . . ."[20]

The elements of jazz in which immediacy and spontaneity seem to be most conspicuous are improvisation and syncopation, but Adorno holds that these features are mere ornaments, "add-ons" to the standardized commercial product that he thinks is the essence of jazz, and that they are added on for the ideological purpose of masking its naked commodity structure.[21] Jazz is social authority packaged to appear as libidinal freedom. Blackness itself presences as an absence in jazz; it too is a mere commodity fetish, indicating all the more the black person's colonization by the very context within which he deludedly asserts his individuality: "the skin of the black man functions as much as a coloristic effect as does the silver of the saxophone."[22] Since jazz offers only the deceptive semblance of liberation, the pleasure taken in it by both producers and consumers is *au fond* a masochistic and sadistic pleasure in one's own alienation from oneself, in the "othering" of one's own instincts and in the "othering" by others of theirs.[23] For Adorno, jazz is thoroughly modern, then, not in its aesthetic, but in its having been engendered by the dialectic of Enlightenment through the mechanism of suppression.[24] Recalling in some ways Marcuse's idea of "repressive desublimation," Adorno holds that the "jazz subject" is not quickened by the liberation of old and repressed instincts; instead it presents only a static, standardized, and petrified mask that testifies to its domesticated, controlled, and mutilated instinctual structure.

As for jazz's supposed "progressiveness," its genuine *aesthetic* modernity, Adorno takes what is musically progressive in it to be plagiarized from European impressionism and to be simply pasted on, rather than developing organically from out of the musical material itself as it did for Claude Debussy, Maurice Ravel, and others. So jazz makes false claims both to the Dionysian archaic and to that which is truly modern.[25]

Locating its origin, and just as speciously, its essence, in a combination of salon dance music and military march music, Adorno sees jazz as inextricably circumscribed by the authoritarian control of the eight-bar cycle and the machine-like steady beat.[26] Even jazz at its best—the so-called hot music of, say, Louis Armstrong, in which it appeared that the lyrically self-asserting individual soloist willingly and autonomously engaged with the collective—is really a music in which the individual is sacrificed to the mechanistically contrived collective. Adorno finds it no accident that the Western composer whom he took to be most sympathetic to jazz,

Stravinsky, placed human sacrifice at the center of his principal work, *The Rite of Spring*.[27]

Adorno maintains that the social authority of the prescribed metric law, manifested by a rigidly maintained basic beat, is never effectively challenged by jazz syncopation. Indeed he likens jazz syncopation to sexual dysfunction and *impotence*, to premature and incomplete orgasm, to what is at best a gesture without a meaningful purpose.[28] Like Benjamin's bourgeoisie taking pleasure in its own alienation, and presumably like black vaudeville performers taking pleasure in their own clownishness, in "acting the fool," the jazz subject takes pleasure precisely, for Adorno, in its own weakness.[29] As a sort of preemptive strike, and to the tune of the superego's sadomasochistic dance, the jazz subject enacts a moment of self-castration, achieving its power through an internal split whereby it identifies with a repressive social authority over itself. But this is all the latent content of the dream that is jazz; its manifest content, the text on which we are encouraged to enact a hermeneutic of suspicion, is the myth of the empowered individual democratically engaged with the collective, and unconstrained by social authority. This text, however, enacts the symptoms of the neurotic; the nonspontaneous, ritualized, and mechanical behavior of the neurotic has for Adorno a musical parallel in the thoroughly conventional nature of jazz music. Jazz expresses the thoroughly mutilated status of oppressed black humanity.[30]

Inspired by Marx's analysis of the commodity and no doubt also by the centrality to industrial production of the Fordist principle of interchangeable parts, Adorno avers that the formal elements of jazz have been prefabricated in accordance with the capitalist requirement that they be exchangeable and interchangeable.[31] With this thesis of what I shall call the "detachability" of jazz's characteristic features, Adorno implies that a jazz performance cannot have the organic integrity of a genuine work of art, for it will always be a whole fully reducible to its arbitrarily arranged, interchangeable parts.

Further, since for Adorno the details of a jazz performance are interchangeable in *time*, jazz cannot be governed by an imperative of temporal articulation and development. Since its elements are arbitrarily fungible, its progression in time lacks the organic developmental inevitability of concert music; its essential temporal nature is stasis.[32]

One might feel compelled at this point to object, "Given what is at issue in a genuine jazz performance, actual jazz practice is virtually unrecognizable in Adorno's descriptions." Today it is argued increasingly that the object of Adorno's ire was not what we refer to today as "jazz," but rather what was the popular music of his time, which was not necessarily even American music.[33] We should thus attend to what was in Adorno's "ear" when evaluating his jazz essays, and, given the musical context of 1920s Germany, what was in his ear was a peculiarly German interpretation of commercial dance music (*Tanzjazz*). No American jazz band visited Germany prior to 1924, and virtually no recordings of the major black American jazz artists were available at any time during the Weimar Republic years.[34] Among the white bandleaders, Paul Whiteman was especially important, and if, as one writer suggests, we listen to a typical Whiteman performance, much of what Adorno says in "On Jazz" hits home.[35] But as late as 1953, when what is translated as "Perennial Fashion—Jazz" was published and Adorno had spent over eleven years in the United States, Adorno's critique remained virtually unchanged. Moreover, he insisted to the end on the underlying unity between the "hot" jazz characteristic of the first rank of African-American practitioners and the "sweet" jazz or dance music of the 1920s.

III. "Talking Back" to Adorno

Perhaps most damning are Adorno's charges of jazz's atemporality, its lack of organic integrity, and its thoroughly mechanical nature. I wish to respond to these charges by briefly taking up in turn his critique of jazz's temporality, his assertion that jazz syncopation is a mechanical contrivance that gives lie to its claim to rhythmic freedom, and his claim that improvisation is a similarly mechanical practice masquerading as individual expression. I shall then turn to a brief account of the criteria that jazz practitioners *themselves* take to be salient for the evaluation of a jazz performance, the sort of account that Herder exhorts us not to ignore.

On the issue of temporality, repetition in jazz is often a means to impart movement. One need only listen to the deployment of riffs (repeated background melodic phrases that are rhythmically oriented) in the work of Count Basie to see this (for example, his "One O'Clock Jump" on *Count Basie: The Complete Decca Recordings*, Decca GRD-3-611). As opposed to this, repetition in Stravinsky, for example, *does* impart a sense of stasis, of having suspended time, of a musical "meanwhile" (for example, in *The Rite of Spring*, the *ostinati* in "Danses des Adolescentes"). While repetition is arguably an important strategy in black culture, one should be attentive to the various uses to which it can be put.[36]

As far as Adorno's critique of syncopation (his insistence on the performer's submission to the domination of a uniform basic beat) is concerned, he seems unable to acknowledge that a regular beat is the condition of the possibility of syncopation. Such a beat provides the coordinate system or context within which rhythmic experimentation can intelligibly take place. As Søren Kierkegaard pointed out in his discussion of the interesting, it is precisely our expectations that form the ground for the unexpected.[37] The established and recurring beat configures or articulates the very temporal horizon that allows syncopated rhythms to have *meaning*. In fact, it is the recognition of this that allowed one critic to *fault* Ellington for variations in tempo in his "Black, Brown and Beige," for those variations undermined the possibility of syncopation.[38] And unless one claims as Adorno implausibly does that such musical intelligibility is necessarily equivalent to the utterly undemanding accessibility required by the market, then the case to be made for jazz syncopation's necessarily authoritarian character cannot be made—at least not in the way that Adorno seeks to make it.[39]

Adorno further alleges that jazz's musical spontaneity is fatally compromised by its rigid adherence to bar lines and its slavish restriction to the chord structure of the popular songs that form its basis. While it can be argued that excessive intelligibility flirts dangerously with cliché and that genuine art is ambiguous, we obviously cannot dispense with intelligibility altogether, and there are a number of important enabling conditions of musical intelligibility. Chord progressions in a jazz performance constitute one of those enabling conditions. So it is not the case that the harmonic structure need be seen as a restriction on the genuineness of improvisation; it is rather an enabling condition of the intelligibility of the improvisation, of its being recognized as a move in the game—as opposed to an arbitrary gesture—that makes sense. Further, the chord structure provides a metalinguistic frame that enables members of an ensemble to communicate with each other, to respond to one another and to participate in a common project. The touchstone of harmonic structure is one of the conditions of jazz's being the "sound of surprise," to adopt Whitney Balliett's suggestive description, without its degenerating into the arbitrariness of noise. Based upon my limited experience attempting to play jazz, I would argue—in a way reminiscent of Michelangelo's declaration that it is the sculptor's charge to liberate the figure from the block of stone in which it is potentially present—that performing jazz is, among other things, a matter of finding the music in the chord. Originality is to be sought, at least in the first instance, in what the musician fashions within the "constraints" of form and material, in the distinctiveness of the story that can be articulated using the vocabulary of the tradition. Does adherence to the sonata form render all Western concert music of the classical period interchangeable?

We recall Adorno's account of the relationship between the individual and the collective in jazz performance, his conviction that in such contexts genuine individuality is sacrificed to the collective. But certainly what is *sought* in such a performance at least is a genuine dialogical or conversational interaction, featuring antiphony (call and response), signifying (humorous and ironic dueling), and so on—an interaction that places a premium on attentive listening.[40] In this way, at least ideally, the dialectic of the individual and the collective is not collapsed, and a genuine communal creation is forged. The soloist speaks the language of the collective, but a language that enables the formulation of one's own statement. Max Roach and Wynton Marsalis confidently assert that jazz is a democratic form of music in that, as Roach puts it, "[w]hen a piece is performed, everybody in the group has the opportunity to speak on it, to comment on it through their performance."[41]

Though it is not central to my argument, it is perhaps worth mentioning here that there is also another dialectic involving the individual and the community that Adorno fails to acknowledge in the black performance tradition, that of performer and audience. One writer refers to this under the rubric of an "ethics of antiphony."[42] One sees this frequently when audiences *participate* in solo performances, be they dance or musical performances per se. In such cases, the audience encourages the soloist, enabling him to transcend what he might otherwise do. This, in turn, produces a finer "spectacle" for the audience, but it is not a pure spectacle in the Greek sense, for the audience too is part of it, egging the performer on. What the spectators behold is a presentation of not only what is best in the performer, but also of what deeply taps into what they as a community are about. That is, this phenomenon is a celebration of both the genius of the performer and of the audience itself. As spectators of the performance, members of the audience are, in part, "reading" themselves. This phenomenon, then, is not constituted by the domination of either the individual (performer) or the community (other musicians and audience), but by the community's being implicated in the performer's own expressive individuality.

For a critical response to jazz, we can easily avoid critiques that, like Adorno's, flirt with insinuating musical unintelligibility as a critical counterpoint.[43] By attending to the criteria that jazz musicians themselves employ in evaluating performances, a recent major study by Paul Berliner provides strong evidence both against Adorno's charge that jazz improvi-

Musical Interlude 53

sation is largely a matter of the mechanical or arbitrary application of clichés and for the claim that there is a language of criticism and evaluation that is internal to jazz musical practice itself. By attending to the criteria that those who engage in the practice themselves employ, Adorno's hermeneutic failure is underscored. Discussing jazz musical values, Berliner mentions nine criteria that are implicitly or explicitly brought to bear in musical evaluations. First, he focuses on the degree to which a performance "swings," that is, the degree to which the variety of an artist's rhythmic conceptions and the stylistic manner in which they are articulated or phrased contributes to giving them qualities of syncopation and forward motion.[44] This consideration directly confutes some of the counts in Adorno's indictment of jazz. Adorno claims that a jazz performance is rigidly governed by bar lines. However, in a competent improvisation there is no such rigid observance. The intentional anticipation of chord changes is one way in which bar lines are blurred. Listen, for instance, to Coleman Hawkins's solo on Ellington's "Mood Indigo" (*Duke Ellington Meets Coleman Hawkins* MCA/Impulse MCAD-5650 JVC-461). Anticipation of this sort is itself an instance of syncopation. Phrasing across bar lines was commonly done by Louis Armstrong and Charlie Parker. Further, the jazz solo typically eschews the repetition of four- and eight-bar phrases characteristic of the AABA song form.[45] In general, mature performers obscure the formal elements that guide their inventions.[46]

Second, in addition to the importance of swinging, there is the matter of the melodic substance of ideas, as evaluated in terms of the economy of expression and of lyricism.[47] Third, one seeks evidence of the artful handling of harmonic dissonance to achieve the appropriate mixture of pitches inside and outside indicated chords for creating interesting melodies.[48] Fourth, it is important that there be a balance between originality, on the one hand, and taste or discretion on the other, where the emphasis is upon avoiding the overuse of conventional jazz vocabulary while respecting the conventions of a given repertory.[49] Fifth, there is an eye to the emotional coherence or integrity of expression displayed in a performance, embodying such qualities as pathos, intensity, urgency, fire, energy, and humor of the ironic "signifying" sort.[50] Sixth, but always in the context of emotional expressiveness and the distinctiveness of the performer's sound, one evaluates instrumental virtuosity and the technical features of musical ideas.[51] Seventh, there is a central concern about the ability of a soloist to shape, and thereby tell, coherent, "organic," and unified narratives through the suspenseful development of ideas and the dramatic shaping of sound, with the effect that the solo moves forward in time with such logic that its "direction seems inevitable" (recall Adorno's invidious comparison of jazz and classical music in this regard), its narrative compelling.[52] Well-known examples of performances meeting this criterion are Armstrong's solo on "Potato Head Blues" (*The Smithsonian Collection of Classic Jazz* [compilation] 16, CBS CD Edition RD 033 A5 19477) and Coleman Hawkins's "Body and Soul" (*Body and Soul*, RCSA Bluebird ND 85717). Eighth, one looks for spontaneity of musical invention, where here is meant the extemporaneity of the performance.[53] *Premeditated* and *conventional* are terms of derision in the evaluation of a jazz performance.[54] To describe an improvisation as cliché ridden or as relying upon patterns is to *criticize* it. So, I would argue, the very language game of jazz practice draws distinctions between the derivative and the original that are important to the jazz community itself. Last, and the most rarely achieved of the desiderata Berliner adduces, is innovation in the sense of the creation of a new performance idiom.[55] This refers to the sort of extraparadigmatic accomplishment achieved by the likes of Louis Armstrong, Charlie Parker, Miles Davis, John Coltrane, and Ornette Coleman. The evolution of jazz practice and the coexistence of different performance idioms or performance schools contributes to there being competing musical values *within* the jazz community and a contest of interpretations that insures the vitality of the tradition and the viability of the music.

It is true that jazz is in some ways more vulnerable to colonization by the culture industry than is Western concert music (though current responses to the growing concern about the graying of the audience for classical music, as well as Adorno's own acknowledgment of the fetish character of this music, make even this a distinction in degree rather than kind). In many ways, the constraining, overly arranged character of some swing bands, the clichés of the hard bop or "soul jazz" movement, some of the banalities of the fusion movement and, today, what is called "smooth jazz," are testimony to jazz's distinctive vulnerability. Indeed, in the ever more prevalent smooth jazz format, the saxophones (and they are almost always soprano saxophones, à la Kenny G) *do* simulate sexual ecstasy, and do so to the rhythm of the electronic drum machine. Here we truly have an example of music in the age of (electro)mechanical reproduction and of a music that is a virtually unalloyed product of the culture industry. But the distinction between what, say, Ellington was doing, on the one hand, and the "machine-products of Tin Pan Alley," on the other, was well known and perceived circa 1936, the time of Adorno's first entry into the fray.[56] Already in 1954, André Hodeir offers an implicit critique of Adorno's claim that a jazz treatment can have only a merely decorative, artificial, or gratuitous effect.[57] Moreover, with respect to composers in the classical tradition such as Maurice Ravel, Frederick Delius, and Claude Debussy, whose works have harmonic affinities to jazz and who no doubt either directly or indirectly influenced Ellington's compositions, a strong case can be made, pace Adorno, for Ellington's harmonic and timbral originality vis-à-vis the impressionists.[58]

In short, Adorno lacks and fails to seek the vocabulary or spectacles requisite to bringing jazz into proper focus; he reads it as *lacking* a taken for granted good, rather than as *possessing* an alternative good, where the latter can be demonstrated to be a genuine musical value.[59] He is thus unable to render a perspicuous and noninvidious comparison between jazz and traditional concert music. For example, jazz and classical music arguably embody competing conceptions of sound, of what are musically appropriate tonal criteria. It is not here a case of one or the other being correct, but of competing conceptions of *the good*.

One of the central points that I should like to highlight now is that by emphasizing *composition* alone Adorno commits category errors in assessing the tradition of jazz practice.[60] In fact, because of these category errors he cannot even see this tradition *as a tradition*, as a set of practices with a developmental history given shape by progressive resolutions of aesthetic problems.[61] It is, no doubt, Adorno's compositionalist bias—privileging melody, harmony, and rhythm as *notated* over *performance*—that naturally inclines him to embrace what I earlier referred to as the "detachability thesis," which leads him to distinguish what he takes to be jazz's Tin Pan Alley center from what he takes to be its merely ornamental surface. This compositionalist bias, along with his corollary embrace of the "detachability thesis," conspire to force him to see jazz structure as—to borrow a phrase from the architect Robert Venturi—a "decorated shed," with the consequence that, musically speaking, all that can count for Adorno is the shed, which is to him a shack. The compositionalist paradigm that informs his way of hearing forces what is central to jazz to the aesthetic periphery. His rhetorical strategy is to effect an inversion by prefixing the expression *mere* to what is essential to jazz's aesthetic nature, to what is distinctive about it, thereby relegating what is essential to it to the artistically superficial and making what is only an occasion for it (for example, the popular song) its essential nature.

From this follow the blind spots that prevent Adorno from seeing, for example, timbral individuality (a performer's "sound") as a legitimate element of musical spontaneity. The frequently made observation that he largely ignores musical instrumentation per se points to a lacuna in Adorno's analysis of music in general,[62] but it is perhaps even more fatal to his jazz analysis than to his account of Western concert music; for in jazz practice, musical spontaneity is often constitutively mediated through idiosyncratic instrumental timbre or sound. In Ellington's classic "Concerto for Cootie" (*The Blanton-Webster Band*, RCA 5659-2-RB), the improvisation within this thoroughly composed piece is almost exclusively timbral, with Cootie Williams deploying a broad spectrum of tone colors.[63] To focus upon composition alone here is to thoroughly miss the point. More generally, a varied timbral palette and an expectation that soloists will develop a unique personal sound are acknowledged to be prominent among African-American musical values.[64] (Within a couple of bars, one can fairly easily distinguish the light and fluid alto saxophone of Johnny Hodges from the tartness of Jackie MacLean, or from the heavily blues-inflected sound of Cannonball Adderly; or, on the tenor, the breathiness of Ben Webster from the hardness at the center of the tone of John Coltrane; or, on the trumpet, the lyricism of Miles Davis from the jagged rhythmic sensibility of Dizzy Gillespie.) Moreover, vocalized tonal qualities and pitch inflections are staples of jazz practice.[65] Adorno can see such modifications of "objective" sound as at most a "whimpering which is helplessly testing itself."[66] Given that criteria for tone production tend to be standardized in the *classical* repertoire (at least in comparison to jazz), less is lost if in *its* analysis musical instrumentation itself is not thematized.[67] But such an elision is fatal to jazz analysis. This category error or failure to fuse horizons takes the form of not understanding *performance* and the evaluative categories relevant to it as the appropriate rubric for responding to jazz.[68] Adorno quite explicitly refused to acknowledge that the categories of performance and sound were those that were best suited for bringing into focus what is most distinctive about jazz and, in his graphocentrism, continued to subordinate them to that of composition.[69]

IV. A Path Not Taken

Jazz retains and foregrounds the improvisatory character of the social, economic, and cultural strategies of a people who, at critical junctures in their history, were forced to "make themselves up" as they went along. The tunes that Adorno maligns, that form the basis of much jazz performance, are often only *occasions* for improvisation. And those improvisations sometimes constitute a parodic *response* to the banality of those very tunes.[70] The relationship of a jazz treatment to the original tune is more analogous to the relationship of an analytical cubist painting to its subject matter than it is to the relationship of a "detachable" decorative overlay to an unadorned structure. The jazz improvisation treats the original's melodic and harmonic structure as raw material that it decomposes and reconfigures in novel and, if successful, *meaningful* ways. This bears deep affinities with what the critic Albert Murray discusses as the "riff style" of African Americans.[71] (There are also undoubtedly ties to the African aesthetic of creation for the moment, wherein masks are created to be "danced" in significant rituals and then not infrequently tossed aside.) Jazz's spontaneity and hence critical negativity must be sought here. Adorno's Frankfurt-School colleague Herbert Marcuse was much more sanguine about jazz's potential for critically negating "affirmative culture." Through its possibilities for revolutionizing perception, Marcuse includes jazz, along with the twelve-tone composition of Schoenberg's school, as a vehicle for the dissolution of the prevailing mode of perception.[72]

In "conceding" jazz's origins in the African-American folk tradition, Adorno goes on to say that "Negro spirituals ... were slave songs and *as such* combined the lament of unfreedom with its oppressed confirmation."[73] But are the songs of slaves necessarily slavish songs? Espousing a different basis for an aesthetic, Ralph Ellison insists that it is not the case that a slave cannot be a man but that "the enslaved really thought of themselves as *men* who had been unjustly enslaved."[74] For Adorno, art's truth registers the unhappy consciousness of a utopia denied. Autonomous music expresses the suffering attendant upon the recognition of the impossibility of the achievement of true individuality. For Ellison and Murray, art's truth lies in its heroic affirmation of individuality *in spite of* the chaos that threatens to swallow it. Referring to jazz musicians he knew as a boy, Ellison writes, "The delicate balance struck between strong individual personality and the group during those early jam sessions was a marvel of social organization. I had learned too that the end of all this discipline and technical mastery was the desire to express an affirmative way of life through its musical tradition and that this tradition insisted that each artist achieve his creativity within its frame. He must learn the best of the past, and add to it his personal vision. Life could be harsh, loud and wrong if it wished, but they lived it fully, and when they expressed their attitude toward the world it was with a fluid style that reduced the chaos of living to form."[75]

Murray suggests that "the nature of the creative process [is realized in an exemplary way in] the affirmative disposition toward the harsh actuality of human existence that is characteristic of the fully orchestrated blues statement."[76] Its affirmation is not, however, the affirmation of which Adorno accuses it. It is not that the "jazz subject," in Murray's and Ellison's estimation, is engaged in practices of self-deception, leading this subject to think that the social dialectic of the individual and the collective has finally reached a satisfactory resolution. For Murray's and Ellison's jazz subject, there are no illusions about having achieved utopia. The idea of satisfactory resolution has little purchase—life is "always wrong." This jazz subject faces with utmost clarity utopia's perpetual postponement. The struggle to wrest individuality, and hence meaning, from the chaos is never ending. And if life is always wrong, the incessant registering of suffering that Adorno endorses becomes a kind of "false utopianism" bereft of a true tragic sense of life, like deconstruction's ceaselessly repeated refrain of meaning's indeterminacy.

While it is beyond the scope of this essay to stage a full-fledged confrontation between these contrasting aesthetics, the Murray-Ellison position does have a hermeneutic advantage in this case. Something akin to the methodological role played by the principle of interpretive or hermeneutic charity is very much to the point here. I refer to the idea that, as a regulative principle, a field linguist has to assume that most of the assertions made in a yet-to-be-translated language are true, and a student of culture has to assume that most of the behavior in a culture of interest is, at least minimally, rational. Just as we should be skeptical of a translation procedure that renders most of the utterances in a target language false, or most of the behavior irrational, we should be suspicious of a cultural-aesthetic account that makes of an entire artistic tradition an aesthetic dysvalue, that renders it meaningless in the sense that its significance is exhausted by its systemic function. It redounds to the credit of the Murray-Ellison position that it allows the richness, integrity, and— dare I say it in these postmodern times—*humanity* of the jazz tradition to come to the fore and into focus, and to do so without our sacrificing critical standards. In making this claim I do not intend to give their position a blanket endorsement, for in its existential and ahistorical resignation before the absurdity of human existence it has the potential to encourage social and political, if not aesthetic, quietism. Moreover, and though this is by no means a necessary consequence of the position, I question some of Murray's judgments about which musical practices ought to be allowed into the "jazz canon." And Adorno's unwavering focus on sources of manipulation in late capitalist societies *is* all to the good, despite the questionably totalizing nature of his claims about the "liquidation of the individual." Still, like all theories, Adorno's aesthetic theory is implicated in a dialectics of blindness and insight. And when it comes to jazz, its blindness is all too apparent.

It is perhaps a genuine question whether jazz and Western classical music can be brought into focus at the same time. Nonetheless, if we are not prejudiced by narrowly compositionalist blinders, the demonstrable overlap in musical values between the two traditions—an intersection to which Adorno was not attentive and that is insured in part by jazz's hybrid status and perhaps to some extent by its Du Boisian "doubleness"—would enable a mediated transition from one focus to the other, and thus a fusion of hermeneutic horizons in the sense I would advocate. One element of the set of intersections would no doubt be the idea of *rubato*, or of taking liberties with tempo without changing the basic pulse. This is an acknowledged interpretive practice of classical musicians and is obviously a feature of the jazz repertoire. Another would be attentiveness to sonority—that is, to musical sound per se.[77] Indeed, if Adorno had not concentrated so single-mindedly on composition, he might have had a fuller appreciation not only of jazz but of the classical tradition as well.

II
THE UNFINISHED PROJECT

3
Critical Theory and the Politics of Recognition

Having considered how some historically influential responses to matters of cultural difference have contributed to framing the issues that I wish to address, I now proceed to develop and elaborate my position. As I suggested in chapter 1, I wish to sublate the positions associated with Arnold and Herder in order to develop a conception of a critically effective humanism that, unlike Theodor Adorno's, will also accommodate difference. I view Jürgen Habermas's Critical Theory, especially in its current stage of development, to be a step in that direction. Accordingly, for a more sophisticated approach by a Critical Theorist to the problem of preserving humanism in face of the fact of difference than Adorno provides—as well as one that does greater justice to the intersubjectively constituted nature of the self and of the role of language in it than do the noteworthy recent attempts mentioned in the Introduction of Luc Ferry and Alain Renaut—I turn to Jürgen Habermas. In a wide-ranging analysis of discursive democracy, Habermas has made it a central concern to find principled ways of acknowledging the claims of the distinct cultural groups comprising modern societies. I find in Habermas's work an important, though ultimately limited, resource in my attempt to reconstruct humanism in the wake of the postmodernist critique of subjectivity.

I make my argument in two stages, devoting this chapter to the first and chapter 4 to the second. I begin it by considering a model of conversation inspired by Habermas's well-known conception of practical discourse. (Though Habermas has been roundly criticized for being unable to accommodate matters of difference within such a conception, I have argued elsewhere that, though there is a level of analysis at which he is vulnerable to such a charge, his characterization of ideal practical discourse does nevertheless have considerable potential for helping us to structure public dialogues that pay respectful attention to difference.[1]) The second stage of my argument—described in the following chapter—complements this by articulating a more hermeneutically informed model of conversation than Habermas provides. I begin my discussion in this chapter with a brief summary of Habermas's discourse theory of normative legitimacy, then turn to consider some of his recent remarks made in response to critics, and finally consider his explicit intervention into current debates on multiculturalism and the recognition of cultural minorities. It is in this latter intervention that he exploits the resources of his conception of discursive democracy for the respectful accommodation of matters of difference.

To stage one: if empirical or scientific speech aims at truth, then practical discourse or social, political, and moral discussion aims at what Habermas calls a "generalizable interest."[2] Habermas denies that all needs or interests are merely subjective and, therefore, that they would necessarily lead to irreconcilable conflict when groups with differing interests must share the same social space. Those interests that *are* irreconcilable in this way he refers to as "particular interests." Opposed to purely particular interests, generalizable interests for Habermas are those that can be communicatively shared, those that can reflect an unforced consensus about what *all* could want. (A genuinely particular interest is one that fails to be shareable in this way.)

It is important to emphasize that generalizable interests are not simply found or discovered, but are rather shaped and forged in discussions among, in the ideal case, all persons concerned.[3] Both the social norms regulating and reflecting interests or needs and the interpretation of the needs themselves form the subject matter of practical discussion. That is, need interpretations are among the items of discussion. For Habermas, there are certain requirements that ideally govern such discussions, the requirements of what he calls the "ideal speech situation." These requirements are meant to guarantee that a participant need not accept any interpretation of her needs in which she cannot recognize what she truly wants. Such a dialogue situation is structured then by conditions that insure that no participant be coerced into giving her consent to an assertion against her will, conditions that insure that everyone is free to engage in various speech acts—to make assertions, to challenge others' assertions, to question, to reveal their inner feelings, to suggest rules for the discussion, and so on. Also included among the ground rules for the ideal form of such a discussion are conditions insuring the freedom to move from a given way of framing a discussion to increasingly abstract ways of framing the discussion and to *alternative* ways of framing a discussion—that is, to call into question and modify the originally accepted conceptual framework. For example, in a discussion structured by a particular normative ethical framework, participants are free to move to a metaethical discourse that calls that framework into question. Since the interpretation of needs and interests is constrained by the discursive framework in which those interpretations are articulated, it is important that the chosen framework not be inappropriate to express what we really want. For example, could women's need for self-respecting fulfillment find an appropriate interpretation in a framework structured by a simple opposition between responsible domesticity and corrupting ambition? This feature of practical discourse, its reflexive aspect, is important for my purposes because it allows for the negotiation or forging of a framework that might accommodate seemingly opposed points of view. This points to the importance of there being a common language in which the needs of everyone concerned can be given a voice and gain a respectful hearing.

The point then of practical discussion is to search for ways to frame the needs of everyone concerned in such a way that common or generalizable interests can be found. The idea of generalizable interests then suggests *one* possible basis for the discursive construction of community, albeit perhaps of a rather thin form of community founded on overlapping interests.[4] Nevertheless, it is important to keep in mind that on this view, an interest is *presumed* generalizable or shareable until proven particular, and that proof would have to take the form of a dialogue whose outcome cannot be judged a priori.

As useful as Habermas's account is, my project goes beyond it in that I shall claim that what he calls sheerly particular interests (or now existential or ethical commitments) are *also* amenable to conversational negotiation, a negotiation whose terminus need not be consensus, but rather mutual understanding and edification. For my purposes, consensus is *not* projected as an ideal, except at the metalevel where participants in discourse collaboratively seek to articulate and acknowledge mutually available and noninvidious descriptions of each other. For all of his commendable relativization of the distinction, when discussing practical discourse Habermas remains mired in the false dilemma of seeing our options as limited to *either* a generalizable, discursively redeemable, consensus *or* a sheerly particular, idiosyncratic, private, and ultimately pluralistic congeries of fundamental commitments. But, as I shall argue, the achievements of mutual understanding and edification need be neither. Though Habermas has among his own theoretical resources the notions of "aesthetic" and "therapeutic" critique, he does not seem fully to consider their ramifications for the idea of practical discourse.[5] Nor does he exploit them to illuminate what can be achieved via communication processes between existential or ethical positions.

For a more perspicuous account of the promise and the limitations of Habermas's project insofar as they bear on my interest, I turn to some of his recent work, in which he responds to criticisms prompted by the increasing salience of matters of cultural diversity. Habermas refers to the setting in which current philosophical thought must find its purchase as "postmetaphysical"; by this he refers to the historical stage at which cultural traditions have become reflective in the sense that competing worldviews cannot simply *assert* themselves against each other, but rather are compelled to *justify* their claims to validity self-critically.[6] In acknowledging the explicitly *interpretive* self-understanding of modern, postmetaphysical world conceptions, Habermas's understanding of *metaphysics* is very close to Martin Heidegger's in that it refers to systems of thought that do *not* acknowledge their interpretive status and that dogmatically claim to reflect an "order of things" that is legislative for human will and action. For Habermas, it is important to distinguish the postmetaphysical condition of modernity from the putative stage of *postmodernity*. For while in the former case competing worldviews raise reciprocal validity claims understood to be subject to redemption, in the latter case competing worldviews would be understood to be enacted in indifference to or with suspicion toward claims to validity.

Modern worldviews, then, have associated with them the reflexive awareness that there are alternatives to them, and hence reasons not to be dogmatic about their status. Habermas adds, explicitly, that such world conceptions also make validity claims. But in what sense can they be understood to do this, and what scope can we give their claims for validity? Given Habermas's current distinction between the right and the good—between questions concerning moral obligation and questions concerning the nature of the good life—and given that the plurality of answers to questions concerning the good are anchored in the plurality of worldviews, the validity claims raised by world interpretations cannot be reduced to any of Habermas's traditional triumvirate of truth, truthfulness, and rightness. What then are these validity claims about?

Habermas, in an appreciative discussion of John Rawls, refers to modern worldviews as being subject to the "burdens of reason."[7] However, such worldviews cannot of course be subject to the pressure of reasons in the abstract. Reasons and reasoning must proceed from premises, and if the relevant premises are in turn anchored in comprehensive worldviews, different and competing worldviews will give us different and competing premises (except, of course, in the special case of an overlapping consensus). That is, comprehensive worldviews might be more appropriately understood as the frameworks *within* which validity claims are made. In order for Habermas to counter successfully a Rortyian ironical redescription of modern worldviews as simply "contingent final vocabularies," none of which can make a noncircular appeal for its own justification, Habermas must say more about what the redemption of these claims to validity would consist in. Given his wider commitments, this would take the form of articulating the connection between learning processes, on the one hand, and world disclosure, on the other—a connection that Habermas criticized Heidegger for failing to respect. And Habermas would make this connection, in part, by assuming the tradition invariance of the identification of the problems addressed by learning processes, by presuming that there is a nontrivial level of description at which all social actors mutually identify the *same* set of problems across cultural traditions. This is, I shall argue, one of the problems in Habermas's more recent work, and it is a problem whose recognition would lead us to question his strategy for unpacking what is meant by maintaining that world interpretations make validity claims.

Habermas seems unwilling to acknowledge the extent to which different socially and culturally defined groups may not face the same problems or may not find the same problems to be *salient*. As a consequence, he can conceive of a comparative evaluation of competing tradition-based resources for problem solving only by reference to a *commonly held* and *defined* set of problems rather than with reference to how well the resources provided by competing traditions measure up with respect to a set of problems identified in ways that are relatively peculiar to a given tradition. Thus, in his response to Alasdair MacIntyre, Habermas seems mistakenly to believe that we can have rational evaluation of competing traditions *or* noninvariant social problems, but not both. Accordingly, he is obliged to understand, again mistakenly in my view, MacIntyre's position on the rational evaluation of traditions as implying the necessity of irrational conversion when a given tradition comes to prefer resources from another tradition to its own, as opposed to that tradition's understanding its resources as having been *rationally* discredited in terms of its own standards of rationality.[8]

I *do* appreciate Habermas's evocation of a bilingually extended identity in the course of his polemic against MacIntyre. Yet, rather than describe this "fusion of horizons" in terms of a "convergence between 'our' perspective and 'theirs' guided by learning processes," as he does, I would describe it in terms of a convergence on or a consolidation of what I shall in chapter 4 refer to as a "situated metalanguage," a collaboratively forged language that permits noninvidious and mutually acknowledged representations of self and other.[9] It is only in terms of such a metalanguage that the different perspectives of "ours" and "theirs" can first even be articulated and common problems, where they exist, identified. Only then can we talk about the possibility of convergence guided by learning processes. Again, Habermas maintains—very problematically I think— that social and cultural problems are shared and identified in the same way across cultural/linguistic boundaries. Or that "our" perspective and "theirs" will always be operating in the same register. Or that such problems are self-announcing across cultural/linguistic horizons.

As a way of acknowledging the difficulty of rationally adjudicating competing conceptions of the good under contemporary conditions of globalization and multiculturalism, Habermas invokes a distinction between the moral and the ethical, which corresponds roughly to his earlier distinction between the domain of generalizable interests and that of particularity, respectively, but without the latter distinction's invidious intent. The term *moral* refers to what can be justified universally, while *ethical* refers to what has only local purchase.[10] But there is considerable ambiguity in Habermas's deployment of this distinction. Sometimes he writes as if "morality" captures the rational core of competing conceptions of the good, their "overlapping consensus." In this sense, morality would operate in a different register from the good or from competing ethical claims; morality would thus be neutral with respect to such claims. The moral and the ethical would have their purchase at different categorial levels and hence, in principle, would not conflict. Accordingly, the universality of the moral point of view, where one is concerned with questions of the rightness of procedures and their outcomes, would not conflict with the particularity of the ethical point of view, where one is concerned with questions of authenticity and existential self-understanding.

Yet Habermas acknowledges the possibility of instances where questions of morality and ethics do not remain neatly separated in different categorial or conceptual registers—cases where morality is not neutral with respect to the good, cases where an acknowledged moral obligation conflicts in a presumably irreconcilable way with an existential self-understanding, or with what has been called an "identity related difference."[11] A paradigm case of this sort of conflict would be the experience of citizens of a procedural liberal democracy whose self-understanding is informed by theocratic fundamental commitments. But first, to what extent could such a moral claim be acknowledged as placing a person whose interest in authenticity is not accommodated by it under an *obligation* to respect its validity? How could a person or group be *morally* required to recognize a norm that entailed abdicating their interest in cultural authenticity? This question is especially pressing, given Habermas's account of what constitutes a morally justified norm—that is, one that fulfills what he calls "condition U." Condition U is fulfilled when "*All* affected can accept the consequences and the side effects its *general* observance can be anticipated to have for the satisfaction of *everyone's* interests (and these consequences are preferred to those of known alternative possibilities for regulation)."[12] If the vocabulary in which a person's identity is made salient cannot be accommodated in a moral consensus, do we want to say that such vocabularies are not morally relevant, that they should be registered only at the level of the good? The problem is that Habermas wants a principled way of accommodating matters of difference by reserving a conceptual space for them in his architectonic. But as he himself acknowledges, such matters often refuse to remain on the reservation. When faced with a conflict between the right and the good, how do we rationally adjudicate it? The framework for such an adjudication cannot of course be that of moral discourse, for that would be blatantly question begging. In cases where it has become clear that we have to do with conflict between competing ethical positions drawn from different contexts of self-understanding, as in the abortion controversy, Habermas has recourse to the language of fair compromise and, perhaps, though he does not mention it in this context, of aesthetic critique.[13] However, the issue that concerns us here is not, at least on its face, one of competing ethical commitments, but rather the hybrid competition of the moral versus the ethical. If principle U does not have the status of a trump card, are we to entertain the plausibility of an "existential opting out of the moral"? Does the absence of a rationally guaranteed bulwark against such "seepage," the absence of a metaframework for addressing such issues, point to an important lacuna in Habermas's thought?

One response that Habermas might make to what I have here suggested is to point out that identity is itself conversationally negotiable, that one can always raise the question of whether social or cultural identity can be reconfigured without being destroyed in such a way that it may harmonize more completely with a reformed moral consensus. The point would be, then, to *enlarge* and *expand* the overlapping consensus through reciprocal, mutual discursive reflection on the existential claims brought to the table. Accordingly, Habermas might say that we should be as wary of dogmatically using identity as a trump card as I suggested we might be about principle U. And, as I shall indicate later, not only would I have a great deal of sympathy with this response, but it is also consistent with my reading of Habermas's position on the conversational forging and negotiation of interests. But his discussion of this matter does not take this form.

Rather, what he seems to suggest here is that I would be mistaken to understand him to want a principled distinction or a distinction *in kind* between the moral and the ethical, a distinction that is more than an analytical distinction between different aspects or facets of an issue, a distinction that allows for an a priori parsing of *which is which*.[14] There is no principled distinction then between what counts as the *content* of a moral, as opposed to ethical, issue. Such a distinction will have to await the outcome of a discourse. This relativization of the distinction between the moral and the ethical would then permit Habermas to say that identity-articulating vocabularies are not morally irrelevant qua identity-articulating vocabularies, but that some such vocabularies may, as a matter of fact, "pass" (as being generalizable or as warranting public acknowledgment) and be allowed into the club, and some will not. It cannot be decided a priori which aspects of a tradition-bound self-understanding can be incorporated into a moral consensus and which aspects will end up being relegated to the merely existential.

However, from the moral point of view, from the vantage point that most engages Habermas's interest, existential or ethical claims are *at best* candidates for generalization; in the idiom of the philosophy of science, they are claims emerging from the context of generation that are candidates for success within the context of justification. This has two troubling consequences. First, this focus upon the moral, which in turn is understood in terms of what can command general assent, tends to marginalize material that fails to meet that standard and thereby threatens to deprive us of world-disclosive and world-informing resources that we might not otherwise entertain as live options. Habermas's focus is too restricted to give us a satisfying account of how we can fully exploit the transformative possibilities in cultural material that lies beyond the confines of a potential moral consensus. That is, his base is too cramped for what concerns me in this book. My idea of pedagogical representations, developed in the next chapter as part of an attempt to do justice to the *public* salience of such cultural material, is intended as an emendation of Habermas's account.

Second, and perhaps despite his intentions, the moral/ethical distinction ends up informing invidious distinctions among cultural identities. Insofar as inharmonious views of the good life are among the interests to be regulated in moral discourse, consensus will require, in the operational sense, a "shearing off" of the irreconcilable residue. Will this process not always play itself out in favor of participants who are willing to make the requisite distinctions allowing for a separation of the right from the good? Or whose notion of the good furnishes an autonomous sphere for the right? Habermas avers that moral discourse requires "distancing oneself from the contexts of life with which one's identity is inextricably interwoven."[15] Yet some are thereby called upon to distance themselves more and in different ways than are others. Will not potential participants who are unwilling to make the requisite distinctions, or for whom those distinctions do not represent live options, be asked to give up more in terms of their identity-informing commitments than others? For instance, those whose ethical self-understanding is such that it is only with extreme difficulty and at considerable existential expense that they can entertain a principled distinction between the right and the good would be at a distinct disadvantage when compared to cosmopolitan liberals. It will not do to make it a condition of participation that one avow such willingness, or disavow unwillingness to do so. If it did, how could Habermas envision the possibility of someone who in the course of ingenuous participation acknowledged a moral obligation that he could not fulfill under pain of self-abnegation? Surely, Habermas would not claim that all of those who view this distinction with suspicion can be as easily dismissed as can members of what he calls "fundamentalist cultures."[16] And for similar reasons, Habermas cannot say "we" are all moderns now. It is starting to look suspiciously like what is at issue here are two competing conceptions of the good where one is given pride of place, rather than a matter of the right versus a conception of the good.

In a related objection, Thomas McCarthy points out that questions of the right cannot be completely separated from questions of the good, from the very values and interests whose harmonization Habermas's conception of practical discourse was devised to secure.[17] As a consequence, the principles in terms of which competing values are to be adjudicated could themselves be just as subject to dispute as are the values in contention. Habermas's reply to McCarthy seems to beg the question in that it presupposes the very distinction between good-based reasons and right-derived reasons that McCarthy has questioned.[18] And given Habermas's own admission that the condition of multiculturalism has the effect of driving questions of the right to more and more abstract levels,[19] we should look again at the rational potential and resources inherent in the claims for the good that are posited in the worldviews that compete for our attention.

I would not shy away then, as is Habermas's wont, from genuine conflicts between versions of the good. Moreover, taking versions of the good per se as commanding our rational appraisal will help to answer the question I posed to Habermas earlier—namely, in what sense do world conceptions make validity claims? I believe they are validity claims in a more indirect way than are truth or rightness claims, but that they are validity claims nonetheless; they are not immune to criticism. One can always ask, What way of framing the world is good, given the projects a people is engaged in, given their interpretations of who they are, and given the people with whom they are likely to interact? (The move away from the merely local is especially important given the globalization of society.) Understanding modern worldviews to have such a hypothetical status is another way of saying that the confrontation of world-disclosing frameworks may throw into relief, in a symmetrical fashion, what each side may come to acknowledge as defects in its practices, aspects of its practices whose interrogation and possible transformation may allow its social agents to flourish more fully.

My discussion thus far has been pursued for the most part within the register of ethics and culture. Habermas's concern, however, lies primarily at the level of law and politics. This point of departure helps to explain his work's relative indifference to some of the concerns I raise. However, the kinds of question this orientation inclines him to ask, the site from which he chooses to begin, implicate him (unavoidably perhaps) in a dialectic of

Critical Theory and the Politics of Recognition

insight and blindness. What gets eclipsed thereby is an adequate acknowledgment of the potential for reciprocal learning processes that are fueled by the cognitive, moral, and aesthetic resources of competing existential/ethical contexts.

The concern that authorizes this restricted angle of vision is explicit in Habermas's recent intervention in the "politics of recognition." It takes place in an essay entitled "Struggles for Recognition in the Democratic Constitutional State," a response to Charles Taylor's reflections on multiculturalism. In the essay, Habermas pursues the question of whether the universalist emphasis upon *individual* rights necessarily conflicts with *group-based* demands for recognition. Given Habermas's current concern with practical reason's role not only in the justification of norms but also in the *application* of moral norms in concrete situations,[20] he can now explicitly maintain that not only is it a mistake to construe the universalistic interest in granting priority to basic rights as being at odds with the public recognition of concrete forms of cultural expression, but that such an interest actually *requires* the encouragement and promotion of the viability of such cultural expression. He holds that not only does an individualistically construed theory of rights not conflict with demands for the recognition of collective identities, but that such a theory, correctly understood, actually requires such recognition, for among the protections afforded individuals must be the recognition and protection of the intersubjective contexts from which their identities are forged and which sustain their capacities for agency.[21] For example, consistent with this concern would be the institutionalization of maternal leave policies to address the factual preconditions for women to be able to take advantage of equal opportunity. And Habermas accordingly endorses extensive protections of nondominant cultural groups in the form of government subsidy of minority cultural initiatives, various infrastructural benefits, and so on.[22] In this way he splits the difference between liberalism and communitarianism. While seeking to protect basic rights he nevertheless, in Herderian fashion, acknowledges the communal basis of identity formation.

Full autonomy requires not only the equal freedom to realize private life projects, but also the freedom for conversational participation in and negotiation of the social and legal norms regulating the application of principles of equality. Hence, Habermas speaks of the internal connection between public and private autonomy.[23] Here is where the conversational negotiation of need interpretation that I mentioned earlier comes into view and where the implication for need satisfaction of the acceptance of norms is thematized. Because there is an internal relationship between respect for individuals and respect (in the sense of legal recognition and protection) for the cultural sources of their identity formation, the Kantian notion of moral equality has to be extended to the equality of respect accorded to cultures within which individual identities are forged.[24] On this account, then, the protection of cultural groups is underwritten by legal demands for the protection of individual autonomy and not, as Habermas thinks Taylor believes, from estimations of the presumed excellence of one's culture of origin.[25]

The legal systems in democratic constitutional states are codetermined by the universalistic procedures of posttraditional morality from "above" and by the cultural self-understanding of particular legal communities from "below."[26] So the application of universalistic procedures is shaped by a nation's cultural self-understanding, by its political culture or ethos. Yet insofar as the political culture that informs the articulation of legal systems should remain neutral with respect to the various ethical and cultural communities comprising the nation, the former axis of integration, political integration, can be analytically uncoupled from the "thicker" social integration manifested in the "local" solidarities of particular cultural and ethnic affiliation. However, as a nation becomes more multicultural, the "complexion" of the overlapping consensus—the agreement underwriting the political integration that undergirds the allegiance to constitutional democracy—will be altered.[27] This might be described as a "capillary effect" whereby cultural material from newly included social and cultural groups rises to refashion the identity of the political community as the context for the application of universalistic principles changes.

Since the moral pressure for group recognition is fueled by the categorical demand to protect and enable individual autonomy, the moral significance of group recognition is determined by the degree to which such recognition furthers or hinders such autonomy. This puts Habermas in a position to endorse the public recognition of social and cultural difference but also (and correctly, in my view) to worry about the oppressive potential of what can be called "identity politics"—that is, the tendency to embrace overly prescriptive, and therefore restrictive, accounts of ethnic/cultural membership and to assume that such membership is definitive of one's identity.[28]

This is all to the good. But it is important to note that only two sorts of learning process are authorized by this approach. First, there are those "corrective" processes that encourage the requisite transformations of political self-understanding to accede to the "base line" perspective of acknowledging the principled distinction between the right and the good. The cosmopolitan West has already undergone such a process. We know from Habermas's larger project that he adduces rational reconstructive arguments to demonstrate the developmental superiority of the standpoint of modern procedural universalism.[29] So this clearly asymmetrical learning process is one to be undergone by "them," not by "us." Next are the processes that result in alterations to the discursively achieved collective will formation, alterations produced as a result of arguments made by previously marginalized groups to transform the way in which universalistic norms are applied. (The need interpretations that inform these alterations are embedded in concrete social and cultural contexts; they are shaped by diverse cultural self-understandings and commitments.) It remains the case, however, that only under the aspect of that cultural material's relevance for fashioning a public political consensus does it come into our purview. Thus, in neither case is there thematized a conceptual space where genuinely symmetrical *cross-cultural* learning processes that exceed the political (so defined) can occur.

The way that Habermas frames his discussion, then, has the effect of bracketing concrete cultural self-understandings and modes of world disclosure—and the interpretive and evaluative discourses addressing them—except insofar as they are relevant to questions of political and legal regulation. Now I grant that his principled exclusion of evaluative presumptions, his taking them out of play for the purposes of determining social recognition, is a salutary gesture insofar as it avoids placing marginalized social and cultural groups on the defensive when making their demands for social recognition. Here Habermas explicitly distances himself from Taylor's invocation of the presumed excellence of a "petitioner's" culture of origin. I have, however, two concerns about this framework. First, as I have been suggesting throughout, it prevents our bringing into focus the reciprocal learning processes guided by critical evaluations within the register of world disclosure. This deprives us of the sort of challenging encounter that edifies us concerning the nature and limits of our own presuppositions, that challenges us to *re*view the world we had taken for granted. It deprives us, for instance, of a lively sense of the variety of humanly viable conceptions of the moral relationship of the individual to the community, or of the relationship between the cognitive and the symbolic, or of the relationships between religion and a variety of domains such as art, science, politics, and the law. That is, the way in which Habermas frames his discussion fails to do justice to his own assertions regarding the validity claims made by worldviews.

Second, this way of framing the discussion underplays the significance of the fact that such marginalized groups must, according to Habermas, mount an *argument* that the prevailing institutionalization of the principle of equal rights fails to accommodate their legitimate need interpretations. Thus, rational evaluations of legitimacy and of claimed failures to accommodate legitimate needs have to be made. Habermas rightly emphasizes not only the unavoidable necessity of all those affected by a given norm having the opportunity to give voice to the implications of its general observance for their needs and identities (within which, to be sure, the signs of social and cultural specificity are clearly to be discerned), but also the necessity of *justifying* their assessments of those implications in public discussion.[30] So there is clearly an evaluative moment that is *internally* related to the public acknowledgment of a failure to accommodate a legitimate need. Habermas has himself explicitly thematized this evaluative moment elsewhere when arguing for the internal connection between understanding and evaluation.[31] So, despite his attempt to distinguish himself from Taylor, an evaluative moment is unavoidably implicated in his position.

In addition to the concerns that I have raised here, it could be argued that a more *explicit* focus on the role played by the cultural materials involved in this evaluative transaction, and on the fact that modes of argumentation and of self-presentation are also strongly culturally indexed, would strengthen Habermas's explicitly *political* theory in the face of critiques (such as Iris Marion Young's) aimed at his overly restrictive assumptions concerning the style of political discourse. Young—whose work I take up in chapter 5—makes the claim against Habermas's conception of deliberative democracy that it fails to attend to the "cultural specificity of deliberative practices."[32] Her discussion suggests the ways in which storytelling and narrative can make salient, in ways that strictly argumentative discourse cannot, the value commitments and underlying structures of meaning that inform the very need interpretations that are subject to political negotiation. Moreover, a greater sensitivity to the cultural register per se would render Habermas's theory more in tune with the actual hermeneutic interpretive processes that should operate at the heart of constitutional discourse itself in multicultural societies.[33]

For Habermas, questions of "difference" remain questions of "application," of the application in varying contexts of universalistic principles. Aspects of difference not relevant to questions of application, the aspects that speak to issues of meaning and world disclosure, are effectively taken out of play. Habermas's categorial framework cannot accommodate the dimensions of difference that would give those contexts that are meaning-informing per se a public character. He restricts his purview primarily to what can garner a public consensus in favor of its recognition and consequent protection. In doing so, he occludes the hermeneutic learning processes fueled by confrontations with alien cultural materials—aesthetic, metaphysical, ethical, and so on—that, while perhaps protected, are not engaged to see what radical self-questioning they may provoke. It is one thing, and a very good thing indeed, to protect the stranger. It is quite another to risk learning from her.

4
Situated Cosmopolitanism

> The unity of a literary language is not a unity of a single, closed language system, but is rather a highly specific unity of several "languages" that have established contact and mutual recognition with each other.
>
> —Mikhail Bakhtin, *The Dialogic Imagination*

In chapter 3, I developed the first stage of my argument for a postmetaphysical humanism in the form of a response to the recent work of Jürgen Habermas. I was led to seek a broader scope for the public salience of matters of difference than his framework allows. Habermas's concern is with harmonizing the interests of persons sharing the same polity. My own interest is in a broader conversation, the ideal virtual dialogue that can take place interculturally—though with contemporary processes of globalization it too can take place within a single polity—and that ranges beyond the political per se. For all of the manifest virtues of Habermas's conception of discursive democracy, and especially its concern for the respectful accommodation of matters of difference registered in its challenge to the strand of contemporary liberalism that eschews public acknowledgment of the distinct cultural identities of members of multicultural societies, I have argued that his intervention is not fully satisfactory. It does not offer a sufficiently distinct alternative to the liberal conception of an overlapping consensus, and, accordingly, Habermas's framework cannot fully exploit the transformative potential inherent in cultural material that lies beyond the borders of such a consensus. Moreover, as a consequence of this, I have argued that Habermas is unable to redeem adequately his own assertion that modern cultural worldviews implicitly raise validity claims.

And now, the second stage of my argument. If we suitably modify Habermas's conception of practical discourse by attending to its manifest hermeneutic inadequacies, its equivocations about matters of cultural identity, and its problematic distinction between the moral and the ethical, the possibility of a richer conception of community comes into view. Put simply, communicative discourse should be informed by an ideal of mutual understanding. The achievement of this mutual understanding requires what can be called a "reversibility of perspectives," not in the sense of my collapsing myself into you or you into me, but in the sense that I try to understand—but not necessarily agree with—what you take your life to be about, and that you do the same for me. I hasten to point out, pace some postmodernist social thinkers such as Iris Marion Young (whose work I consider more fully in chapter 5), that the reversibility of perspectives does not require mutual identification or even necessarily take such an identification to be an ideal. What Young rejects, for example, is the ideal of actually *adopting* the other's point of view, the other's culture and values; she rejects the presumption of having "gone or of being able to go native."[1] And she thinks that such mutual identification, which Young identifies with the reversibility of perspectives, is an illicit attempt to find commonness, and is either impossible (because of unbridgeable differences) or undesirable (because it would reproduce a homogeneity at odds with diversity).[2]

Yet such reversibility does not threaten to extinguish difference, though it may well *transform* difference. As we engage in a reversibility of perspectives, our experiential horizon, composed of background assumptions and values that shape our interpretations of the world, can be broadened in such a way that those assumptions and values can be situated as just one possibility alongside the different assumptions and values of a formerly unfamiliar culture; as J. G. von Herder has perceptively demonstrated, they can be situated as shaping just one way to be human. The result of the conversation that effects the incorporation of a novel understanding of the world would be what Hans-Georg Gadamer would call a "fusion of horizons" in which something *new* gets acknowledged. With the notion "fusion of horizons" Gadamer refers to the product of an interaction between a text and a reader or between members of two cultures such that a new meaning gets produced, a meaning that cannot be reduced to the horizon of either of the two cultures but incorporates some of each. In a fusion of horizons, our vocabulary for discussing political, social, and cultural life alike gets expanded.

Respectful understanding of another is *nonstrategic, critical* understanding. We want to put ourselves in a position to take seriously the reasons and the reasoning of the other. Though this will require an appreciation for how things look from the inside of the other's hermeneutic situation, it does not require, nor does it encourage, identification with the other—that is, the *adoption* of her point of view. None of this will require that we be able fully to insert ourselves, cognitively and emotionally, into the "perspective of . . . others differently located."[3] Instead, what is involved is a *mutual* dialectic of recognition where each side has an understanding of what the other *takes* herself to be doing, an understanding of the descriptions under which the other would place her own actions, and each side can raise critical questions about the other's position. Each side will be able to issue to the other reciprocal rejoinders. If understanding required the adoption of the other's perspective, how could we ever *criticize* the other? I shall address in more detail this nonrelativistic moment of critique presently.

My understanding of the other is linguistically mediated through a language that is intelligibly related to my own. I cannot simply "jump over" my own language completely into the other's; but this does not necessarily lead us down the path to the opposite "vice," namely, an objectionable ethnocentrism or competing ethnocentricities. Through mutually respectful interaction, parties engaged in practical discourse attempt to forge a language that is neither just the self's nor just the other's, neither solely mine nor yours.[4] We attempt to forge a common language, or sets of common languages, that will have as categories dimensions of experience that reflect the space of human concerns and possibilities. In order to engage in a mutual location or triangulation of each other, we will require a language whose constituting categories *beg questions from neither side*. The point is to forge a language that permits a *mutually* acknowledged and perspicuous representation of what is salient in each position, a language within which the difference between contrasting positions is, at least initially, noninvidiously represented. For a given dimension of experience—for example, that having to do with our understanding of the moral relationship of the individual to the community, the relationship between the cognitive and the symbolic, or the relationships among religion and a variety of domains such as art, science, politics, and the law—we then seek to indicate the *alternative* positions on a common scale that you and I, ego and alter, occupy.

I wish now to specify further the nature of this to-be-forged language. I understand this project to involve the sort of expanded vocabulary that I would view as a type of metalanguage. It would be a "situated metalanguage" in that it would be comprised of redescriptions of all parties participating in the negotiation; these redescriptions would be acceptable to all, and would mediate the differences each wishes the other to recognize.[5] And there can be at least as many of these situated metalanguages as there will be dyadic cultural encounters. Further, none should be understood as a final vocabulary, as a final or unrevisable accomplishment. The consolidation of such a metalanguage would represent the practical achievement of having forged sufficient common ground for the purposes of mutual recognition at hand. The status that this metalanguage has in my project is both that of an *ideal* and of an *idealization*—an *ideal* in that like Habermas's celebrated "ideal speech situation" it counterfactually projects the *equal opportunity* of parties on both sides of the negotiation to contest and consent to proposed frameworks, and an *idealization* in that, for purposes of exposition, my discussion of it may at times *provisionally* abstract from the fact that all cultures are sites of struggle over what form an adequate representation of them should assume. As an ideal it can serve as a point of appeal in terms of which we can criticize and analyze distortions (as the result of the operation of power, for instance).

Except in its descriptive sense, where it is opposed to theism, humanism has almost always been understood as an ideal, as an articulation of that to which it is proper that we aspire. The point of this metalanguage is to enable noninvidious and mutually critical cross-cultural representation. Still more fundamental, such a metalanguage or its functional equivalent serves as the coordinate system in terms of which difference can be represented; for the intelligibility of the very *idea* of cultural difference requires a common grid wherein the points of difference can even be *articulated* as different perspectives on a given issue, let alone reconciled. The point of such a representation is to find what Gadamer calls *die Sache*, or the fundamental concern about which "we" and "they" differ but not differ so much that there is no overlap in paradigmatic examples. (The absence of such overlap would be the point of incommensurability.)

The scheme that I have in mind can be represented by the following diagram, where for each row of the n x 1 matrix of *Sachen*, there are two contrasting n x 1 matrices of response, the v's and u's, each such matrix representing n competing positions on a given Sache *within* a given culture, the Bakhtinian heteroglossia within cultures:

$$
\begin{array}{ccc}
v_{11} & Sache_1 & u_{11} \\
\bullet & & \bullet \\
\bullet & & \bullet \\
\bullet & & \bullet \\
v_{n1} & & u_{n1} \\
v_{12} & Sache_2 & u_{12} \\
\bullet & & \bullet \\
\bullet & & \bullet \\
\bullet & & \bullet \\
v_{n2} & & u_{n2} \\
v_{13} & Sache_3 & u_{13} \\
\bullet & & \bullet \\
\bullet & & \bullet \\
\bullet & & \bullet \\
v_{n3} & & u_{n3} \\
& \bullet & \\
& \bullet & \\
& \bullet & \\
v_{1n} & Sache_n & u_{1n} \\
\bullet & & \bullet \\
\bullet & & \bullet \\
\bullet & & \bullet \\
v_{nn} & & u_{nn} \\
\end{array}
$$

It is undoubtedly the case that the Sachen cannot be defined, except vaguely, in complete independence of the contrasting sets of responses to them. To some extent they are what gets referred to in one or another distinctive cultural vocabulary. On the other hand, the Sachen are not to be understood to be exclusively or exhaustively defined by any such vocabulary; this would be the situation of incommensurability that would subvert the very idea of a common metalanguage. Further, the contrasting vocabularies represented by the u's and v's that are featured in the metalinguistic scheme comprise not only what people explicitly say but also the implicit background assumptions and practices that sustain the

Situated Cosmopolitanism

patterns of meaning that are deployed in what is explicitly said, background assumptions of the sort that Charles Taylor calls "intersubjective meanings."[6] Moreover, just as the various strands of a given culture's response to a particular Sache—as represented by the various rows of the u and v matrices corresponding to that topic of concern—will be subjected by indigenous agents to competing assessments of relative priority and weight, there will be different estimations of the priority and weight of the various Sachen themselves by members of contrasting cultures.

In thinking about the first case of interpretive conflict, the case of heteroglossia internal to a culture's boundaries, it might be useful to think of each u or v matrix—each of which represents a culturally distinctive response to a particular topic—as representing a system that reflects shared points of appeal. These distinctive manifestations of shared points of appeal are in part what give cultures their distinctiveness. Given that they are linguistically articulated, jointly shared symbolic expressions, they also set the terms for culturally sanctioned and mutually intelligible agreement and disagreement (as different social actors within a given culture give the various rows of the corresponding matrices differing priorities, weights, and interpretations). The rows of each such matrix, then, collectively structure the relatively porous system within which cultural negotiation takes place.

For an example of this first case, of internal heteroglossia, we can turn to a recent, rather innovative ethnography that can serve to illustrate a number of the points I wish to make in this chapter.[7] In her study of the Meratus Dayaks, a marginalized people in the Indonesian rain forest, Anna Tsing offers compelling evidence against entrenched habits of viewing "out-of-the-way" cultures as isolated from the wider contexts in which they are situated, as static, and as homogeneous. She focuses on a shared point of appeal among the Meratus known as *adat*—which refers to customary law, ritual conventions, and other formally articulated norms. In giving an account of its invocation in a series of disputed marriage claims, she points out how adat is an essentially contested concept among the Meratus. Although it invokes order and tradition and there is some agreement about what kinds of rules can satisfy the conditions of adat, it is discussed competitively, is continually reinvented, and is constantly the subject of negotiation and renegotiation.[8] The adat-sanctioned response to a Sache is essentially, then, a plurality of responses. To illustrate the second case, that of cross-cultural variation in the assessment of the significance of Sachen, and to do so briefly, one might simply note that, all things being equal, "Westerners" may arguably grant technological progress a higher priority relative to an existential concern with meaning than others might.

A fairly common occurrence of the use of the sort of lingua franca that I am gesturing at in this chapter is one in which a reasonably complete metalanguage is already at hand in situations where speakers are unable to translate directly from one another's "home" languages but are each able to speak a third language into which each translates her "home" language. In the third language, each represents perspectives to the other that would otherwise be articulated in the respective home languages. (I had this experience in Dubrovnik, Croatia, where upon arrival I, who speak no Italian, found myself having dinner with an Italian academic who spoke little or no English but who, like me, spoke some French.) In general, this will of course require an elaboration of what the metalanguage typically provides, and there will undoubtedly be material that cannot be represented as precisely in the third language as it would be in the respective home languages, but, assuming that empirical conditions of fluency in the third language are met, one can come arbitrarily close to representing adequately one's intentions.

I return now to the topic of identifying and representing cultural contrast. Identifying contrasts *presupposes* the identification of a Sache, an "X", a fundamental concern. A contrast can only be properly understood as the condition of there being two (or more) ways of addressing X. Failure to assume a topic of concern makes the notion of contrast unintelligible. Failure to identify the *appropriate* topic—this is, of course, always open to interpretive and dialogical contestation—can lead to category mistakes and false contrasts. For example, if one assumes, as did Habermas, that certain mythical narratives were attempts to *explain* natural phenomena, then one gets a "contrast" between mythical narratives and scientific narratives.[9] Indeed, one gets an invidious contrast in that mythical narratives must then be viewed as failed or outmoded *scientific* narratives; but this may be a *false* contrast because mythical narratives may be addressed to an entirely different concern or topic—to the issue of identity, for example. This is an instance of what I identified in the last chapter as Habermas's tendency to assume the cultural invariance of the identification of salient problems, or that such problems are self-announcing across cultural horizons. Such mythical narratives may be symbolic or expressive means of recovering a people's sense of important and sustaining meanings. We should then properly look to contrasting ways of addressing *this* concern. Or, as the philosopher Peter Winch points out, it is a mistake to see the Zande magical rites made famous by Sir Edward

Evans-Pritchard as irrational technological practices, as Sir James Frazer would, rather than as something more like the prayers of supplication that the West, too, takes seriously.

These examples further highlight what is, I think, an interesting and telling phenomenon. There are many cases where there is a relative asymmetry between the employment of causal explanations versus hermeneutic understanding in rendering an account of "their" practices versus "ours," cases where we feel obliged to *explain* the actions of those who are different but seek to *understand* those who are relevantly similar to us. This asymmetry is, I believe, *a* measure of the degree to which we have failed to discern an appropriate Sache and to identify a genuine, noninvidious contrast. For example, in the case of mythical narratives, Habermas can identify them as reasonable in context, but, assuming the rationality of the agents for whom the myths have purchase, he is obliged to *explain away* the difference between "us" and "them" by reference to the deficient state of their factual knowledge relative to ours. It is assumed here that once this deficit is repaired "they" will agree with us. The asymmetry arises here because there is no corresponding need to explain "us" in this way. On the other hand, if we think of, say, magical rites as analogous to prayers, then any explanations we would feel called upon to provide in order to account for their practices, and for their difference from us in this respect, we would logically feel obliged to provide for *ourselves* as well.

If (as I shall argue we should) we take the metalinguistic scheme to represent not only different perspectives on given issues but also *competing claims* about those issues, then the u's and v's will represent positions in contest. The "settled opinion" of one side will contest that of the other. In general, the outcome of such a contest will be one or some combination of three possibilities: one, the rejection, if not absolutely at least relative to a particular context, of one perspective in light of the "settled consensus" of the other; two, the transformation through a learning process of one or both sides of the dialogue through such an encounter; and three, a *reframing* of the terms of the contest through the postulation of a topic of concern that is distinct from the one originally taken to be at issue.

In the course of this discussion, I will treat each of these possibilities. At this point I am interested in what we can call "pedagogical representations," representations of the other from which both parties to the dialogue can learn. Such learning processes may involve both the second and third possibilities just mentioned—that is, both a transformed vision of a given topic and a revised outlook achieved through the postulation of a different topic, one to which what were initially considered deficient responses on the part of the other can be seen as appropriate responses and indeed even as responses worthy of emulation. Learning can accordingly take the form both of discovering new and promising ways to address a given concern or Sache and of the recognition of other concerns to consider. Indeed, we are likely to get *enlarged* understanding and learning only when we can identify *genuine contrasts*, by which I mean nondistortive representations that, as Taylor felicitously puts it, "allow us to see two goods where before we could only see one and its negation."[10]

A contrast pries us open, beckoning us "outside" ourselves, only when the new element can be seen to be *legitimate*, a legitimate move in the game; its legitimacy is always a matter of our being able to see it as an *understandable-in-context* response to a concern (a concern that we either *do* have, *could* have, or can see how we *should* have). Thus, *a* methodological maxim for adducing the background concern or topic at issue is that we should attempt to answer the question, In what game is theirs an intelligible move? This is *one* of the enabling conditions of bringing the other into proper focus. However, the satisfaction of this maxim still leaves open the possibility of misidentification. Misidentifying the Sache can allow us to view a practice as being reasonable in context—as Habermas did in the case of mythical narratives—without our seeing it as having any claim on us, without our having reason to think we can learn from it. (Of course, such misidentification is not the only reason that "their" practice may have no claim on us; we may have the Sache right and find "their" response simply abhorrent, perhaps as in the case of the headhunting of the Philippine Ilongot.) We may legitimately think, that is, that "they have good reasons for what they are doing, but we have better reasons for what we are doing because we know better than they do." This can happen—we can view a practice as reasonable in context without its having a claim on us—because our assessment of what is a good reason will be a function of what we assume the purpose of their practice to be. And for a given assumed purpose, we may believe that—although their practice constitutes a reasonable response—we have better resources for addressing it than they do. Accordingly, our representation may display them as reasonable in context but not as, in Taylor's terms, possessing a "good," something from which we could learn. So the methodological significance of our representing their practices and expressions as a good is that such a representation can provide a "correction" to the implicit assessments of reasons and of fundamental concern that we made in our original rendering of them as reasonable in context.[11] (Here we move beyond the hermeneutic undertaking authorized by Herder.) This "second order" principle of charity, not necessary for rendering an intelligible interpretation or representation, is nevertheless an important heuristic principle for insuring that we have fixed upon the right Sache, and so for producing a hermeneutically adequate pedagogical representation. It exhorts us to find the most compelling *connection* between response (the u's and v's) and Sache.

Gadamer speaks to the issue that I have framed here by way of what he calls an "anticipation of completion."[12] By this phrase he means to imply that an adequate understanding must presume that the practices, claims, and so on that are to be understood are to be construed not only as reasonable in context, but *also* as reasonable, true or valid *überhaupt*.[13] After having genuinely attempted to interpret others in this way, our inability to do so might legitimately lead us to seeing their practices as, at best, only reasonable in context. But to begin with the notion of seeking only contextual intelligibility is perhaps to be blinded to the real topic at issue and, more important, to forfeit the opportunity to learn from them. This discussion, then, supports the methodological warrant for my interpreting you, representing you to myself, under the aspect of "what can I learn from you" so that I "interpret to the strongest case that can be made" for your position. It is through discovering the real strength of your position that I can learn.[14]

As useful as Gadamer's insights are here, there is an angle of vision from which we can see that they too are limited. Gadamer's tendency to focus on the tradition that both text and interpreter share reveals a lacuna in his approach to the matters that concern me here, for this focus tends to occlude the problematic and deeply contested nature of Sache identification—that is, the identification of the topic that will allow us to make the best case for a given response—in cases where one cannot rely upon the commonality provided by a shared tradition. In such cases, the problematics of Sache identification are brought to the fore. It is my concern in this book, as it were, to "rotate" the relationship with which Gadamer is preoccupied—namely, the vertical relationship of an authoritative tradition to an interpreter—so that it becomes a horizontal relationship between interlocutors. This will mean that, in general, we will be unable to take for granted a shared tradition and the advantage that it gives us of already being "in" on the cultural conversation and the topics being addressed. In cross-cultural conversation, we may often be able to rely upon only the expressive potential of language in general (on the fact of what John Searle calls the "principle of expressibility," that anything that can be meant can be articulated in language), our hermeneutic talents, and, crucially, the free response of intercultural interlocutors to our proposals.[15] Accordingly, the presumption of authority that Gadamer accords tradition I want to locate in the reciprocal recognition of interlocutors, but in a way that is not blind to the real asymmetries between dominating and dominated languages.[16]

My position entails that I view the perspective of another culture as having a *claim* on me, as in fact being something like a validity claim about something that is of concern, a Sache, to me. As Georgia Warnke nicely puts it, "This means both that our situation circumscribes the meaning an object can have for us and that its truth [the claim of another culture] provokes us to reconsider that situation and move to a new understanding of it."[17] Finding the appropriate topic of concern and consequently discerning just what claim is made on me will require more than my interpretive powers, which will by themselves yield only hypotheses. This points to the methodological importance of dialogue. In dialogue, both self and other can challenge where they are located on the spectrum of responses to a given concern; they can challenge the way in which the spectrum is articulated; and they can challenge the spectrum itself—that is, the logical space or dimension of experience that we took to be best for perspicuously representing our differences. The point, then, would be to get the other to say, "That's really me," and for us to see in *that* representation a *genuine* proposal of a human possibility for ourselves as well.

The telos of the "unfinished project" is thus not agreement—though on occasion this might occur—but mutual understanding; the goal is to achieve systems of contrast for all the various horizons that allow for the perspicuous representation of the other. Such a dialogue will initiate symmetrical learning processes that will expand, *on both sides of the dialogue*, notions of the kinds of games people play (the kinds of concern that are humanly addressed) *and* notions of the different, and sometimes better, ways of playing them.

By so highlighting the symmetrical nature of these encounters, I am not claiming that for any two cultures it will turn out that both sides will occupy positions of equal merit with respect to every topic of human concern. Ultimately, there may turn out to be asymmetries between them with regard to specific topics—for example, with regard to rendering a reliable, technologically pregnant account of natural processes, or coming to terms with the inevitable. For if we take seriously the very idea of learning, with its ineliminable implications of progressive development, we would certainly have to allow that, for a given and sufficiently narrowly defined concern, some positions are more likely to be fruitful than others. So, by *symmetry* I do not refer so much to the *outcome* of such an encounter as I do to the mutual dispositions of participants in dialogue to proceed as if they could learn from, and be challenged by, the other.

These symmetrical learning processes are at the same time processes of familiarization and of defamiliarization or self-estrangement. In and through dialogue, not only might "they" become more familiar to "us," but we may well become more "strange" to ourselves, seeing ourselves as we might appear through spectacles fashioned in part by them.[18] In such a negotiated mutual understanding you may come to alter the way in which you understand yourself, and I undoubtedly may find that listening to you leads me to alter my own self-understanding. (But again, I would argue, we need to *understand* the other in order to know where to place her, in order to know what difference her "difference" makes, to know *that* she is different in some respect and *how* she is different.) It is this hermeneutic encounter with the other that enables us to become more explicitly aware of who we are—and we may not fully like what is revealed through the mirror provided by the other—and enables our awareness that we occupy only one of the positions in the space of human possibilities; that is, it enables an awareness of difference.

Furthermore, the newly forged common language within which this encounter comes to expression need not be seen as hegemonically usurping the original indigenous languages. Rather, think of it as a dialect in the making, or perhaps as a specialized vocabulary of each, standing to each much as the languages of science and mathematics stand to natural languages. Such an emergent common language can serve as the basis for a decidedly noncommunitarian form of community—one that many postmodernist writers overlook—that is structured upon an ever-expanding shared vocabulary for discussing and representing, though *not* for standardizing, moral and cultural identity. Furthermore, this is explicitly *not* a universal metalanguage of the sort that would erase or assimilate cultural diversity. It does not, therefore, have the status of what the German philosopher, Bernhard Waldenfels, calls the "third person position" that effaces difference and alterity.[19] This negotiated metalanguage—marking an emergent moment of common humanity as it enables the articulation of difference—is a *situated* metalanguage that is reflexively constituted by difference.

I suggested earlier that this conception of understanding does not entail an objectionable ethnocentrism. When I understand another, I transcend what I took for granted but not in such a way that what I took for granted cannot be located and articulated in terms of the framework necessary to comprehend, locate, or articulate the new. In short, I *expand* my experience, not transcend it. For many postmodernist writers there is a tendency to think that we either understand an experience in terms of a rigidly given "paradigm" *or* we understand in terms of one that is absolutely distinct from it. We thus have either a rigid ethnocentrism or irrational conversion. But in order to understand the new we are sometimes required to *expand* intelligibly a given paradigm or to decisively reconfigure it. When performed on both sides of a conversation, this produces an expanded metalanguage that stands in an asymmetrical relation to *both* of the original languages.

What conditions our access to the fundamental concerns of others? It is in light of what are concerns and issues for us that we are able to understand a form of life other than our own. That is, unless we can locate the logical spaces or dimensions of experience that are addressed by the practices situated within the foreign form of life—and we can do this only through modeling upon what can be logical spaces or dimensions of experience *for us* (love, sexuality, religion, power, natality, mortality, etc.)—then we cannot understand it. I take this to be the point of Gadamer's claim, with an approving nod to R. G. Collingwood, that "No assertion is possible that cannot be understood as an answer to a question, and assertions can only be understood in this way."[20]

I would argue that analogy plays a crucial role here. When we seek to identify the topic in question and to make the best case for a response to it, we will ask such questions as, What category of phenomena, or what topics, do *we* treat similarly, or address in the way—or in *some* way that can be intelligibly connected by us to the way—that *they're* addressing X? And when guided by such questions we adduce such a category that we then *hypothetically* project upon them, say, the category of "art," we shall ask, *Is* there, *for them*, a category of objects that they treat (both linguistically and nonlinguistically) in the way—or in *a* way that can be intelligibly connected by us to the way—that *we* treat things we call "art"? In both cases, in both the generation of a topic and in its justification, we are relying on analogy. In the first case, we are asking, Which of the topics with which we are familiar is analogous to what they're addressing, such that the best case can be made for what they're doing? In the second case, we are asking more generally, *Is* there for them something analogous to our X?[21]

Situated Cosmopolitanism

There is thus a sense in which some degree of ethnocentrism is epistemologically unavoidable. To see others as engaged in, say, argumentative practices or morally relevant practices requires *our* experience with those kinds of practice as a touchstone. And we can be sure, to pick morality, that if another culture's criteria for the application of moral terms demonstrated *no* overlap with ours, we would have no reason to think that they were engaged in moral discourse at all. The interpretation that yields a Sache and contrasting approaches to it is, in the last analysis, ours. But I take this to be relatively harmless, and for two reasons. First, we can distinguish, on the one hand, what I would call the "transcendentally" necessary ethnocentrism (our unavoidable, though nevertheless criticizable, appeal to our notions of rationality and cogency or to what we deem can be intelligibly related to them—in my attempt to see your perspective as a live option, I am going to try to see it as one chosen with reason, that is to say with what could be reasons for me) from the residue of contingent, empirical, and possibly invidious ethnocentrism, on the other. We can combat the latter by acknowledging the crucial importance of dialogue (with cultural others) aimed at mutually acceptable descriptions of the Sache and of its correlative contrasting practices.

Second, who "we" are is always subject to revision, for our identities are best viewed as phenomena open to nonfatal contestation in that certain elements of the set of features that collectively constitute one's social identity may be revised as a result of critical reflection without resulting in the loss of identity. The conversational practices of redescription and fusion that I have been advocating can broaden our sense of human possibilities without fatally threatening identities. The threat to cultural distinctiveness need not be feared if we acknowledge that identity is a cluster concept in that few if any beliefs or professions of value, taken singly, are essential to an identity. Our identities, then, need not be construed as being *identical* to our *prevailing* purposes, goals, and projects.

To take but one example (one that resonates with my earlier discussion of Meratan intracultural dialogue), as Akeel Bilgrami has argued forcefully, being a Muslim is not necessarily to accept the strategic framing of one's identity put forward by some of one's fundamentalist coreligionists;[22] such an identity can be critically reconfigured. Bilgrami points out that Muslim communities are defined by competing values, of which Islam is one, and further, that Islamic identity is itself negotiable.[23] Thus, while I would not support Iris Young's postmodernist call for a fractured, decentered self, I do join her in rejecting the valorization of rigid identity preservation. Similar to Young, but in a somewhat different context, Yael

Tamir argues that "[a]lthough cultural choices are neither easy nor limitless, cultural memberships and moral identity are not beyond choice," and they can be made the subject matter for a politicized discussion oriented toward bringing these emotional processes to discursive consciousness.[24] Cultural identities are as much forged as found. They are fields of contestation and negotiation, often of struggles to expand existing and socially acknowledged logical spaces in order to accommodate the intelligibility of styles of group membership that were previously marginalized. And the hybrid, heteroglossial, argumentatively renegotiated "subject in process" taking part in these discussions need not be a fragmented, schizophrenic self.

A hermeneutically self-aware ethnocentrist, one aware of her transcendental ethnocentrism, would hold others up to the criteria that her lights reveal, but not in a way that dogmatically precludes the possibility (or desirability) that her standards may change, that she could learn from others. To be hermeneutically self-reflective implies, for me, an openness and a willingness to take seriously the conjecture that there is a disjunction between one's own standpoint and the regulative ideal of the "good life." On the other hand, the postmodern relativist's refusal to judge can betray a refusal *to be judged*, a refusal both to make claims *on* others and to be claimed *by* those others. Our openness to the claims of the other places our identities in relief. And the critical renegotiation of identity can take place on both sides of the conversation table. For all of these reasons, I understand my project as an articulation of a *situated* cosmopolitanism.

Why should this project commend itself to us? The encounter with an alien tradition illuminates our own presuppositions. Such an encounter may well provide answers to our questions that are different from those with which we have become comfortable. And, as I have suggested, lying behind those different answers may be different presuppositions about certain issues (for instance, about the relationships among science, art, and religion, or between the individual and the community) than those we have taken for granted. In a cosmopolitan culture with critical-reflective pretensions like our own, at its best a postmetaphysical culture that views its perspectives and practices as *hypotheses* for living, as claims amenable to testing and correction, it might be argued that the conditions for cultural survival and flourishing require the survival and flourishing of alternative systems of value to enable the critical perspectives that paradoxically underwrite cultural self-assurance, somewhat in the way that falsifiability is a condition of the "health" of scientific claims.[25] It is for this reason that we should view the perspectives of other cultures as claims on our own.

Implicit in my discussion are two levels at which dialogue operates; first there is the dialogical construction of the metalanguage itself, and second, the dialogical interaction that makes use of, is enabled by, the ongoing processes of metalanguage construction. (In my view, Gadamer does not focus sufficiently on the first level, on the problematics of Sache identification.) To give a brief, and schematic, idea of what might result at the second level, where mutually transformative processes can take place on the ground provided by such a metalanguage, I would like to consider the well-known debate over care and justice initiated by Carol Gilligan's *In a Different Voice*. The debate is structured by a contrast between understanding relations and obligations between moral agents in terms of contextual notions such as those of equity, care, and responsibility on the one hand, and understanding them in terms of noncontextual principles of abstract equality and rights on the other. So, greatly simplified, we can think of a cultural "we" that is defined in terms of a concrete ethics of care, where the social bond is understood to be comprised of fields of concern that are *internally* related by care and an ethics of responsibility, and where the self is defined through relations with others. By contrast, we can think of a culturally defined "we" that owes its identity to a vocabulary centered around the notion of rights, where social reality is understood to consist of isolated atoms that are only *externally* related through contracts based upon rights.

That not only a mutual understanding but also a generalizable agreement is conceivable here, issuing in something new as opposed to the assimilation of one "we" to another or to an unmediated moral schizophrenia, is suggested by Ronald Dworkin's reading of "the right to equality." His reading might be a key to how we could accomplish the preservation and combination of the horizons of care and rights, of equity and equality, in such a way that we could see how a general agreement on this matter might look. I have in mind here Dworkin's understanding of the right to equality, not as the right to equal treatment, but as the right to treatment as an equal, which is the right to be treated with the same concern and respect as anyone else.[26] Treatment of others as equals requires, on his terms, not an abstraction from, but a sensitivity to, the contexts and needs of others. The achievement of such a fusion of horizons would be a step toward the production of the sort of mutually transformative redescription of moral identity that I have in mind.

The model of understanding that I am proposing, emphasizing as it does hermeneutic charity and pedagogical representations, does not leave us powerless to respond critically to the forms of life that we wish to understand. To see this, we need to attend to the sorts of claims being made within the vocabularies represented by the u's and v's of my diagram. Every form of life can be understood to make the following validity claim: its practices are the best way for it to flourish; that is to say, they represent the best way for it to address the Sachen. Of course, cultures do not make *only* this sort of claim. They also make aesthetic-expressive claims about who they are, though, as I have suggested, even such identity claims are subject to critical renegotiation. For the moment, however, I wish to focus on the claim that, given its identity, each culture implicitly makes the claim that its practices provide the best avenue for its flourishing. This sort of culturally rooted validity claim provides the occasion for a cultural critique informed by the presumption of what I shall presently refer to as "second-order rationality." The most insular forms of life can be understood implicitly to make the claim that their practices are the best way for *them* to flourish. More cosmopolitan cultures will, in addition, not only view the practices of less cosmopolitan ones as invitations or hypotheses for the fuller flourishing of the cosmopolitan cultures—as if other cultures, more and less insular, were to say, "Try or consider our practices from the point of view of your flourishing and see how they work; see if they improve for you the way in which you address the Sachen"—but will also tend to view their own, cosmopolitan, practices as invitations to others. In any case, that such a validity claim is made, even if only implicitly, by all cultures provides grounds for non-question-begging critique.

There are at least three sorts of critical question that can be raised, corresponding to three senses in which we can say the others' view of what they are doing is a subjective view. First, there is always the question of whether what an agent thinks she is aiming at is what she is *really* aiming at (we can all be victims of illusions, of arbitrarily limited conceptions of what really matters to us, and of delusions; and it may not be incoherent to claim, as did Sigmund Freud, that an entire culture can be so victimized with respect to a particular domain of experience). Second, there is the question of whether what we want as individual subjects or as members of a given group is just or can be accommodated within a just society. Third, and perhaps less contentiously, we can of course also raise questions related to a purely immanent critique, a critique articulated from within the purview of the other's standards of rationality and/or central vocabulary, and these questions of course will require an *understanding* of the cultural context from which the other's claims emerge. Thus, the project I am advocating countenances both pedagogical and *critical* representations.

That the model that I have proposed does not promote, or even countenance, a promiscuous relativism can be demonstrated in a number of ways. Here I shall address the third type of critical response by providing a brief counterargument to Richard Rorty's claim that the only way to take seriously the distinction between the merely socially or culturally sanctioned, on the one hand, and the valid, on the other, is to be a Platonist, is, I would interject, to be the sort of metaphysician that, like Rodney Dangerfield, gets no respect. This, I think, is mistaken. We can understand the appearance/reality distinction to mark a distinction between what even *everyone* in a culture happens to think—and indeed, thinks honestly and after considerable reflection—and what is true for them.

Such a distinction does not require that we appeal to anything beyond the standards of rationality and/or central vocabulary of a particular group. Rather, it depends simply upon our recognition that we can sometimes be brought to see that practices of justification that we may have heretofore relied upon may be arbitrary and/or untrustworthy. And there is no reason to think that others cannot be brought to see this as well. To *convince* someone of the untrustworthiness of their practices is ipso facto to provide them with a *reason* to consider alternatives. I refer here to justificatory practices as being arbitrary or untrustworthy in the sense that they turn out not to be truth tracking or truth sensitive in the way that members of a given community thought they were, or in the way in which they previously had no reason to disbelieve that they were, where *true* is understood to mean *true within a given language*. By this, I mean that there are cases where persons can be brought to see that there is (to them) no *intelligible* connection between, on the one hand, the reasonableness of their holding a particular claim or of holding it to be true, and, on the other hand, the outcome of what they take to be procedures for evaluating it and other such claims, for they might be brought to see that those procedures are "loaded" in such a way that their outcome is prejudiced. By "loaded" I mean that the procedures, because of a flaw in their design, may yield an outcome that would support (or disconfirm) a claim even if the claim were false (or true), a flaw that could be detected and assessed from *within* the purview of the standards of rationality and/or central vocabulary of the group in question. These are cases, like the discovery of an unbalanced scale in an economic transaction, where the outcome of a justificatory procedure will have been *exposed* as an artifact of the procedure and not of the procedure's truth-tracking sensitivity, and is therefore not to be taken as a reflection of the truth or falsity of what the claim asserts.

This is obviously the sort of thing that occurs when an experimental design in the sciences is criticized, but it can also happen in the case of the interpretation of a sacred text or of a political constitution. Recognition of such cases authorizes us to say, for example, that even if *all* of the contemporaries of Aristarchus—the third-century B.C.E. astronomer who is reputed to have claimed that the earth revolved around the sun—denied his claim, and even if Aristarchus himself was convinced upon reflection to recant, they universally believed what was false *for them*. The form of rationality that I have implicitly referred to here is a form of rationality that I take to have transcultural, or cross-cultural, or culturally invariant standing. It is what I would call a "second-order rationality" that we are entitled to impute to everyone—that is, an inclination to reform one's practices in the direction of more rationality when one's lack of rationality is pointed out to one in terms with which one is conversant.[27] I should emphasize, however, that this exploitation of the transcultural presumption of second-order rationality depends upon a prior hermeneutic understanding of the cultural context in which the disputed practices are situated; we would need to know what the aims of the disputed practices are, which topics they are addressing. Only such an understanding would allow the sort of critical representation that I have here elaborated.

What the discussion in this chapter suggests to me is the possibility of a *historicist* notion of humanity as an unfinished project, as something forged or made as the result of historical negotiation rather than found or discovered as a preexisting essence. Of course, we must also choose from among the newly revealed human possibilities which ones to actualize, and that choice will be made in light of standards, in light of criterial properties of the "good life" as we, by appealing to the "best" in us, see it. Such standards are themselves historical products; the hermeneutic encounter will thus allow for comparative evaluations of the newly revealed human possibilities in terms of tentatively consolidated but revisable standards. The criterial properties of the "good life" may be altered for us in a number of ways as a result of such an encounter. The new culture may highlight features of the good life that may have been forgotten, marginalized, or perhaps never even acknowledged by us. Such encounters invite a critical awareness of standards long taken for granted. As a consequence, the symmetrical learning processes that inform such negotiations will lead to an expansion of both our *vision* of human possibilities and of the *standards* for evaluating them. The "yet to come" of humanity as an unfinished project will then include both versions and criteria of the good life.

Postmodernism's distrust of such an appeal to the human and, consequently, to humanism arises from its understandable skepticism toward what can be called *essentialist* notions of humanity, toward concepts of humanity that claim to reflect an independently existing reality; but postmodernists err in assuming that such essentialist notions are the only viable ones. (The same false assumption is made by both Enlightenment humanists and their postmodern critics: the connections that bring us together are *found*, not *made*. Since no found set of connections embraces what they take to be salient about us all, the postmodernists are wont to reject such connections altogether. Since the Enlightenment humanists—at least at their best—think we share equally and in the same ways what is salient about us—namely, reason, the capacity for language, and so on—they are quite complacent and happy with what they find. But both err in restricting themselves to the found.) As such, the fact of difference does not threaten humanism in my view. To the contrary, difference and its noninvidious representation is the motor that drives the learning processes wherein competing viewpoints are brought to an awareness of their respective limits and of what in others might be of profit. Such an enlarged understanding is for me what humanism, understood as a regulative ideal, is about.

An important challenge to this conception of humanism concerns the *limits* of the redescription and change invoked in my discussion of a historicized notion of humanity. What sorts of limits or controls prevent a "we," willing to take its part in the drama of humanity as an unfinished project, from being swept along and swallowed up in the rush to fuse horizons in such a way that it loses its identity or relinquishes what matters to it most? I propose the following notions as features of a framework that would accommodate this concern: First, the virtual or ideal "we" of a humanity that is a negotiated, unfinished project functioning as an *ideal* community, a notion that makes a virtue of being open to the other and of being willing to take seriously the conjecture that there is a disjunction between one's own standpoint and the regulative ideal of the "good life"; and, second, a notion of *self-recognition* functioning as a boundary condition for the conversation wherein the negotiation takes place. Of course, what counts as the proper description of the self is open to contestable interpretation, and there can be contestable judgments about what counts as a modification of identity as opposed to an abdication of identity. The notion of self-recognition is meant to invoke a dimension of experience where the foregoing questions are pressed. Thus, taking the risk genuinely to raise the questions—Am I playing the right game? Are my purposes the right ones?—need not entail the risk of losing oneself.

5
"Postmodern" Rejoinders

In this chapter, I turn an eye toward some of the salient contemporary perspectives from which my project is likely to be regarded with suspicion. I consider some influential thinkers—two philosophical writers and a loosely affiliated group of cultural anthropologists—who are noted for their concern with the implications of alterity and with the deeply problematic status of representations of the other. In responding to their provocations, I am afforded the opportunity to elaborate my position further. Iris Marion Young is prominent among these thinkers, and she, indeed, appears to contest much of what I have argued for.[1] In the next section, I argue that Young's position and, especially, her metaphor of "listening across distance" actually subvert the understanding of "understanding." I then turn to Robert Bernasconi's critique of hermeneutic understanding, and conclude with a brief discussion of what some so-called postmodern anthropologists diagnose as the "crisis of representation."

I

In a recent book and in a number of essays, Iris Young has provided perhaps the clearest and most explicit analysis of the idea of communicative understanding from what might loosely be called a postmodernist perspective.[2] In "Communication and the Other," for example, she is especially eager to explore ways to emancipate the theories of communicative ethics and of deliberative democracy, associated with Jürgen Habermas and others, from what she perceives to be their fetters of cultural bias. She wishes to do so in order to realize more fully the considerable potential these ethical and political projects have for helping us to think about conceptions of justice that are sufficiently expansive to accommodate matters of difference. For instance, Young challenges the claim, sometimes made by theorists of deliberative democracy, that bracketing political and economic power is sufficient to make speakers equal.[3] Indeed, I believe that she is quite right to point to the ways in which, despite the best intentions, full social recognition is often denied to the speech of persons conventionally identified as members of socially marginalized groups. Young's point is that simply removing the power to threaten or coerce is not sufficient to ensure an equality of chances to assume dialogue roles. She rightly advocates that we attend to the "cultural specificity of deliberative practices" and to "the way that power sometimes enters speech itself."[4] It can do so, among other ways, through an internalized sense of having or not having the right to speak, where that sense is determined by an awareness of prevailing social assessments of differing *styles* of speech, and where those styles are as often as not constitutive of one's social identity.

Young writes that among the modes of speech that are singled out for invidious treatment by deliberative theorists are greeting, rhetoric, and storytelling.[5] In general, she believes, such theorists are markedly more favorably disposed to speech in which the logical connections between assertions and the reasons brought forward to justify them are perspicuously displayed than they are to elliptical styles of speech where premises and/or inferences are characteristically suppressed or remain implicit. And this may be so. However, one might argue that dimensions of communicative action—greetings, for example—that cannot in principle be assessed in terms of validity conditions (such as truth, moral appropriateness, and sincerity) or in terms of their promise as proposals for reconfiguring one's view of the physical, social, moral, or aesthetic dimensions of the world should not be construed as bearing propositional content relevant to the issue at hand. They should not even, like the symmetry conditions of Habermas's ideal speech situation, for example, be construed as content-constitutive conditions of speech. They should instead be viewed as facilitative boundary conditions of communication, conditions like civility or reaching agreement on the shape of a negotiating table. As Young acknowledges, such dimensions would then refer to conditions that lubricate, enable, and promote communication. Insofar as this is the case, such dimensions would not so much be channels through which communication takes place as conditions that promote the freeing of those channels from obstruction. Though Young's emphasis upon such dimensions of the speech situation is, as I have suggested, salutary, one wonders whether an acknowledgment of their significance—for instance, of the significance of "care-taking, deferential, [and] polite acknowledgment of the Otherness of others"—is actually logically or conceptually incompatible with the views of the deliberative theorists she criticizes, or whether those theorists simply fail to emphasize it and would happily endorse it if asked to.

On the other hand, insofar as deliberative theorists denigrate figurative speech—and again it is not clear who *in principle* would rule this out—they might well be guilty of an objectionable proscription of potentially world-informing and -transforming speech of the sort that I mentioned above, speech that challenges us to *re*view the world that we had taken for granted. Insofar as rhetoric names the art of being able to "reflexively attend to the audience in the speech," as Young suggests, deliberative theory arguably *should* accommodate styles of speech that acknowledge the situatedness of speakers.[6] But we can distinguish, on the one hand, a rhetorical style or style of persuasive speech that aims at communicating what is true, valid, or insightful to a particular, situated addressee, taking into account what will be meaningful for that addressee, from, on the other, such speech that aims simply at bringing the addressee to accept what the speaker wants by making an appeal to the addressee with cavalier disregard for, or that intentionally bypasses, the dimension of deliberation, wherein the redemption of claims to truth, validity, or insight is at issue. There is no reason to believe that deliberative democracy is remiss in withholding validation per se from speech acts that are purely perlocutionary or strategic in this latter sense. Of course, it is often necessary to get and maintain the listener's attention, and perlocutionary rhetoric is useful for this purpose. But this brings us only to the *threshold* of communication, to the antechamber of dialogue.

Finally, storytelling or narrative can make salient, in ways that strictly argumentative discourse cannot, value commitments and underlying structures of meaning that, though they emerge from specific concrete contexts, from specific "sites of difference," can nevertheless be edifying for all. To the extent that theories of deliberative democracy do not acknowledge the potentially public importance of this material, material that Habermas sometimes refers to rather dismissively as "existential" matter, such theories are indeed the poorer for it.

So for Young, if the failing of interest-based democracy is that the preferences of the marginalized can simply be outvoted, then the failing of deliberative democracy is that the channels through which the marginalized are forced to speak and be heard (if indeed they are heard at all, given social tendencies to withhold recognition from certain styles of speech and expression) are such that what gets communicated is often truncated and homogenized. The putative consensus arising from such a deliberation, she thinks, is therefore likely to be a mere artifact of those unreasonably limited channels, and *real* difference will not have been given its due, will not have had its "say." Young agrees that it is a virtue for citizens to transcend private, exclusively "self-regarding perspectives on political issues, and take a broader more objective view," but rejects the deliberative theorist's claim that such a move requires finding "common interests . . . [and] mutual identification [among discussion participants]."[7]

What especially seems troubling to Young, here and in her more recent essay, "Asymmetrical Reciprocity," is the notion of mutual identification, which she identifies with the ideal of the universal exchange of roles, which Habermas defines as the "principle that constrains *all* affected to adopt the perspectives of *all others* in the balancing of interests."[8] It is this ideal of the reversibility of perspectives—the reciprocal "willingness to reason from the others' point of view, and the sensitivity to hear their voice"[9]—that is the object of Young's suspicion, that indeed she takes to be unserviceable even as an ideal.

However, as I suggested in my introductory comments in chapter 4, I am not sure that I fully understand or share Young's worry about this idea of the reversibility of perspectives or the sort of mutual understanding that it encourages. I argued there that to champion the idea of the reversibility of perspectives is not necessarily to be complicit in a conspiracy to erase difference. Why would Young persist, then, in the belief that it is neither possible nor morally desirable to reverse perspectives with others? To the extent that she finds it undesirable because of the tendency to reach closure too quickly, hers would be an argument against the *abuse* of the project to reverse perspectives, not an argument against the project itself. However, by interpreting *reversibility of perspectives* to mean *mutual identification*, she seems to wish to make a stronger claim, to wit, that the ideas of symmetry and reversibility *conceptually* imply a contrary to fact sameness among persons at the expense of differences.[10] But this is of course precisely what I have denied. Properly understood, the desire for a symmetrical relation with another or for a reversibility of perspectives does not *deny* difference; instead, as I have argued, it enables an *awareness* of difference.

I now want to ask, Why not think of this idea as a heuristic, counterfactual ideal that functions by exhorting us to be especially hermeneutically open to those whose lives are different from ours, and to be willing to engage in conversations about what is just and worthy of consideration in our common lives? The "reversibility of roles" should be thought of as a device for ensuring that a claim made by a particular social group has a claim on all of us, that it be recognized as a general claim. This would compel us both to make perspicuous the hermeneutic and social contexts implicated in such a claim *and* to make a genuine and open-minded effort to assess the extent to which such a claim is generally compelling—that is, the extent to which it has purchase beyond the specific hermeneutic context of its generation. Such a general claim is one that *addresses* us, one that ultimately invites our reply. It is a claim that *we* should take seriously as a candidate for a perspicuous description of the world, one that renders salient features that should command our respectful attention.

It does not mean per se that the claim is true or legitimate; it is a *claim*. But it is couched in terms that should be granted the status of candidates for "semantic authority." To be accorded candidacy for semantic authority is to be accorded semantic *recognition*, to be taken seriously enough to investigate the possible value of construing reality in its terms. To treat a claim as general is to treat it as a speech act that imposes a mutual burden: the addressee assumes the obligation of taking the claim seriously enough to enter, along with the sender, a dialogically constituted space of reasons and reasoning in considering its general applicability; the sender assumes an obligation to justify the claim or a particular application of a term or to persuade the addressee (again, in a mutually forged justificatory language) of the usefulness of so applying the term. To treat a claim as general in this way is to take it up in such a way that we are willing genuinely to risk having our view of things challenged, without of course there being any guarantee that we will be so persuaded. General claims remain defeasible, criticizable claims. So understood, the reversibility of perspectives would not be in conflict with Young's notion of communicative democracy, but would instead, I should think, be the ideal articulation of it.

It is true, as Young suggests, that asymmetrical relations of power can occlude the other's presentation of self by exacerbating the tendency of the self in power to project itself onto the other. But this is just to say that a high degree of hermeneutic modesty and tentativeness should attend such interpretive encounters and that, as far as possible, special attention has to be given to uncovering, "taking into account," and attempting to neutralize such power relations and/or their effects. Hence, the importance of the ideal of letting the other respond freely. However, Young's claim is that the ideal of symmetry (given her understanding of it) *masks* power differentials and thus has an ideological, mystifying, or obfuscating status. The greater the power differentials, the more likely it is that the self will see itself reflected in the other, making it more difficult to know the other *as* other. Young also implies, not unreasonably, that this can go on behind the back of, or be beyond the reflective control of, the self. Self and other, then, are implicated in a structural configuration that conditions and constrains possibilities for mutual understanding.[11] I would contend, however, that when properly understood as the ideal of mutual recognition the ideal of symmetry would have this ideological status only insofar as we have presumed symmetry to have been achieved rather than as a yet-to-be-realized goal—that is, only insofar as symmetry is an assumption rather than an ideal. We can resist reifying ideological distortion by adopting an attitude of hermeneutic suspicion toward our own interpretive achievements, toward our representations of the other.

Young extends her argument to differences that are not mediated by relations of power.[12] In the first case, that of power, Young argues that projections subvert possibilities for mutual understanding. In the latter case, it is the inaccessibility of the other's subjectivity, of what Martin Heidegger calls its "mineness" (*Jemeinigkeit*), or of what Laurence Thomas refers to as its "subjective imprimatur," that gets in the way.[13] For *I* cannot have the other's subjective experiences and memories. Human experience is more than information *about*, or descriptions *of*, it; it is the actual *having* of it.[14] In the article that Young refers to, "Moral Deference," Thomas actually rests his argument on the claim that I cannot fully represent to myself the *experience* that you have from your—different—*social* location. Young wants to extend the argument to claim that I cannot put myself in your position, and hence understand you, because the position is *yours*, for you and I will inevitably have different "life histories, emotional habits and life plans."[15]

In this context, Young's argument establishes both too much and too little. Even if we neutralize power and restrict our attention to conditions of social equality, irreducible differences of subjectivity remain. This would imply that even with *identical* "objective experience" (from, say, replaying a virtual reality script or, less fantastically, from having similar events befall us), there would still remain an unbridgeable distance that, for Young, would thwart understanding, for I would not be able to have your experience of those events. If in this case I cannot be said to be capable of understanding you, then this would seem to be a *reductio* of Young's implicit conception of understanding. That is, there is something troubling about a conception of understanding that leads to the claim that persons in situations of social equality cannot understand each other simply because of what can be quite unremarkable differences in life histories and so on. So, either there is no understanding (she establishes too much), or subjective difference is not an insuperable obstacle to what we would count as achieved understanding (she establishes too little). There is no reason to think that I can share with another only that which I *already* have in common with her, as Young's discussion of difference and overlapping interests suggests.[16] As I have argued, I can also participate in forging a language within which I can share to a greater or lesser degree precisely what differentiates me from her.

Young, therefore, illegitimately conflates the quite reasonable claim that "I cannot know what it feels like to be you" with the claim that "I cannot understand you." She seems to interpret *understanding* to refer to the idea of empathic understanding or empathic identification, ideas that Hans-Georg Gadamer so trenchantly criticized Wilhelm Dilthey and Friedrich Schleiermacher for promoting. As I have maintained, to understand another is not necessarily to "feel with" that other, but rather to understand the *descriptions* under which she places actions, events, and situations. My understanding of the other is linguistically enabled. The difference of different life histories is what we attempt to bridge by the back and forth of hermeneutic dialogue, which is always open to revision and on the lookout for premature closure.

In addition to conflating empathic identification with understanding, much of Young's argument here is predicated upon the view that advocates of symmetry and reciprocity think that *imagining* oneself in the position of others is sufficient.[17] But this is, of course, precisely what motivated Habermas, for example, to *dialogize* Kantian ethics. If the other is not talking back, what else *can* I do but project?

Young's position is in general deeply informed by Jean-Paul Sartre's analysis of self-other relations. Language, generally construed, is our access to the viewpoint of the other. Sartre points out that language is an objectification such that when the self interprets the other's language, it will not necessarily *interpret* it as the other *means* it, so that a gulf remains between the self and the other. But the point of dialogue and reciprocal rejoinders is to bring interpretation and meaning into a kind of equilibrium. What is achieved thereby is not the adoption of another's standpoint in any literal sense but an acknowledgment of the descriptions in terms of which the other articulates her world. Language is crucial here, and Young does not seem to acknowledge it sufficiently. She still has as a target the "straw man" of what Gadamer refers to as the romantic hermeneutics of Dilthey and Schleiermacher—the ultimately incoherent imperative "to suspend our perspective" or positioning.[18] Of course, the point is *not* for me to jump out of my skin into yours, but to be able to represent how you see things in terms of a language that is intelligibly related to my "home" language, yet also in such a way that you can assent to it. Thus, this kind of Sartrean argument is irrelevant to a model of communication that does not depend upon the possibility of *identifying* with another.

Young further claims that the specific *temporality* or narrative history of persons prevents symmetry. Some of a given person's background meanings may be shared or communicated to others, but not all, Young claims, because of the necessity of retelling one's story in different contexts.[19] But this also makes subjective history inexhaustible to the very person whose history it is, for our autobiographies are always subject to retelling and reframing to *ourselves*. Further, much of an agent's history is effective or operative "behind the back" of the person whose history it is, so that she cannot be granted epistemic privilege; in fact, in many cases an outsider may actually be *better* positioned to give an account of such background meaning. For such an outsider may have at her disposal a set of categories or contrasts that permit a more perspicuous representation of the agent's commitments than the agent herself may have. (And there is such a legitimate monological interpretive *moment* in any genuine dialogue. This interpretive moment, the provenance of the cogency of our sometimes being able to say that "we know them better than they know themselves" and vice versa, must still be open to a discursive response by our interlocutor, though the process of such confirmation will of course be much more complicated than eliciting a simple yes or no.)

The metaphor of "understanding across distance" that Young invokes in her discussion of these matters is, I believe, a misleading one.[20] Language does not only cross boundaries or span difference; it also *reconfigures* boundaries and *transforms* difference, and therefore also the borders separating and defining self and other. It is not the case that boundaries (selves) are fixed and that language serves as a two-way ambassador carrying messages back and forth. Young seems to presuppose the *givenness* and *irreducibility* of the distance derived from difference. Another way to put the point of my criticism here is to say that the boundaries are not given in the sense of being self-announcing. That is to say, they are in part artifacts of the distinctions language brings to bear rather than *given* sites from which language emanates. As G. W. F. Hegel noted in his discussion of the "dialectic of the limit," simply to be aware that my position is a position among others is already to reconfigure the limit or boundary.

Young maintains that communication is a creative exercise in which each side learns something new, and I heartily endorse this view.[21] But she implicitly suggests that if we understand communication as taking place across *commonality*, then we cannot have access to the new. However, I would argue, the "new" is simply inchoate and unintelligible unless placed in a frame of meaning that is intelligibly related to our own.[22] To understand the new as a new "X," as the new *under a description*, is to place it in a framework of intelligibility. And the mutual forging of this framework of intelligibility, intelligibly related to our home framework, is itself in part the creation of which Young speaks. As my framework gets enlarged in this way, my resources for self-description get enlarged and my *self* accordingly gets reconfigured, my boundaries redrawn. Again, Young makes the assumption that the common language is already *given* or *found* rather than *made*.

In the final analysis, understanding requires resources for the articulation of a novel experience, a way of framing what the experience is of or about, a way of bringing it under a description, and a way of *our* bringing it under description. It does not require that people differently situated actually be similar, but it does demand methodologically that we find analogical relations of similarity if we are to understand others. It is precisely through devising such similarities of analogical relations that new things can *intelligibly* arise for us.

Young's asseveration that understanding the new requires transcending that which is familiar to us—"transcending my own experience," or "getting out of ourselves,"—is self-defeating.[23] We will have learned something new when we can say, " I used to think that X was the only way to approach S, but now I see that Y is also a way to approach it," or that "S, which heretofore had not been an object of my focal awareness, is a concern worthy of my attention." These are some of the possibilities allowed by an expanded common language or metalanguage standing in an asymmetrical relationship to both of the originals. As I argued in the last chapter, when I understand a novel experience of the world, I go beyond what I took for granted, but not in such a way that what I took for granted is thereby erased. Instead, the latter is sublated in the new framework designed to comprehend, locate, and articulate the new. My experience is *expanded*, not transcended. Young thus betrays the unfortunate tendency I have mentioned toward thinking that our options are restricted either to a rigid ethnocentrism or to irrational conversion. As I have suggested, however, this is a false dilemma. As I argue in the "Musical Interlude," Theodor Adorno could not properly understand jazz within his narrow compositionalist paradigm. But his paradigm could be expanded, sublated, without its being completely set aside. Indeed, pace Young, if I were to "suspend [all of] my assumptions in order to listen,"[24] I would never hear anything but noise, would hear nothing intelligible. It is often true that, at first, the genuinely new will be experienced as noise, as be-bop or John Coltrane's music once were, for the requisite categories for assimilating it are not yet at hand. Operating with the presumption of openness, that it will be worthwhile, we set about reconfiguring and expanding our horizons in order to experience the new as meaningful. But this means bringing it into focus *for us*, from our (expanded) point of view.

The ideal of what Young calls the *copresence of subjects*—presumably another metaphysical illusion—may indeed be unrealizable. It is true that we always understand from within our hermeneutic horizon and that we are therefore vulnerable to all sorts of category error when seeking to understand others. But it cannot be settled a priori just what the limits to our understanding might be in a given situation, and it behooves us to try to push our understanding as far as we can. We cannot know what meanings are unshared or unshareable until we have made the hermeneutic attempt to understand the situation of the other, to become cognizant of how she experiences or interprets social life, to have access to the descriptions under which she understands her actions and those of others. (And, of course, she must be able to participate as a free interlocutor in the process of our seeking a perspicacious representation of her situation.) And indeed, there may already be more community, more that is shared, than we think. Glancing briefly at matters of race, for example, white middle-class Americans might find, culture of poverty theorists notwithstanding, that they share a great deal more with poor blacks in regard to values and aspirations than they would otherwise think.[25]

"Postmodern" Rejoinders

It is thus far from the case that an awareness of difference should be *opposed* to understanding. It is understanding, and understanding alone, that enables an awareness of difference under a noninvidious description. Once one has made the real attempt to understand, *then* one can speak of genuine differences. How are we even to *know* that others have different values from ours without a hermeneutic investigation, an attempt to understand from the inside? Accordingly, I think that it is unhelpful abstractly to oppose, as postmodernist writers like Young sometimes do, a recognition of the fundamental opacity of the other, on the one hand, and an ideal of complete transparency or fusion, on the other, making the stakes "all or nothing," complete transparency or irremediable opacity.[26] We can acknowledge the ways in which the other will always transcend any given understanding that we may achieve by saying that the fusion of horizons, or the forging of the appropriate metalanguage, is a potentially infinite task, by declaring that it will remain an unfinished project. The systems of contrast within which we represent our salient differences can always be contested, and contested from both sides of a conversation. The recognition that full transparency may be an unrealizable ideal does not make it unreasonable for us to hope and strive to allow some light to shine through a glass darkly.

To foreclose the importance of such a project's success at the outset and not to act *as if* it *could* succeed in significant measure is to fail to take seriously, to fail to respect, the rational agency of those who might share our moral community. For such respectful recognition would require our making the same attempt to maximize the reasonableness of what they say and do that we would expect them to make in our case, and to not dismiss them as inscrutably different. The conversational and interpretive practices that I am advocating require striking a delicate balance between critical discrimination and hermeneutic modesty. Yes, there is no doubt a limit beyond which we cannot go, and our hermeneutic hubris and presumption should be chastened with humility, but why *in any way* sanction our setting such a limit at the outset? This is to say nothing of the *theoretical* hubris required to maintain that we can say a priori and in principle exactly where the line should be drawn separating the understandable from that which cannot be understood. I think that it is important, then, both to preserve a *sense* of difference, in order to guard against premature interpretive closure, and to maintain an ideal of understanding that urges us to recognize and take seriously our common humanity.

In general, I think that postmodernist writers like Iris Young tend to operate with a conception of mutual understanding that is so demanding that such an understanding could not be understood to take place even, as I suggested earlier, between persons from similar cultures and social backgrounds. Heeding Hegel's admonition that if one has a criterion for knowledge that renders knowledge impossible one needs to discard one's criterion, we need to reconsider Young's understanding of "understanding." We do know some things, we do understand each other on occasion, and, moreover, we often do so in challenging contexts, in conversations that, even though with close friends, involve "discourse across distance." So I take those experiences to be a *reductio ad absurdum* of the rather defeatist conception of mutual understanding with which Young operates. Moreover, the latter, challenging, contexts will almost always involve the creation of a metalanguage, that is, a reconfiguration of conceptual fields or an expansion of the system of salient contrasts on both sides of the conversation.

I want to end this section with a discussion of the idea of community. Young is hostile toward the very idea;[27] her hostility is based, I would argue, on an unexamined *communitarian* conception of community. I say this because I have offered, in chapter 4, a way of thinking about community that is not subject to the charges of homogeneity and exclusionism. Now, why is "community" so important? The idea of the "reversibility of roles" that I took to be central to my idea of community should be thought of as a device for ensuring that a claim made by a particular social group has a claim on all of us who share a society with them, that it be recognized as a general claim. Surely to understand another is to have come to perceive more than that she is different, and I think that, pace Young, we need to ask more of ourselves than to understand that there is much that we do not understand, if the other is genuinely to feel *heard*. Though I know that this is not Young's intention, I fear that taking opacity to be such a salient feature of others will too quickly and easily legitimate a dismissive attitude toward the actual *claims* of the other even as we seek to accommodate her expressed interests. The image that comes to mind is what used to be the stock situation comedy character of the beleaguered husband thinking to himself "I just don't understand women" as he uncomprehendingly does his best to accommodate what he understands to be his wife's preferences in order to insure domestic tranquility; or the Frenchman who thinks to himself, "I just don't understand Arabs."

We want to respect the claim of the other for the *general, public* semantic authority of her descriptions of social life. We do not want to treat such descriptions as reflecting merely, say, the woman's perspective, or the black perspective. This is part of what it means to accord everyone equal respect, it seems to me. And indeed, we should treat those claims as criticizable; this too is one of the consequences of that respect. Failure to seek to understand, and to take such claims seriously *as claims*, is to fail to give the other her due. I worry about treating sexual harassment and police brutality as merely descriptions of social interaction from the points of view of women and blacks, respectively, with no presumption that these descriptions will have *general semantic authority*. Such a restriction would allow these issues to be understood as simply idiosyncratic matters of "their perception," where *their* perception has unfortunately become *our* collective problem, a problem to be handled strategically, rather than understood as a matter of what their perception *reveals* about our *common* social reality. In the idiom of the philosophy of science, these descriptions should be contested as observation statements, not as idiosyncratic theoretical statements.

What is needed is an expanded common vocabulary, either one that will enable the articulation of generalizable interests or, failing that, one that will allow the articulation of genuine, noninvidious difference, a vocabulary upon which we can begin to wrest the idea of the human community from the ashes, one that will keep us mindful of the ways that being in touch with the humanity of each contributes to the humanity of all.

II

I would next like briefly to consider the work of Robert Bernasconi, a leading Continental philosopher who has made important contributions to our understanding of the complex nexus of race, culture, and philosophy, and who—in an essay entitled " 'You Don't Know What I'm Talking About': Alterity and the Hermeneutical Ideal"—has brought considerations inspired by Emmanuel Levinas's reflections on alterity to bear on the issues that concern me in a strikingly illuminating way. If Young's position addresses those aspects of my project that are inspired by Critical Theory, then Bernasconi addresses its distinctively hermeneutic aspects. In brief, he challenges the adequacy of hermeneutic theory to render an account of cross-cultural understanding.[28] Focusing primarily upon Gadamer, Bernasconi suggests that the conception of understanding that animates hermeneutics is reflective of what can be achieved when one interprets texts drawn from one's own tradition, and that this is the case because it is with such situations that Gadamer himself was most familiar.

Dwelling with the object of one's interpretation in a common tradition has the hermeneutic advantage of underwriting agreement on the questions to which the text is an answer or on the topics or Sachen that it is addressing. Hence, in Bernasconi's estimation, the priority that the question or topic enjoys in Gadamer's hermeneutics, for it is the touchstone of successful interpretive achievement. Consequently, Gadamer does not pursue other, non-topic-centered, ways of conceiving what it is to understand the other.

This "prejudice in favor of the topic or subject matter" is objectionable, Bernasconi thinks, because the goal of understanding on this hermeneutic view is to overcome the otherness of the other, is, by enacting "the prejudice of representing difference or otherness as a problem to be resolved," to assimilate the other to the self.[29] With an exclusive focus upon the *topic* being addressed, the other *person* drops out of the picture, and in this sense, Bernasconi maintains, alterity is not given its due. Ultimately, Bernasconi is concerned that an understanding of the other that is underwritten by hermeneutics is tantamount to a projective misunderstanding, a misunderstanding with which we found Young, too, to be concerned.[30]

This is a sufficiently daunting impediment to doing justice to the alterity of persons and texts from our *own* tradition. However, in situations of intercultural dialogue, because we cannot presume the continuity of traditions—and we could do so, Bernasconi avers, only through the necessarily violent establishment of a "world civilization"—we are at a *double* disadvantage. Not only are we unable to presume a common tradition's promise to orient us with regard to the "right" questions and topics of address, but we are miserably ill equipped to respond to expressions of cultural others that are not intended to address a topic in the first place, for hermeneutic theory necessarily occludes the latter.[31] Bernasconi's essay thus carries a double implication: that the gulf between self and other within a tradition is different in kind from that between selves from different traditions; and that otherness in general, the claim of the other—whether local or intercultural—necessarily gets short shrift from approaches indebted to hermeneutics. In chapter 4's discussion of Sache identification as well as in my discussion of Young, I have spoken to the first concern. I want here to focus my attention on the second worry, that by focusing on the topic, alterity is not given its due.

I should like to begin by contesting Bernasconi's use of *assimilation* to refer to the necessarily distortive refashioning of the heterogeneous material of alterity to fit a previously established matrix, grid, or mold, to refer to the sort of polishing away of rough and characteristically distinctive edges of which Derrida accused philosophy in his "White Mythology." As the basis of an alternative to this idea of assimilation as erasure, the conception of understanding that I have proposed does conceptually involve an act of assimilation; but the act of assimilation involved is a dialectical one in that it is highly unlikely that the matrix invoked at the beginning of the process will prove adequate to its end. What Bernasconi, and Young too, seem to overlook is, as I have argued, that *we may have to change* in order to "situat[e] the other meaning in relation to the whole of our own meanings or situat[e] ourselves in relation to it."[32] That is, they are captive to the falsely dichotomous picture of "theirs *or* ours," where "ours" is by implication taken to rigidly resist transformation. It is true that our semantic matrix can be stretched only so far before it snaps, that is, before it ceases to be, in any meaningful sense, ours. Yet, as I have suggested in chapter 4 in a discussion of the heteroglossia of cultural identity, who can say beforehand what the elastic limit of any given horizon is? There is no line establishable a priori that demarcates what is internal to a self-description from what is necessarily external to it, and this attests to the possibility of a contingently, though not indefinitely, expandable sense of who "we" are. Why not think of alterity, then, as the provocation to extend our horizon in order to perform the feat of mutually situating "their" meanings in relation to ours? I should think, then, that this would accommodate Bernasconi's concern to recognize genuine alterity's capacity to put *me* radically into question.[33]

This would authorize the following gloss of "radical alterity," of that which, in principle, resists homogenizing assimilation. Think of "radical alterity" as playing the role in interpretive understanding that the "thing in itself" plays in the neo-Kantian account of understanding. That is, unless it is illegitimately hypostatized as the autonomous, self-subsistent unassimilable per se, what the term *radical alterity* quite plausibly refers to is the fact that no understanding of the other is final, complete, not subject to further revision, and so on. There will always be more to say, as the other's presence continually challenges any settled interpretive achievement. That is, *radical alterity* refers to the idea that understanding the "other" will always be an "unfinished project." It evokes what has not yet been "assimilated" through understanding.

Bernasconi objects that this makes of alterity merely a limit case.[34] His concern, therefore, is not with that which *has not* been understood, or even with that which *cannot* be understood, but rather with that which *is not* to be understood, insofar as understanding is taken to presuppose there to be a topic in question. And there are clearly such purely "expressive," as opposed to "referential," dimensions in human communicative interaction. For example, there is no topic being addressed in a greeting. As I suggested in the last section, the speech acts that effect greetings have no propositional content associated with them; there is no topic being addressed upon which interlocutors can agree or disagree.[35] Bernasconi gives the example of "small talk," the sort of chat about nothing in particular that facilitates interpersonal contact. Similarly, the sort of speech acts that John Searle denominates "expressives," including apologies, expressions of congratulations and of gratitude, because they are purely expressions, and not reports on the world—be it the inner, psychological world, or the external world—are not to be construed as answering a question or addressing a topic.[36] Considerations such as these encourage Bernasconi to think of radical alterity as that about the other's presence that not merely contingently but *in principle* transcends thematic or topical embodiment. The other challenges not only our biases and limitations, but also our very assumption that a topic, to be addressed by raising criticizable validity claims, is at issue at all.[37]

From this it follows that if we treat the other's expressive intervention as a claim about a topic, then we will have thereby committed a rather straightforward category mistake. And, as I have acknowledged, such an expressive dimension is a recurring feature of communicative action. I do worry, however, and in a way that I have highlighted throughout this study and especially in the last section, that an overweening focus on this aspect of communicative action, to the exclusion of others, will compromise respectful treatment of the other by deemphasizing her claim on us to recognize her semantic authority. This, it seems to me, is part of the price we pay for taking, as Bernasconi does, this subjectivist/expressivist model as the paradigm case of alterity.

The model that I have elaborated in this study allows, and even invites, the other to call us to "alter [our] lives." In order to see this more clearly, we need to return to the discussion in chapter 4 of the problematics of Sache, or topic, identification. By not thematizing sufficiently what it is for a comprehensive worldview to make a validity claim and by tending to understand the concept of tradition in a way that does not allow the deeply problematic character of topic identification to come to the fore, Habermas and Gadamer, respectively, fail to put us in a position to appreciate fully the potential mechanisms for transformative self-questioning that are inherent in the very process of topic identification. To this extent, I believe Bernasconi is right to question the ability of Gadamer's conception of

"Postmodern" Rejoinders

hermeneutics to do justice to alterity. However, this transformative potential, which Bernasconi, too, fails to give its due, is *explicitly* highlighted in my account of the construction of a situated metalanguage. In the course of a dialogical encounter, our differently situated interlocutor may entreat us to rank the various topics of common human concern differently, to interpret them somewhat differently, and perhaps to configure their relationships differently. I have argued that a crucial feature of topic identification is an interpretation to the "best case." In doing so, we may discover that the topic that we thought to be in play is not at issue, and that the topic that we discover to be at issue is one to which we had not given priority in our own lives, and one that shows itself to be more compelling than we originally assumed.

While cultures are not monolithic wholes, I would urge that widely based, socially shared understandings of the relative priority of various *Sachen*, of the interpretations of individual topical concerns, and of the configurations of relations among topical concerns can be understood to be among the expressive features that are distinctive of cultures. And these features can provide the occasions for the sorts of claim—implicitly made by other cultures—that can lead us to put ourselves into question. These features point to a moment in intercultural encounter wherein we are led to change ourselves, when we do, not by our having been convinced that we were mistaken about a subject matter, but by our having been invited to alter our views about the relative importance of various subject matters or about the relations among them.

For example, our encounter with mythical narratives—which when viewed in their proper contexts may be revealed not to be deficient explanations, and thus competitors to our scientific claims, but rather to be expressive dramatizations of social identity—may lead us to be more attentive to the identity informing contexts of our own lives.[38] Or, consider again Peter Winch's encounter with Zande thought, which led him to reconsider the role that an orientation to that over which we have no control, to the inevitable, ought to play in a human life.[39] Think again of my reconstruction of Anna Tsing's account of Banjar/Meratus relations, where the Meratus's implicit critique of the ideal of self-sufficiency could be seized upon as an invitation to the Banjar to change their lives (chapter 4, note 10). Consider, further, encounters with culturally different interlocutors who do not differentiate between the aesthetic and the utilitarian, or between the beautiful and the sacred, as sharply as many of us in the West are now accustomed to do—encounters with interlocutors who could be found on the African continent or among the aboriginal people of Australia or, for that matter, in rural America or during the Middle Ages in Europe.[40] From all of these we may learn; they may all provide occasions for a profound "re-visioning" of our settled notions about topical priority, topic interpretation, and topic configuration, and, consequently, for "re-visioning" the lives we think it worthwhile to lead. Naturally, not all encounters with alterity will persuade us to change our lives. For instance, if we are unwilling to relinquish our commitment to the sorts of enormously powerful and technologically exploitable learning process that are institutionalized in modern science and underwritten by the ideal of the strict segregation of the cognitive-instrumental domain from that of the moral-practical, the religious, or the aesthetic-expressive, then it is not likely that we will be persuaded to question seriously the value of such an idealized segregation, at least in relation to that narrowly defined commitment. Of course, while it is beyond the scope of this study to pursue it here, it should be pointed out that even this is by now a controversial claim, as is indicated by ongoing debates in the field of science studies about the putative multicultural status of science.[41] In any case, the aim of understanding in my view is not necessarily to reach a consensus with the other on a subject but rather, as I put it earlier, to be in a position to see the other's position as a good, which once discerned will be the occasion of a vivid sense of loss in the event that it turns out to mark a path that we decide not to take.

What is to be addressed and the address itself, both the expressive articulation of what topics are worth addressing and how they relate to each other on the one hand, and the modes of addressing those topics on the other, are moments of cultural expression. Insofar as Gadamer does not fully thematize the vexed nature of topic identification, the first expressive moment of cultural identity—the moment that is revelatory of topic significance and configuration—is not brought to light. And this is one of the limitations of traditional hermeneutics that has seldom, if at all, been remarked upon. The manner in which what Habermas refers to as "postmetaphysical worldviews" can indirectly raise validity claims is also related to these concerns of topic significance and configuration. And, as I have suggested, since Bernasconi does not thematize the moment of self-questioning associated with the concerns of topic configuration, priority, interpretation, and so on, he misses what is perhaps most distinctively valuable and achievable in intercultural encounters.

Of course, there remains the distinction between the category error of taking someone to be speaking to the wrong topic and that of mistakenly taking her to be speaking to a topic when she is not addressing a topic at all. Further, as Bernasconi points out, there are certainly configurations of self/other relation that, by their very nature, would seem to preclude the possibility of understanding the other—for example, that of oppressor to victim.[42] And here he raises the stakes by suggesting that genuine alterity is that which poses a challenge of the most radical sort, to wit, that one cannot understand without ceasing to be oneself.[43] The cases Bernasconi invokes here are cases where the status or identity of both self and other is constituted solely by the asymmetrical relationship of self to other itself, where the other's status or identity just *is* its place in such a relationship, cases where the self relates to the other *only* via the projection of an invidious representation and where the self *is* only the subject of such a projection. *Being* a racist, for example, just *is* to operate with an invidious understanding of the target of one's attitudes. But, surely, this is not the only mode of relating to the other. These cases, where alterity is exclusively the product of invidious representation enforced by asymmetrical power relations, can be distinguished from those where there is more to alterity than this, even if those power differentials are nonvanishing as such. Better put, perhaps, alterity can be parsed into a moment that is an effect of power and a moment that is not. The otherness of other cultures, for instance, certainly is not *exhausted* by their place in a power dynamic, nor is the otherness of a good friend who is quite different from us. We can be more to others than those in whose eyes they are deviations from our norms, and others can be more to us than deviations from those norms. To claim otherwise is to deny to cultural others, and to others in general, their own integrity as embodiments of alternative ways to be human. This is what underlies, for instance, the arguments made by Ralph Ellison and Albert Murray against those who would reduce African-American culture to a mere by-product of oppression. And recognizing this is another way of acknowledging that we can understand cultural others without ceasing to be ourselves—though, again, not perhaps without being transformed selves, selves whose biographical episodes form a series each of whose moments can be intelligibly related to what preceded it.

It is perhaps not terribly exciting to acknowledge it, but it is simply the case that being put into question is a matter of degree, and so too is the alterity that occasions such an interrogatory moment. It is therefore implausible to claim that unless one addresses a mode of alterity whose understanding requires the interpreter to cease being herself, one has not addressed alterity at all. Given that my orienting concern in this study is the dialogical construction of pedagogical representations, my aim is not at all, in Bernasconi's terms, to assimilate the other, but to learn from her. This in turn implies that the model that I have adduced for mutual understanding is in a fundamental way oriented toward the novel in experience. It is a Hegelian truism that my own views—both about various subject matters and about the relative importance of and relationships among subject matters—can be thrown into question and tested only by differently situated others. It is therefore a constitutive feature of my model to seek out alterity. It would indeed subvert the very aim of my project to too readily assimilate the unfamiliar to the familiar, to too hastily domesticate the uncanny.

In Bernasconi's way of proceeding, the most intractable cases of understanding are used to set the standards for determining whether understanding has been accomplished; they mark the virtually infinite threshold condition to which understanding must rise if it is to count as genuine. This optic leads him to focus on how *little* can be understood. Like the ideal of the mutual transparency of copresence for Young, perfect understanding becomes the measure in terms of which all accomplished understanding is invidiously dismissed. The glass is always half empty. Only if one surveys the terrain from the standpoint of a posited ideal of complete mutual transparency would the recognition of the "misunderstanding that pervades all understanding" lead to the devaluation of the project of gaining all of the mutual understanding that we can. As I have argued elsewhere, this optic, like that of deconstruction, is haunted by the image of an understanding that is always infinitely deferred and in terms of which anything achievable must be found wanting, and, in being found so wanting, tends to be dismissed as a mere simulacrum.

In the end, Bernasconi and I have different concerns. Motivated by a Levinasian anxiety that the otherness of the other will not be given its due, Bernasconi's primary intent appears to be to preserve a moment of otherness *for its own sake*. His point of departure then is the unassimilable and its discontents, and he is concerned with foregrounding alterity's points of resistance to what he sees as the erasure of assimilative understanding. I, on the other hand, am interested in how much can be understood, in how full the glass can be. And given my understanding that "understanding" involves a moment of becoming other to myself, both in the sense of seeing myself from the perspective of the other and of the self-transformation required by and resulting from understanding the other, my concern is with the infinite and perhaps paradoxical project of anticipating the overcoming of the alienness per se of the other, while embracing her always residual otherness as an occasion for further growth, for furthering my self-othering, my self-*alter*ation. Were we to adopt the starting point of thinkers like Bernasconi, it would be difficult to see how we could give an account of how this process of *Bildung* could get off the ground. It would be short-circuited from the start.

III

In closing this chapter, I would like to address the implications for my project of the skeptical and relativistic thrust of what has been called "postmodern anthropology." Perhaps what most clearly distinguishes those gathered under this umbrella is their insistence that ethnography be regarded more as a literary than a scientific genre. Being greatly influenced by contemporary intellectuals' sensitivity to the complicity of truth and power, the spokespersons for this highly self-reflexive cultural practice—like the philosophers I have discussed—often seem to despair of achieving veridical cross-cultural understanding. And this from people whose very *business* is cross-cultural understanding. How cogent is their position? Are they merely coparticipants in the zeitgeist articulated by the philosophers, or do they have an angle of vision not yet considered? And if the latter, how important is it for what I am attempting here? In the course of my discussion, I wish, however briefly, to explore the question: Given my primary concern with learning from others, what has truth got to do with my project, either the truth of our representations of others or the truth, as in "authenticity," of their self-representations? (And I do not think that this can be dismissively settled by definitional fiat, by pointing out that, strictly speaking, we cannot be said to have "learned" what is false.) Actually, since my project has the status of a regulative ideal, it authorizes our proceeding with what may be counterfactual presumptions of good will and sincerity, though it offers resources for detecting violations of these conditions, and though I have also argued that there are reasons internal to a culture's own interest in self-assurance that would incline it to align itself with the ideal. That said, if the philosophers raised the issue of the philosophical coherence of our hopes for a mutually enlightened humanity (unsuccessfully, in my view), the anthropologists, insofar as they are offering something distinctive, are perhaps questioning how realistic that hope is.

In the case of the veridical representation of others, the anthropological theorists who believe that the human sciences are experiencing a "crisis of representation" can be argued to be subject to an artificial anxiety that can be attributed to postmodernism as a whole. The feeling that representation is in crisis seems to be the consequence of taking seriously the fact that cultural data will always underdetermine cultural representations and the descriptive categories used in such representations.[44] But to refer to this situation as a crisis seems too strong. That theoretical accounts are underdetermined by the data they are adduced to explain has long been recognized in the philosophy of science and, indeed, in scientific practice without leading to epistemological despair. That is, some who subscribe to the "crisis of representation" thesis may well have so stringent a criterion of objectivity, of veridical or authentic cultural knowledge, that they too must see all attempts at understanding as necessarily falling short.[45] Their heightened, even *hyper-*, sense of self-reflexivity can be paralyzing. They tend to view the very necessity of a metalanguage's bridging distance to portend an obfuscation, producing "them" for "us," or as testimony to the incommensurability of our standpoint and theirs, rather than as the acknowledgment of an enabling condition of our understanding them. The crisis of representation thesis, thus, may well reflect what Gadamer criticized as an overweening concern about the avoidance of error, a concern that leaves little room for adequate attention to the enabling conditions of knowledge.

In general, I would argue, the epistemology of postmodern anthropology—at least of some representative versions of it—rests upon a deficient view of scientific representation and of the role of language in it. If science fails, it is not because of its inability to "reconcile the competing demands of representation and communication."[46] For scientific representation, like all representation, is representation under a description; that is, it is linguistically mediated and thus inherently communicable. It is true that there once reigned an empiricist self-understanding of science that dreamed of finding a language for science that effaced itself as a language, but that is a dream well lost. In its emphasis upon a dialogically negotiated discourse that emerges from the mutual participation of both anthropologist and "informant," and in its emphasis upon the value of ethnography for inspiring us "to restructure experience and the conduct of everyday life," postmodern anthropology exhibits traits that I would obviously applaud. But in their concern to distance themselves from representation and to understand ethnography as a purely literary genre, many of the thinkers who pursue this practice do so seemingly without having confronted current thinking about either language or science.

It is of course true that "reality [cannot] be explicitly projected in text," if by this one means captured in all of its aspects in a single textual framing.[47] Textual frames are always underdetermined by "reality" since reality is not self-announcing. But this does not mean that reality will always completely elude our textualizations, however partial those textualizations may be, particularly if they are dialogically constructed. For instance, when "we" take "them" to be addressing X, they may not take themselves to be addressing X, or to be doing so primarily, but *insofar* as they can plausibly be construed to address X, our representation of what they have to say about it can be adjudged true or false, just as in the case of scientific representation, descriptive claims can be shown to be more or less adequate with respect to the linguistic framework within which they are articulated.

Little in what postmodern ethnographers adduce in the way of argument makes the case for the "failure of the whole visualist ideology of referential discourse."[48] More precisely, nothing brought forward is particularly damaging to the idea of *referential* discourse. For if by "visualist ideology" is meant the commitment to the aperspectivality and full transparency of *theoria*, with its associated "view from nowhere," then few if any today would take that seriously. Nevertheless, the idea of representation within what is acknowledged to be a language, and hence to be one among possible others, is alive and well. Once one has acknowledged that facts are, in part, linguistic artifacts, then one can recognize that what counts as a fact can be essentially contested without giving up on the idea of representation itself. It is just these linguistic frames that are subject to the conversational negotiation and testing that I have discussed throughout this essay.

The postmodernist claim, as noted by Stephen Tyler,[49] that ethnography is "just literature" rests upon two highly questionable premises: one, the belief that the "pure seeing" of *theoria* is constitutive of scientific representation; and two, that the science/literature distinction exhausts the possibilities for intellectual practice. Hence, it is argued that if ethnography is not a matter of the representation of brute, uninterpreted data purely observed, then it must be a literary genre. It is as if the putative incommensurability of the language of the "truly" other with our own licensed an almost solipsistic fictional production without constraint.[50] Given such a view, it is difficult to understand why an anthropologist should bother to talk to *real* others except as a means of generating more "chance happenings" later to be integrated into the fictional narrative that is an ethnography.[51] As far as the culture in question is concerned, such ethnographies proceed as if there were no "there" there.

Clearly not even a "dialogical anthropology," to use a current expression, would seem to satisfy such theorists.[52] This is because even a dialogically generated cultural self-representation would not be self-announcing; such a self-representation, too, would require *our* interpretation and would be subject to questions with regard to the adequacy of our interpretation. Further, such a self-representation, given the occasion of its generation, is likely to be framed in categories that are not wholly indigenous to the population whose representation is in question. Surely, however, this line of thought would amount to a *reductio* of their position, for all conversations to some degree will require such practices of mutual interpretation. Much of what I say in criticism of Young's conception of "understanding" is *mutatis mutandis* applicable here. Dialogical assent is of course no *guarantee* that we have a faithful representation of a culture. There can be self-deception, strategic manipulation, and so forth. But, I would argue, it is ultimately a necessary condition of a fair and faithful representation. We may well require a *depth* dialogue of the sort that the hermeneutics of suspicion represents in order to get at what is "really" going on. On the other hand, we can learn from even a strategic self-presentation what is valued by cultural others, or what they think should be valued, or, certainly what *they* think *we* value.

Then, what *about* the issue of strategic representation? Even if we can to a mutually acceptable degree determine what others mean by what they say, how do we know that they really *believe* what they say, or would believe it in the absence of strong psychosocial incentives, incentives directly and explicitly tied to individuals' strategic interests? We can draw an analytic distinction between the general social processes of the construction and modification of cultural tradition and its representations on the one hand, and "objectification" as an explicit and self-conscious strategic political process on the other.[53] This distinction would seem to license a "hermeneutic of suspicion" with regard to *self*-representations of a culture just as we are wise to enact such a hermeneutic of suspicion with respect to allorepresentations of a culture. And the reasons and prospects for a hermeneutics of suspicion enacted on the self-representations of a culture are not significantly different from those for an "ideology critique" of an allorepresentation.[54] My concern with pedagogical representations, representations from which we can learn, implies a presumption against viewing the other's self-representation as invidiously strategic. Thus, reference to their possibly strategic intentions is suspended in the first instance. In Habermas's terms, there is a presumption of sincerity, truth, and normative rightness, but not in his more purely counterfactual sense that these are the standards to which we unavoidably appeal, but in the more substantive sense that we actually grant to our interlocutor the presumption that these standards have in fact been met. Here we might say that the criterion, though not the meaning, of "the most adequate representation" is "the representation in which the best case is made for what they do." One might say that such a strong methodological principle of charity informs our definition of a genuine conversation, that the standards, as far as the participants are capable of it, are met and that each trusts that the other is meeting them.[55]

Yet, given that self-representations clearly can be and—as the anthropologist Renato Rosaldo advises me—perhaps typically are strategic in some sense, it is incumbent on us to attend to this possibility. So, the question remains, If culture is always constructed, how do we maintain a distinction between a mystification, or an ideological and strategic objectification on the one hand, and nonideological representations of self on the other? First, we have to acknowledge that strategic representation is a matter of degree. Such representations are responses to a situated addressee, responses that range from the relatively innocent attempt not to offend or to hold the addressee's attention, to calculated attempts to negotiate an actual or perceived power differential between speaker and listener. Though most cases fall between the two extremes, there are cases of representation that seem to be strategic in the strong sense, for example, the case of some contemporary versions of "Afrocentrism" (which offer highly prescriptive representations of an essentialized black cultural subject) or the case of so-called Islamists (who proffer highly prescriptive accounts of Muslim identity).[56] Second, the interests that occasion strategic representations are unlikely, except in extreme cases, to be distributed *uniformly* across individuals in a culture. The *representativeness* of such strategic self-images can then be interrogated through dialogue with a representative variety of such individuals, knowing full well, of course, that what counts as a representative variety is a matter for interpretive contestation. Nevertheless, one would do well to start with representations parsed out in terms of the demographic categories of class, ethnicity, and gender. Further, one should be on the lookout for signs that would trigger a hermeneutics of suspicion, signs such as observed conflicts between speech and behavior, conflicts of interest within the culture, observed indices of perceived or actual power asymmetries between interlocutors within the culture, and so on.[57] Further, I would argue that such a broadened conversation should be informed by the counterfactual query, "What might your response be if it were not constrained by your fears?"—particularly in cases where there are reasons to believe there to be a connection between fear of reprisal and self-representation.

However, even if we can draw an analytic distinction between general processes of social construction and transformation and those of strategic objectification, where the objectifications do not serve the general interest, it does not follow that all cases of strategic objectification will appear on a radar screen oriented toward detecting instances of what Habermas would call "suppressed generalizable interests" (and not only for the hermeneutic reasons that I have mentioned elsewhere,[58] but also for logical reasons); for in some cases the strategic ends of objectification may be to promote a genuine generalizable interest within a culture. Secrecy and deception would be understandable strategies to deploy if a culture as a whole felt itself under siege, for example.[59] Then the question becomes, What would it mean to enact a hermeneutics of suspicion when objectification serves a generalizable interest? (By the way, this would seem to point to an aspect of the account of cultural self-representation not envisioned by Habermas, to wit, that such expressions may be subject to the validity claims of moral rightness as well as to demands of authenticity and sincerity.) In the case of nongeneralizable objectification, what would occasion our suspicion are questions about the representativeness of self-representations. And we regard our suspicions as being dialogically testable. But if there are no reasons to doubt the representativeness of the representations, what then? Would it not then become a fairly naked issue of who has the right to control cultural representation? Without wanting to dismiss this always important question, it can be pointed out that much of interest can be gleaned from a comparative inquiry attending to how a given culture represents itself to different others at different points of intercultural contact. In this way, we could gain some sense of the role that even generalized strategic interests play in cultural self-representation. It should be remembered, too, that cultures generally are sufficiently heterogeneous that this case is a special and limiting case. So, we are always entitled to ask, though always within a context of hermeneutic modesty, Which such objectifications really are in the general interest? Various indigenous justifications for the practice of female circumcision are obvious cases in point here.

Going further still, the reason we would want to make a distinction between even a strategic self-representation that did in fact reflect a generalizable interest, on the one hand, and what is "authentically" or "really" going on, on the other, is that it is likely that *only* those cultural patterns that *actually* inspired and sustained a civilization over time will be the cultural patterns that we can learn from. (Of course, patterns that are items of "false consciousness" might have such sustaining power, but presumably once exposed, they would be deprived of that power, and, at any rate, we would not be inclined to learn from them once they had been so exposed.) Clearly much remains to be said here, but that would take us beyond the scope of this essay. I shall bring this discussion to a close by noting that, as the anthropologists George Marcus and Michael Fischer recently put it, "If . . . the knowledge which anthropology offers of cultural alternatives cannot be conceived according to conventional notions of scientific precision and certainty, then on what authority can it offer itself as a critic of its own society"?[60] It is in this way that questions of truth, of the "authenticity" of representation, become important for my project. Though absolutely essential, they remain subordinate to the issue of pedagogical value, however. Within the ambit of the pedagogical interest, truth is of value, not to confer a competitive advantage in negotiation but to warrant the reliability of a potential source of edification. And, as I have argued, there is a trade-off between the putative competitive advantage conferred by strategic representation and the potential gain in insight afforded by less disingenuous representation. Self-representations in general no doubt contain moments of each, aspects of both the strategic and the nonstrategic. Insofar as the strategic aspects are occasioned by real asymmetries of power, our attention is directed beyond the realm of philosophy to that of politics, where we imagine ways to address these asymmetries where we can.

Fischer and Marcus offer, in many respects, a compelling account of the contribution that anthropological understanding—and in particular what they call "critique by ethnographical juxtaposition"—can make to the critique of one's home culture.[61] Theirs is thus an important research program for my purposes. However, the brief for their program is deficient in one important regard. They claim that their projects of cultural critique via cross-cultural juxtaposition are antiseptically value free.[62] Such a project, however, would flirt with incoherence, and on two counts. First, one cannot consistently operate with a concern for allowing other cultures to be fairly represented, to have their voice heeded, and suspend that concern—that is, fail to at least take it to be *a* desideratum, even if only one among others—when it comes to taking account of the way in which other cultures in turn treat *their* least powerful voices (those of their women, minorities, and so on). This is a moral judgment that, while it may be regarded as question begging, is nevertheless unavoidable and "unsurpassable" given the original concern with fair representation. On the question of female circumcision, for example, a concern for fair cultural representation would make it exceedingly difficult to avoid the concern for the affected women's point of view, as that perspective would perhaps be articulated under the ideal counterfactual conditions where the connection between undergoing such rituals and the quality of life chances (for marriage and so on) has been severed. Second, one cannot coherently perform cultural critique by ethnographical juxtaposition alone, because critique will always require criteria; otherwise, one would not know in which direction the critic's arrow should be aimed. The practitioners of such criticism must take a stand on what they take to be of value in the cultures they are contrasting; otherwise one has mere difference, not critical counterpoint. I end with these observations concerning the methodological inescapability of evaluative perspectives to highlight the nature of the symmetry requirement that is presupposed by my model of cross-cultural conversation—a requirement that demands equality of respect for the other's practices and claims as *candidates* for acceptability, but not equality in their *ultimate* acceptability—and thus to underscore its status as a model for mutually *critical* conversation.

Epilogue
Toward a Humanistic Multiculturalism

I

I conclude this study with a focus on its implications for the concerns of multiculturalism, particularly as those concerns have expressed themselves in the United States. Multiculturalism is a highly overdetermined phenomenon. To some degree, as institutionalized from "above," it represents a "substitute program" for genuine racial equality, social justice "on the cheap." Moreover, to some extent from "below," and particularly under such cultural nationalist descriptions as "Afrocentrism," it can be grasped as an understandable reaction to the repeated failure to deliver on the Enlightenment democratic promise of a color-blind society. That is, multiculturalism is firmly inscribed in the domain of racial politics. While not in any way wanting to deny this, I suggest that thinking of multiculturalism from the standpoint of "humanity as an unfinished project" highlights what is of enduring value about the movement. In order to show this, I shall exploit the analogy between the idea of promising research programs in the sciences and the idea of what I call democratically chosen "promising life programs." The understanding of multiculturalism that emerges from the standpoint of "humanity as an unfinished project" will prove to have an explicitly normative content.

Let me begin my argument by pointing out that a doctrine, like Matthew Arnold's, that privileges "the best which has been thought and said in the world" does not—despite the provincial contexts of its typical invocation—*necessarily* exclude the cultural products of the marginalized qua marginalized, the thought of the other qua other. It would do so only on the assumption that criteria of worth or of value are incapable of having anything other than a merely local validity and application, an assumption that I have challenged in this essay. It is true that such a doctrine sets us up for all sorts of hermeneutical blunders when assessing the "noncanonical" (and my account of Theodor Adorno's jazz analysis is illustrative of this). But it also challenges us to discern what goals the noncanonical sets for itself, to determine how well the noncanonical practice lives up to those goals and, of course, to come to some provisional and open assessment of the goals themselves—of what agendas they serve, of how worthy, interesting, and edifying they are.

In a wide-ranging and much-commented-upon discussion of the vexed state of intercultural recognition, Charles Taylor has argued that we should distinguish judgments of value from expressions of taste and willful acts of solidarity. The latter, in particular—a willful, though well-meaning, act of solidarity—can be, as I suggest in chapter 5's discussion of Iris Marion Young's work, tantamount to a subversion of the respectful recognition that we owe the other.[1] Taylor avows that a favorable judgment rendered on demand—that is, one not informed by the judge's own standards—would be a meaningless gesture. In order to avoid such condescension, we need to understand judgments of worth to be meaningful claims. That is, if a judgment of the value of a cultural practice is to count as a meaningful recognition of those whose practice it is, it must be understood—as G. W. F. Hegel's "master/slave" dialectic teaches us—as a falsifiable claim, as a claim that permits of disputation and that can be redeemed or demonstrated argumentatively.

The very idea of presuming to judge the practices of cultural others, no matter how well-intentioned, has come under attack by thinkers who are understandably wary of its alliance with paternalism and cultural imperialism. For instance, in response to Taylor, the feminist theorist Linda Nicholson claims that Taylor not only untenably opposes reason and meaningful judgment, on the one hand, to power and will, on the other, and does so in an absolute fashion, but also that he implicitly licenses invidious distinctions between those "peripheral" cultures whose

Epilogue: Toward a Humanistic Multiculturalism

practices require justification from the "center" and those whose practices do not.[2]

Taylor himself acknowledges that a position, like Michel Foucault's, that projects the constitutive connection between power and knowledge would license the dismantling of the distinction between judgment and will.[3] But, here, Taylor concedes too much. The distinction between will and justification that Taylor wishes to maintain can be retained, if suitably redescribed. That is, as Nicholson herself seems to acknowledge, one does not have to subscribe to what she rightly views as a false opposition in order to retain the distinction in an effective way. One can, with Foucault, assume that argumentation and validity claims are always already situated within a knowledge regime constituted by power or, with Hans-Georg Gadamer, that they are inserted within a tradition as its historical effects. Even if we grant this, we can still meaningfully distinguish between having *reasons* (drawn from that regime or tradition) for a belief and being *forced* to adopt a belief. We can still meaningfully distinguish between reasons for a judgment and fear, prejudice, or habit as a basis for issuing a judgment; between a regime's or a tradition's *ideal* of a good reason and what is in fact *accepted* as a good reason; and further, between challenging or questioning that tradition and passively accepting its limits.[4] In other words, reasons are relevant, even if not conclusive. And autonomy is not irrelevant, even if it is to be understood as a contextual property.

However, the second worry implicit in Nicholson's criticism—the reference to the invidious selection of the cultural groups whose practices require justification—is more troubling, for why should members of a group, whose practices were thought sufficiently "weird" that they were singled out for justification, accept the prevailing framework dictating who gets judged, and by whom? Why should they be the supplicants, submitting to being judged by a tradition whose framework has made no conceptual space for them and whose objective validity they would have every right to contest? That is, why should they acknowledge in this form those who have yet to acknowledge them? Would it not be tantamount to acceding to the astonishing arrogance of those who had arrogated to themselves the right to judge? There would indeed be something rather pathetic and demeaning in this. *Please, massa—find me worthy!* On the other hand, as Taylor suggests, it would be an act of patronizing condescension on my part if I were to endorse your practices simply because you demand it of me, without satisfying myself *by my lights*. My judgment of you will mean more to you the more it is informed by your standards of worth, and my endorsement will be less a matter of condescension to me the more I can see your standards of worth as intelligible measures of good *for me*. This is a situation—requiring the avoidance of the Scylla of arrogance and the Charybdis of condescension—that palpably begs for a fusion of horizons. It requires that we put ourselves in a position to see that a meaningful and non-question-begging judgment of worth is one that satisfies the following two conditions: it is freely reached in context; and it is informed by standards appropriate—in the ways discussed in chapter 2—to the range of phenomena being assessed. Such a fusion of horizons between my context and your standards is conceptually feasible because the criteria of rationality that are constituted by power or by tradition are not themselves codified in explicit algorithms or rules whose alteration would be coextensive with their violation.[5] And, consequently, if my argument here is sound, judgments of worth need not exclude a recognition of cultural others in terms that they too would acknowledge. I do agree with Nicholson, however, that there is a somewhat troublingly asymmetrical tenor to the prosecution of Taylor's argument, but I think that this is not fatal and can be addressed by being quite explicit, as I have tried to be throughout this essay, about the purely *indexical* status of the pronouns *we* and *they*, and their cognates. That is, whoever meaningfully utters those pronouns should enjoy the equal opportunity to be the judge or the judged. We are dealing here with processes of *reciprocal* recognition.

Naturally, judgments about the value of the goals of cultural practices are the most difficult, and indeed, in many if not most cases, nothing like a *final* epistemic decision should be sought. Of course, however, in situations where it is a matter of garnering resources for the public recognition of particular cultural ideals, the sorts of situation that typically give rise to debates over multiculturalism, practical decisions have to be made. Here, in ways that I have tried to make clear in this essay, it is legitimate for *our* interests to come into play, assuming we have a flexible enough sense of who *we* are and an enlightened enough sense of what our interests are. We want the best that is of interest or that should be of interest to *us*. Here, in making discriminations between the best and the rest, between the worthy and the less than worthy while acknowledging the inadvisability of epistemic closure, we might do well to appeal to notions analogous to "promising" and "unpromising" research programs in science. For the sake of convenience, I shall call them "life programs," and understand such a program to be promising insofar as the values it embodies—be they moral, social, intellectual, political, religious, aesthetic, psychological, or scientific—show potential for facilitating the realization of the (revisable) ideals of the good life, in any of its senses, that actual people have. As the discussion in chapter 2 implies, for instance, increased attentiveness to the values embodied in jazz practice can enhance—can broaden and deepen—one's response to music in general, making of jazz practice an example of such a promising life program in that it can contribute to the fashioning of an enlarged musical mentality.

Many of the conclusions concerning multiculturalism to which I have been led by my development of the idea of "situated cosmopolitanism" resonate, to varying degrees, with some recent articulations reached by rather different routes from my own—to cite three, Thomas McCarthy's idea of "multicultural cosmopolitanism," Homi Bhabha's "translational cosmopolitanism," and Paul Gilroy's "planetary humanism."[6] Central to these conceptions, and to my own, though in importantly different ways, is the idea of culture as a "changing same," but the implications of my project bear a close affinity with a much older formulation as well, that of the distinguished black philosopher Alain Locke.[7] In a note to chapter 2, I have already made reference to Locke's offering a critical counterpoint to Adorno's jazz analysis. In the pamphlet to which I referred there, Locke emphasizes both jazz's "context of generation" in black culture *and* its status in the "context of justification," where he pronounces it "human enough to be universal in appeal and expressiveness."[8] Locke goes on to speak in general of the value, in terms of the enhancement of pleasure, derived from the "widening of taste to a cosmopolitan range."[9] His is an important articulation of the idea of the generalizability of cultural resources in the context of an advocacy of the sort of critical pluralism and intellectual democracy that I here endorse.

This cannot imply, of course, that every cultural good, no matter how compelling it is in its own terms, will be found universally valuable or applicable. The value of a cultural good will be determined by its usefulness in realizing a particular, though revisable, vision of the good life. Our interests come into play here. Just as in the case of research programs, where there are *guidelines* for making discriminations between the promising and the unpromising—as opposed to criteria that can be applied a priori to scientific theories in the abstract—there cannot be rigid criteria here. Promising life programs can span a broad spectrum. At one end might lie simply those with the potential to expand our sense of human possibilities. Perhaps nearby will be found those tableaux drawn from other cultural contexts that for good reason we cannot adopt, but that nevertheless allow for an edifying mirroring of ourselves in terms of the world of the other. For an illustration of this point on the spectrum of possibilities, one that I have used elsewhere in a different context, consider a political liberal who—when her commitment to individualism is redescribed from the angle of vision of a Marxist or a communitarian—may discover implications of that commitment for the conception of the relationship between self and community of which she was unaware. Such a person would not thereby cease to be a liberal, though it is unlikely that she would not be changed by the encounter. At the other end of the spectrum will be those programs that we will see the benefit in adopting to varying degrees.

This approach has the virtue, I would argue, of bringing together Charles Taylor's emphasis upon what is universally *worthy* in another tradition with Susan Wolf's emphasis upon reflecting the variegated strands that make up the *us*.[10] Especially in cases where public resources—spatial, temporal, and material—are contested, each *demos* will have to be a site where decisions are made regarding which cultural "leads" are most promising for pursuit and, once engaged in such a pursuit, to decide, again provisionally, which aims and practices within those cultural paradigms seem to represent promising life programs. The decision regarding promising cultural leads, insofar as it is not purely a matter of private exploration, is ideally to be reached in a discursively democratic fashion—that is, not by a simple majority or plurality.[11]

This brings into focus another version of a false dichotomy, one presumed by latter-day followers of Arnold and their critics alike: to wit, the assumption that one either adopts a stance of critical discrimination that is inevitably shadowed by ethnocentrism and cultural conservatism (e.g., Hilton Kramer and the *New Criterion*) or one adopts the stance of a hermeneutic openness devoid of standards that consorts with a promiscuous relativism. My approach in this book constitutes a challenge to this dichotomy. It challenges the putative isomorphism that both sides accept: "high culture" (the noble) is associated with a settled, established elite "us," and "low culture" (the vulgar) is associated with "them" (the global "subalterns").

One side thinks that since "high culture" can *only* be understood as what happens to be sanctioned by a social elite, that in order to appreciate "them," the high/low culture edifice has to be dismantled (this is the postmodern moment). The other side, thinking it has high culture's stamp of approval ("it's estimable because we like it") feels legitimately entitled, justified, to dismiss the folkways (which it opposes to "culture") of "them." Historically, the consolidation of the high/low culture distinction has almost certainly been informed by some such isomorphism.

Epilogue: Toward a Humanistic Multiculturalism

(Theodor Adorno and J. G. von Herder might represent countertrends, as might even Arnold in his better moments; and with sympathy for both Herder and Arnold, W. E. B. Du Bois challenges this isomorphism by emphasizing the aesthetic merit of the "sorrow songs," of Negro spirituals[12].) But the question is, Must it necessarily be so informed? It is a ramification of my argument that the critical distinction between the estimable and the inestimable should be deployed within the context of a group and its aims—this is the historicist or contextualist dimension of my argument—and that no a priori (de jure or de facto) privilege should be given to any demographic feature of a group in deciding what is to count as "high" or "low." The only legitimate reference to demographic features will be for purposes of "accounting" or "inventory"—that is, to insure that everyone affected (within a given national or regional "we") will have representative participation in the conversational negotiation of what cultural leads to pursue and in decisions regarding what should warrant our attention (and perhaps be taught in our schools).

This way of putting it highlights the centrality of a conception of discursive democracy to multiculturalist discourse. *All* parties to the negotiation bring their cultural predispositions and inclinations to the table. The point will not be to decide, in Arnoldian fashion, which single sort of cultural product will have hegemony over society (a consensus of this sort is not likely to be reached in a multicultural society anyway); rather, it will be, in the course of an ideally open discussion, to agree on a vocabulary for debating likely cultural leads to pursue with society's support.

Such a discussion will no doubt make reference to some analogue of what I have alluded to as "promising life programs." One can develop an argument for a life program's promise in at least two ways: (1) the program is particularly edifying to members of society associated primarily or historically with the tradition from which that program emerged (for example, it initiates, enables, and/or sustains processes of self-understanding) as are arguably, for example, jazz, African art and African dance for many, though not all, African Americans; and (2) the program is edifying and transformative for *all* members of society, as are, in addition to the examples cited above, the wisdom implicit in non-Western religious traditions, in non-Western assumptions about social life, and so on. And, in a hybrid—or what the cultural theorist Albert Murray calls "mulatto"—society such as ours, both arguments are relevant at once.

How can we encourage the production and reproduction of a society that would sustain such a multicultural conversation? By supporting socialization processes that cultivate and provide a rationale for a taste for diversity. By encouraging the situated cosmopolitan sensibility that prizes the encounters with others that enable us to test our assumptions about the "good life." This cosmopolitanism differs from that of, say, a Martha Nussbaum, who understandably focuses on what is *like me* in the other.[13] And I applaud the concerns that motivate her conception of cosmopolitanism. This focus, however, not only tends to decontextualize the other, but also fails to emphasize sufficiently that it is the *different* in the other from which I, given my context of concerns, can learn. And given that my self-knowledge and my understanding of the shared human world is fashioned by the rays refracted through the prism of others, it is crucial to emphasize in processes of socialization that—much as a lack of variation in its gene pool inhibits the viability of a species—a loss in cultural diversity is a self-impoverishment.

This essay's acknowledgment of the dynamic, open, hybrid, and "dialogic" structure of cultural identity argues against "nationalist" styles of multiculturalism. In black nationalism, for example, the idea of organic racial unity—which, when not articulated biologically, is founded upon a unitary conception of racialized experience—plays the roles allotted to language and culture by Herder. This consequent tendency toward hermeticism and highly prescriptive accounts of cultural identity is very difficult to reconcile with the position I have staked out. This renders many current articulations of Afrocentrism, though understandable, nevertheless deeply questionable for me.[14]

There have been many attempts, undertaken with varying degrees of sophistication, to establish the importance for cultural diversity of a racially articulated acknowledgment of others, and thus to demonstrate that racially articulated approaches to multiculturalism should be viewed, not only as "reaction formations" in a racist society, but also as necessary conditions of continuing cultural diversity in an ideal postracist society. One of the more sophisticated is a provocative intervention by a prominent philosopher of science, Philip Kitcher. In an argument to the effect that a taste for diversity would, perhaps paradoxically and even in an ideal nonracist society, require the continuation of race consciousness, Kitcher has averred that the preservation of ethnic diversity requires the social recognition of the biological significance of race, that such preservation requires a racial substrate.[15] He has suggested that, if we want to preserve ethnic diversity, eliminativist attempts to replace the biological notion of race by the cultural notion of ethnicity will fail. Having acknowledged that "race" is a social construct in two senses—that it, to use Aristotle's apt expression, does not cut nature at its joints, and that human "racial" differences are sustained, where they are, by social and cultural decisions regarding the acceptability of reproductive intermixing—Kitcher's position on race is that ethnicity performs the race-preserving work of reproductive isolation. His position on ethnicity is that race and biological lineage are the lines through which ethnicity is handed down, so that the racial transmission of ethnicity performs the ethnicity preserving work of cultural isolation. Consequently, for Kitcher, the systems of race and of ethnicity are mutually reinforcing. This is the case, I believe, because ethnicity has for him two distinguishable features, one exercised horizontally and the other vertically: it acts horizontally in that it serves as a mechanism of reproductive isolation; it acts vertically in that it tends to be transmitted along lines of biological lineage. The horizontal, isolating, feature insures that the vertical biological lines of cultural transmission are also racialized lines.

Kitcher expresses the deep concern that cultural diversity would be threatened if we failed to acknowledge socially the salience of race. Given that, for him, ethnicities contingently seem to stick to races, race-blind mating patterns will ultimately undermine the continuation of distinctive patterns of cultural meaning. I would argue, however, that the continuation of a network of cultural traditions does not *require* a racial substrate or a racialized line of transmission, even when that network of traditions has arisen with, and been historically maintained by, racialized subjects. Cultural traditions could be supported without the bearers of the supported traditions being members of the "race" historically associated with them. I recall here an account of a woman of European descent who, hesitantly to be sure, became the link for the continuation of a medically important healing tradition practiced by native peoples of Central America when the last living practitioner, an old man of Mayan descent, passed it on to her. Closer to home, and despite the controversies it has given rise to around just these sorts of issues, Lincoln Center's jazz program in New York, dedicated as it is to the preservation and vitality of this crucially important aspect of the black musical heritage, could well provide funding to white musicians for this purpose. This sort of initiative would obviate the necessity for the sort of cultural policing required to "keep the natives on the reservation." Mechanisms of cultural preservation do not *have* to be mediated by the concept of race or by a normative pressure that would enforce harmony between race and ethnicity. A tolerant society could support the survival of culturally diverse ways of being insofar as it provided reasons and incentives to each of the groups comprising it to see the survival of the other ways of being as important to itself. And such a society would do so not in the context of forcing members of threatened groups to propagate themselves culturally or by making it difficult for them to make other cultural choices, but by removing impediments to, and assuring the necessary enabling conditions of, such cultural propagation for those who choose to take advantage of it. And, for a variety of reasons—including what I referred to earlier as a life program's promise for enhancing self-understanding—persons from backgrounds traditionally associated with a given family of practices will choose to take advantage of such an opportunity.

Indeed, given overwhelming tendencies to essentialize the notions of both race and ethnicity and to link the two, perhaps we would be better off dropping talk of both (except, and this *cannot* be overlooked, for strategic reasons of the redress of discrimination and for the psychological empowerment of youth in a continuingly racist society). This is especially so if the requisite emphasis on race is ineluctably invidious. In such a postethnic scene we could hold on to a concept of culture wherein we need no longer think of the bearers of a culture as being necessarily connected by biological links.[16] What would make a culture distinctive, what would give it its integrity would be the sorts of overlapping affinities and family resemblances that allowed Thomas S. Kuhn to talk about different scientific traditions, or that allowed me to invoke the idea of a plurality of life programs above—affinities like those between some of, say, Toni Morrison's novels and the jazz idiom, or between, say, James Baldwin's writing and the black church tradition, or between the black church tradition and jazz. The promise of promising life programs need not be detained at the borders bounding traditional ethnic spaces. If a tradition inaugurated by a given group were uniquely dependent upon members of that group for its preservation, what would remain of the blues tradition today? Also interesting to ponder in this context is the significance of the black musician Don Byron's investigations of Jewish-derived klezmer music, and indeed of his role in its *revival*.[17]

A related worry of Kitcher's is that, should we refuse to acknowledge race, the diverse cultural-ethnic heritages might not so much disappear altogether as become so thoroughly mixed that *in the future* we would be left with a society of ethnic hybrids and that this would be tantamount to a potentially stifling cultural homogeneity. Though this engages me in speculation that goes beyond the ramifications of my argument, I must confess that I, too, have worried about this. If I am permitted a brief, explicitly provincial, focus on the United States, it now seems to me that we must ask, however, What else is it to be an Ameri-

Epilogue: Toward a Humanistic Multiculturalism

can in our present historical moment but to be *already* to a significant degree such a hybrid (though, to be sure, we probably each move in circles where that hybridity is given a characteristic inflection, where different changes are rung on the theme)? It is particularly the case, in our postmodern world, that parents in a family are not the only significant cultural parents.[18] This is certainly in part what so bothers the religious Right and what makes groups like the Amish stand out in contrast to the norm. In our highly mediatized society, white suburban teenagers form the majority of consumers of rap music, and young white boys "want to be like Mike [Jordan]." While it is clear that I am no gushing fan of postmodernism—and I believe we must avoid the insipid eclecticism that characterizes the facile and superficial cross-cultural masquerade that appropriates only simulacra of cultural otherness without doing justice to the contexts that give the "exotic" practices their meaning[19]—it seems to me that thinkers like Kitcher tend to believe that only if pure ethnicities are maintained in a state of splendid isolation could they continue to make distinctive contributions. This, however, would seem to restrict us to a purely aesthetic (in the Kantian sense) appreciation of multiculturalism or of "ethnic" difference. In this society at least, the plurality of cultural traditions makes a distinctive contribution because it both informs and addresses us. As I have argued throughout this essay, a tradition with which we are unfamiliar invites us to consider other possible ways of being, other possible ways to comport ourselves in the world, ways that may have been marginalized, forgotten, or even never acknowledged. If we take such invitations seriously, we will look at "our" tradition differently or enact, in varying degrees, a transformation of it. In other words, some degree of ethnic hybridity might well be just what allowing "pure" ethnicities to make a distinctive contribution will result in. And this process, having begun at least as far back as the seventeenth century in this country, does not seem to me destined to lead to a stifling cultural homogeneity, even if increasingly cultural affiliation is uncoupled from phenotype.

In a utopic, postracist society, abandoning racialized discourses may well require us to give up prescriptive notions of identity that allow us to speak in terms of "violating" one's ethnic heritage or to speak of a cultural tradition as somehow belonging to someone simply because it was practiced by people who in some way or other physically resemble that individual.[20] But, pace Kitcher, I do not think that abandoning racialized discourses requires us to abandon the idea of the preservation and enhancement of cultural traditions.

What postmodernists and cultural nationalists alike often overlook is the fact that cultures are not discrete, uniform sites of perfect consensus, but are rather themselves sites of ongoing conversation, of ongoing negotiation and renegotiation. It is the resources provided by this internal heterogeneity and heteroglossia, itself to some degree an effect of cross-cultural awareness, that facilitate cross-cultural understanding and identification. The idea that cultures exist in splendid, pristine isolation from each other was probably always a myth, and it certainly is now. That is, there is considerable scope to the options I can entertain and still be "myself." This in turn licenses the degree to which I can expand my horizons in order both to understand the other *and* to be changed by that understanding. To this flawed conception of culture as a discrete, bounded whole, by the way, can be traced also the license some cultural relativists assume—by reifying and hypostatizing what are always contestable and contested cultural boundaries—to be ethical relativists, to say, in effect, that tolerance for difference must in principle stop at cultural borders and not penetrate them.

II

I bring this essay to a close by suggesting—insofar as I accept postmodernism's critique of the essentialism traditionally attributed to humanism—why I want to retain the term *humanism* to refer to what I am advocating. I have argued for a situated cosmopolitanism that places a premium on ongoing practices of reframing conversations and of forging commensurable vocabularies for discussing differences. I would claim that my conception of a dialogical humanism represents a dialectical sublation of traditional Kantian or metaphysical humanism that retains the distinctively progressive features of that conception while shearing it of the burden of its metaphysical baggage. As I indicated in the Introduction, the traditional conception of humanism allowed us to speak coherently of progress; it enabled a social critique that appealed to a notion of common humanity; it provided a basis for the presumption of the dignity of the individual; and it provided a basis for the pursuit of humanistic learning, for the humanities. The conception of humanism that I have proposed can serve these laudable ends without appealing to a transcendental essence of humanity. To begin with, we can abandon the idea of an abstract, metaphysically sanctioned measure for underwriting progress and yet retain the idea of progress if we think of it in terms of the asymmetrical results of symmetrical learning processes. I have in mind sit-

Epilogue: Toward a Humanistic Multiculturalism

uations where a concrete, socially recognized problem that resists solution within a given framework or language game yields to the resources provided by another framework or paradigm without the loss of problem solutions already achieved.[21] And the framework that enables this progressive development may be either one that is internal to a given culture or form of life or one that is external to it but dialogically encountered.

The utility of the idea of common humanity for social and political criticism is inseparably tied to the question of what might be the basis for the presumption of human dignity. Before spelling this out, I want to review briefly the edifying features of the idea of common humanity as I understand it. Common humanity is not only found but also forged; its content cannot be ascribed a priori. The idea of common humanity highlights, therefore, not only the ways in which others who are differently situated are the *same*—as does humanism traditionally conceived—but also, and most distinctively, what we can learn from the differences themselves. This, to comment briefly on the fourth virtue of the traditional understanding of humanism, its relationship to the humanities, is an important rationale for the pursuit of humanistic learning. The importance of the humanities in our civic culture is due to their revealing, as no other disciplines can, the full measure of worlds and epochs that are orthogonal to ours, worlds that represent differences from which we can learn and that provide a perspective from which our own strangeness can come into view, enabling a more reflective and critical awareness of who we are.

The criterial status of a common humanity proffered by the traditional conception is provided in my project by what I have referred to as the always provisional and revisable, but none the less operative, criteria of the "good life" consolidated in ongoing dialogical negotiations. This places a burden of proof, a critical pressure, upon apparent deviations from the diverse criteria of the good life that have met with mutual acknowledgment. Like an anomaly in science, such an apparent deviation may prove itself to be a resource from which we can learn, and thereby effect an expansion of what we take to be legitimate under the rubric "the good life." Or, it may be rejected as something from which we cannot learn. The so-called local knowledges drawn from cultures less technologically driven than ours, particularly in the area of health care practices, provide examples of the former. And I would argue that many of the practices that are interrogated under the sign of "human rights violation" would provide examples of the latter.

We would fail to learn from the latter sorts of practice because they arguably violate an "un-get-over-able" criterial property of the good life.

I take the recognition of the centrality of the freedom of individuals to assent to or to reject propositions put forward by others to define the minimalist core of any set of criterial properties of the good life that would meet with reciprocal acknowledgment and survive the test of the conversation of humanity, even if the various sets of criterial properties are not jointly realizable because of mutual incompatibilities. This recognition, at least in principle, of individual freedom is inescapable for those who accept my account of humanism. And it is so, I believe, for two reasons, neither of which requires a metaphysical commitment. First, such recognition is clearly a metavalue of cross-cultural negotiation as I have described it. Participants entering into the human conversation have to accept as a defining condition of that interaction the acknowledgment of the other's freedom to falsify and confirm proposed descriptions and languages of description. It would be a bit odd, if not outright inconsistent, to jettison this concern with human dignity in the return home from the brightly lit metapractice of cross-cultural conversation to the cave of ordinary, everyday interaction. For, as I have argued, to do so would be to reify the artificial barrier between inter- and intracultural alterity; the otherness from which we can learn dwells both at home and abroad. Second, as Hegel has brilliantly and convincingly pointed out (as did Karl Popper and Ludwig Wittgenstein in their own distinctive idioms), one's own self-certainty, one's confidence in one's descriptions and evaluations of oneself, is internally related to the ability of the other to reject those descriptions and evaluations. Thus, one's implicit recognition of the freedom of the other is a necessary condition, a transcendental-pragmatic presupposition, of one's confidence in one's own status. So the presumption of humanity, of the dignity of the individual, does not require a metaphysical foundation.

Finally, by way of justification for my retention of the term *humanism* it can be argued that there are elective affinities between my conception and some rather more ancient humanisms. For instance, taking issue with Martin Heidegger's dismissal of Renaissance humanism as another anthropocentric metaphysics, Ernesto Grassi argues that Renaissance philological concerns are focused upon language as the revelation of humanity's *historical* possibilities.[22] In this context, he stresses metaphor's role in forging *new* codes, structures, and frameworks through which there might arise what we could call, following Habermas, non-question-begging generalizable interests. Grassi cites as a paradigm example the standoff between the plebeians and patricians in fifth-century B.C.E. Italy, where both sides were locked into a code that made conflict

Epilogue: Toward a Humanistic Multiculturalism

inevitable. Menenius Agrippa's fable of the belly and the limbs provided a new, "organic" code in which the interests of each group were identified on the basis of the common well-being of the entire organism. The metaphorical activity established a poetically reframed code that attenuated the conflict, by encouraging each side to identify self and other as comprising a "we."[23] This is humanism in the making. Further, though for him it does not have the progressive, developmental character that I wish to emphasize, Quentin Skinner, in his account of Thomas Hobbes's intellectual development, characterizes Renaissance humanism as an intellectual orientation committed to the view that plausible arguments can often be constructed on either side of a given moral or political question. Accordingly, such a view gives pride of place to dialogue, to the willingness to negotiate over rival intuitions concerning the applicability of evaluative terms, to striving to reach understanding in a conversational way.[24] Finally, the Plato scholar Sabina Lovibond offers an interpretation of Plato that suggests that it is the distinguishing mark of the human being to transcend itself, to surpass provincial particularity, to see beyond one's situatedness. To borrow her phrase, we are "forever only *en route* to our humanity."[25]

Notes

INTRODUCTION

1. David Berreby, "The Unabsolute Truths of Clifford Geertz," *New York Times Magazine*, April 9, 1995, 44.
2. Sarah Lyall, "Irish Now Face the Other Side of Immigration," *New York Times*, July 8, 2000, A1, A8.
3. Roger Cohen, "Europe Tries to Turn a Tide of Migrants Chasing Dreams," *New York Times*, July 2, 2000, A1, A6.
4. I am grateful to David Luban, one of my colleagues during my residence at the Woodrow Wilson Center, who, in a challenging response to some of the ideas presented in this study, articulated this concise catalog of the virtues of humanism traditionally understood
5. Vito R. Giustiniani, "Homo, Humanus, and the Meanings of 'Humanism,'" *Journal of the History of Ideas* 46 (1985): 167–95.
6. Ibid., 171–73.
7. Ibid., 172.
8. Paul O. Kristeller, *Renaissance Thought: The Classic, Scholastic, and Humanist Strains* (New York: Harper Torchbooks, 1955), 95.
9. Ibid., 60.
10. Giustiniani, "Homo, Humanus," 193.
11. Ibid., 175.
12. Ibid., 176.
13. Ibid., 177.
14. I discuss this aspect of Rorty's work in my *Technology, Time, and the Conversations of Modernity* (New York: Routledge, 1995), 114–24.
15. I owe this expression to my much missed colleague, Neale Mucklow.
16. Heidegger broadly construes "learning" to include literary *and* philosophical education in general, to be the equivalent of Greek *paideia* ("Homo, Humanus," Giustiniani, 183–84).
17. See, for example, Ernesto Grassi, *Heidegger and the Question of Renaissance Humanism: Four Studies* (Binghamton, NY: Center for Medieval and Early Renaissance Studies, 1983), 43–44; and Sonya Sikka, "Heidegger's Concept of *Volk*," *Philosophical Forum* 26 (1994): 119–22.
18. For a fuller account of postmodernism, see my *Technology*, 136–63.
19. Richard Rorty, *Contingency, Irony, and Solidarity* (Cambridge: Cambridge University Press, 1989), 73.
20. Fredric Jameson, *Postmodernism, or the Cultural Logic of Late Capitalism* (Durham, NC: Duke University Press, 1991), 90.
21. See Tom Rockmore, *Heidegger and French Philosophy: Humanism, Antihumanism and Being* (London and New York: Routledge, 1995) 95.

22. Michel Foucault, *The Order of Things: An Archaeology of the Human Sciences* (New York: Vintage/Random House, 1973), 386–87.

23. Luc Ferry and Alain Renaut, *French Philosophy of the Sixties: An Essay on Antihumanism*, trans. Mary Schnackenberg Cattani (Amherst: University of Massachusetts Press, 1990), 22. See also Jacques Derrida, *Margins of Philosophy*, trans. Alan Bass (Chicago, University of Chicago Press, 1982), 118–19; and Rockmore, *Heidegger*.

24. Ferry and Renaut, *French Philosophy*, xv.

25. Jacques Derrida, *Of Spirit: Heidegger and the Question*, trans. G. Bennington and R. Bowlby (Chicago: University of Chicago Press, 1989), 120–22.

26. Robert Henri Cousineau, *Humanism and Ethics: An Introduction to Heidegger's Letter on Humanism* (Paris: Beatrice-Nauwelaerts, 1972), 52, 98. See also Ferry and Renaut, *French Philosophy*, xxiii, especially note 17; and Rockmore, *Heidegger*, especially 57–58.

27. Coisineau, *Humanism and Ethics*, 66–67, 71–72.

28. Ferry and Renaut, *French Philosophy*, 209.

29. Ibid., 25.

30. See their *French Philosophy of the Sixties* and *Heidegger and Modernity*, trans. F. Philip (Chicago: University of Chicago Press, 1990).

31. Ferry and Renaut, *Heidegger and Modernity*, 84.

32. Cf. Ibid., 5.

33. Charles Taylor, *Multiculturalism and "the Politics of Recognition"* (Princeton, NJ: Princeton University Press, 1992); reissued in expanded paperback edition as *Multiculturalism: Examining the Politics of Recognition*, ed. Amy Gutmann (Princeton, NJ: Princeton University Press, 1994).

CHAPTER 1

1. A comment by Joseph Epstein nicely illustrates Arnold's influence on recent neoconservatism. Writes Epstein, "Arnold could hardly be other than dismayed at our own contemporary scene, where politics is permitted not only to transcend but to shape culture, so that, to cite only the most obvious example, the idea of a central common culture is chipped away to accommodate the claims of several political groupings—minorities, women, the young—as if culture were spoils to be divided up in a smoke-filled room." Joseph Epstein, "Matthew Arnold and the Resistance," *Commentary* 73, no. 4 (1982): 59–60.

2. See Robert J. C. Young, *Colonial Desire: Hybridity in Theory, Culture and Race* (London: Routledge, 1995), 64.

3. Edward W. Said, *The World, the Text, and the Critic* (Cambridge, MA: Harvard University Press, 1983), 11–12.

4. Matthew Arnold, *Culture and Anarchy: An Essay in Political and Social Criticism*, 1869 (New York: Macmillan, 1919), xiii.

5. Ibid., xvi.

6. Ibid., xv.

7. Ibid., 66–68. See also Michael Ragussis, *Figures of Conversion: "The Jewish Question" and English National Identity* (Durham, NC: Duke University Press, 1995).

8. Young, *Colonial Desire*, 88.

9. Arnold, *Culture and Anarchy*, 101.

10. Insofar as he uses race as the final arbiter to set limits to cultural diversity and national identity, the English nation is for Arnold one of cultural hybridity but not of

racial hybridity, and its cultural hybridity is ultimately circumscribed by race. For a general discussion of these matters, see Ragussis, *Figures of Conversion*, 211–33.

11. Arnold, *Culture and Anarchy*, xxxiii, 28–29. Arnold's expression is "larger minded," which is interestingly similar to the notion that Seyla Benhabib deploys, "enlarged mentality" (itself inspired by Hannah Arendt), in the course of an argument for an understanding of "community" that highlights the virtues of tolerance, pluralism, and an appreciation of the viewpoint of the other; see Seyla Benhabib, *Situating the Self: Gender, Community and Postmodernism in Contemporary Ethics* (New York: Routledge, 1992).

12. Arnold, *Culture and Anarchy*, 9.

13. Ibid., 56, 110. The concept of "free play" that Arnold invokes is presumably taken over from Friedrich Schiller's *Letters on the Aesthetical Education of Man* (see Young, *Colonial Desire*, 57) and can be usefully compared with the use Theodor Adorno makes of "autonomy" in his writings on aesthetics and culture. There are also echoes of the Kantian notion of "disinterestedness," where for Arnold it signals an indifference to the particular interests of the various social classes. On Arnold's relation to Schiller, see David Lloyd, "Arnold, Ferguson, Schiller: Aesthetic Culture and the Politics of Aesthetics," *Cultural Critique* 1, no. 2 (1985): 137–69.

14. Arnold, *Culture and Anarchy*, 105–6.

15. Ibid., 111.

16. Ibid., 121.

17. Ibid., 159; emphasis added.

18. Lloyd, "Arnold, Ferguson, Schiller," 138–39.

19. Arnold, *Culture and Anarchy*, 120.

20. See Isaiah Berlin, "Two Concepts of Liberty" in Berlin, *Four Essays on Liberty* (Oxford: Oxford University Press, 1969).

21. Arnold *is* explicitly critical of the idea of class allegiance, of what we might want to call the ideological character of Victorian social and political life. In this sense, we might read him as a critic of ideology. On this, see Eugene Goodheart, "Arnold: Critic of Ideology," *New Literary History* 25 (1994): 419. But on the nonetheless persisting ideological dimension of Arnold's conception of culture, see Lloyd, "Arnold, Ferguson, Schiller."

22. Arnold, *Culture and Anarchy*, 43, 58. Arnold's conception of the relationship between culture and the state, with its clear resonances of Schiller, Herder, and Hegel, makes him a rather Germanic thinker indeed.

23. Ibid., 81, 82.

24. Ibid., 158–59, 161, and Said, *The World*, 28.

25. Arnold, *Culture and Anarchy*, 30–31.

26. Herder is said to have introduced the term *nationalism* in its modern sense in 1774 (Paul Gilbert, *The Philosophy of Nationalism* [Boulder, CO: Westview Press, 1998], 8). By articulating the idea of cultural nationhood, by arguing that the nation is a community bound by spiritual ties and distinctive cultural traditions and that the natural human condition is to be consciously integrated into such a community, Herder provided the intellectual resources for the authorizing ideologies of nationalist movements. The doctrine of national self-determination, closely allied to his conception of cultural nationhood, was the conduit of Herder's considerable influence in central and eastern European cultural nationalism. See F. M. Barnard, "National Culture and Political Legitimacy: Herder and Rousseau," *Journal of the History of Ideas* 44 (1983): 245–52.

Though Herder himself had reservations about the concept of race per se, as distinct from that of culture, the idea of organic racial unity as it was articulated during the so-called classical period of black nationalism, and especially in the work of Edward Blyden and Alexander Crummell, bore strong marks of Herder's influence; see Wilson Moses, *The Golden Age of Black Nationalism 1850–1925* (Oxford: Oxford University Press, 1988), 21–22, 25. In its assumption that the entire race has a collective destiny and message for humanity, in its claims that, in Crummell's words, each race is "destined through its peculiar organization and its place in the world to represent a certain side of the divine image," this movement invoked Herder's conception of a *Volk* (Moses, *Golden Age*, 17, 50). W. E. B. Du Bois, too, picked up on this latter theme, bringing both Herderian and Arnoldian ideas to bear in his conception of leadership; see Robert Gooding-Williams, "Between Masses and the Folk: Du Bois, Culture and Political Leadership," in his *Du Bois and the Politics of Double Consciousness* (Cambridge, MA: Harvard University Press, forthcoming). Further, Herder's ideas on the ways in which folk art both reflects and embodies the spirit of a people were influential in the development, beginning in the nineteenth century, of the idea of a specifically African-American aesthetic and thus of black aesthetic nationalism; see Bernard W. Bell, *The Folk Roots of Contemporary Afro-American Poetry* (Detroit: Broadside Press, 1974).

27. Isaiah Berlin, *Vico and Herder: Two Studies in the History of Ideas* (New York: Viking, 1976).

28. Ibid., 153.

29. Johann Gottfried von Herder, *Reflections on the Philosophy of the History of Mankind*, trans. Frank E. Manuel (Chicago: University of Chicago Press, 1968), 83.

30. Hugh West, review of Herder's *Selected Early Works, 1764–67*, *Central European History* 25 (1992): 462–64. I am also indebted to Hugh West for bringing to my attention the importance of Herder for my project.

31. Johann von Herder, *Sämtliche Werke*, ed. B. Suphan (Berlin: Georg Olms Verlagsbuchhandlung, 1887–1913), XIV, 87.

32. See *Herder on Social and Political Culture*, ed. F. M. Barnard (Cambridge: Cambridge University Press, 1969), 29–30; and Hans-Georg Gadamer, "Herder und die Geschichtliche Welt," in his *Kleine Schriften* III (Tübingen: J. C. B. Mohr, 1972), 116.

33. Herder, *Reflections*, 47.

34. Charles Taylor, *Philosophical Arguments* (Cambridge, MA: Harvard University Press, 1995), 93–95.

35. Intersubjective meanings are the meanings that situations can have for participants who share a cultural horizon. See Charles Taylor, "Interpretation and the Sciences of Man," in his *Philosophy and the Human Sciences: Philosophical Papers 2* (Cambridge: Cambridge University Press, 1985), 36.

36. See Theodore R. Schatzki, *Social Practices: A Wittgensteinian Approach to Human Activity and the Social* (Cambridge: Cambridge University Press, 1996), 116.

37. Herder, *Reflections*, 99–100.

38. Herder, *Sämtliche Werke*, XIV, 149.

39. Ibid.

40. See ibid., XIII, 371, for example, where he discusses the encounter between Europeans and native Tahitians, and the translation of excerpts from his *Ideas for a Philosophy of the History of Mankind*, in Barnard, ed., *Herder on Social and Political Culture*, 313–16.

41. Herder, *Sämtliche Werke*, XIII, 339, and *Reflections*, 76.

42. It is interesting to note that for Herder, technology as well as other forms of medi-

ation between persons and their environments, forms such as the reliance upon the labor of others, are media of enervating transcendence. See Herder, *Reflections,* 13 and Barnard, ed., *Herder on Social and Political Culture,* 316. It would also be interesting to compare Herder's position with Richard Rorty's comments on the radically situated character of moral solidarity and the latter's opposition to the tenability of understanding such solidarity in terms of an allegiance to the species as a whole in his *Contingency, Irony and Solidarity* (Cambridge: Cambridge University Press, 1989). On the contrast between Kant's emphasis on autonomy and Herder's on identity, see Hugh West's *From Tahiti to the Terror* (Chapel Hill: University of North Carolina Press, forthcoming).

43. Herder, *Reflections,* 78, 98.
44. Ibid., 85.
45. Ibid., 57–58.
46. Such a presumption, though with a more hypothetical modality than Herder intended for it, animates the discussion in Charles Taylor's *Multiculturalism and "the Politics of Recognition"* (Princeton, NJ: Princeton University Press, 1992), 66–67.
47. Herder, *Sämtliche Werke,* XIII, 194.
48. Herder, *Reflections,* 99–101. See also Gadamer, "Herder und die Geschichtliche Welt," 112.
49. See Herder, *Reflections,* 86.
50. I have made a similar argument with regard to the implications of Habermas's conception of ideology critique in my "On Habermas and Particularity: Is There Room for Race and Gender on the Glassy Plains of Ideal Discourse?" *Praxis International* 6 (1986): 337–38.
51. Berlin, *Vico and Herder,* 182.
52. See Herder, *Reflections,* 44.
53. See Donald Davidson, "On the Very Idea of a Conceptual Scheme," in his *Inquiries into Truth and Interpretation* (Oxford: Oxford University Press, 1984).
54. See Chris Swoyer, "True For," in *Relativism: Cognitive and Moral,* ed. Michael Krausz and Jack Meiland (Notre Dame, IN: University of Notre Dame Press, 1982), 104, though Swoyer appears to have something different in mind from what I mean here by *accessibility.*
55. See James Clifford, *The Predicament of Culture: Twentieth-Century Ethnography, Literature, and Art* (Cambridge, MA: Harvard University Press, 1988); and Michael Carrithers, *Why Humans Have Cultures: Explaining Anthropology and Social History* (Oxford: Oxford University Press, 1992). In fairness to Herder, it should be pointed out that he did not view cultural reproduction, the cultural continuity effected by the handing down of tradition, as a static repetition of "the same." He saw it rather as an ongoing process of intergenerational transmission characterized by a repetition with a difference, whereby later generations, occupying different contexts of reception, apply the contents of tradition in ways that differ from their forebears; see *Sämtliche Werke,* XIII, 343–48. Nonetheless, these variations were viewed by Herder as changes on a single and characteristic perduring theme. And, at any rate, this potential source of internal variation remained of only very marginal importance in the story Herder wanted to tell about cultural difference; it was not highlighted or exploited by Herder in his overall account of the nature of a *Volk.*
56. See James Tully, *Strange Multiplicity: Constitutionalism in an Age of Diversity* (Cambridge: Cambridge University Press, 1995), 13.
57. Ibid., 10, 70.

58. Berlin, *Vico and Herder*, 195.
59. Ibid.
60. Stuart Hall, "What Is This 'Black' in Black Popular Culture?" in *Black Popular Culture*, ed. Gina Dent (Seattle: Bay Press, 1992), 27.
61. Ibid., 28.
62. See Thomas S. Kuhn, "Objectivity, Value Judgment, and Theory Choice," in his *The Essential Tension* (Chicago: University of Chicago Press, 1977).
63. On the politics of representation within Islamic societies, for example, see Dale F. Eickelman and James Piscatori, *Muslim Politics* (Princeton, NJ: Princeton University Press, 1996).
64. Hans Kohn, *The Idea of Nationalism* (New York: Collier Books, 1967), 431–32, cited in Kwame Anthony Appiah, *In My Father's House: Africa in the Philosophy of Culture* (Oxford: Oxford University Press, 1992), 50.
65. See Mikhail M. Bakhtin, "Discourse in the Novel," in *The Dialogic Imagination*, ed. Michael Holquist, trans. Caryl Emerson and Michael Holquist (Austin: University of Texas Press, 1981); and Ludwig Wittgenstein, *Philosophical Investigations*, trans. G. E. M. Anscombe (Oxford: Basil Blackwell, 1967).
66. Though I have acknowledged the tension between Herder's ethnohistoriographic practice and his implicit theorizing, my concern in this chapter is with the *conceptual* or theoretical ramifications of what I have called "the Herderian tendency." This is not to deny that Herder entertained the possibility that cultures could borrow discrete practices or forms of knowledge from each other. Herder believed, for example, as Hugh West reminds me, that Eskimos and Europeans could benefit from each other's knowledge of science and knowledge about survival in frigid climates. However, Herder's penchant to emphasize cultural coherence does have the consequence of representing various cultures as sealed off from each other.
67. Herder, *Reflections*, 100, 114; and *Sämtliche Werke*, XIII, 343–46.
68. Herder, *Reflections*, 49.
69. On the unique character of standards of perfection, see ibid., 98. It might be of interest to note that Alisdair MacIntyre's account of learning across traditions, in his *Whose Justice, Which Rationality?* (Notre Dame, IN: University of Notre Dame Press, 1988), is premised on the second alternative.
70. Berlin, *Vico and Herder*, 212; see also my *Technology, Time and the Conversations of Modernity* (New York and London: Routledge, 1995), 46–47.
71. See Herder, *Sämtliche Werke*, VIII, 207, 314, 315; XIV, 227; XV, 321; XVIII, 248, cited in Berlin, *Vico and Herder*, 182.
72. See Herder, *Reflections*, 100; and *Sämtliche Werke*, V, 509.
73. See Walter Benn Michaels, "Race into Culture: A Critical Genealogy of Cultural Identity," in *Identities*, ed. Kwame Anthony Appiah and Henry Louis Gates Jr. (Chicago: University of Chicago Press, 1995).

CHAPTER 2

1. On jazz as an exemplar of aesthetic modernism, see Martha Bayles, *Hole in Our Soul: The Loss of Beauty and Meaning in American Popular Music* (New York: The Free Press, 1994), 54–56, 85–103.
2. See, for example, Joseph D. Lewandowski, "Adorno on Jazz and Society," *Philosophy and Social Criticism* 22 (1996): 103–21.
3. For a fuller account of Critical Theory, especially of its Frankfurt School phase,

Notes

see Martin Jay, *The Dialectical Imagination: A History of the Frankfurt School and the Institute of Social Research, 1923–1950* (Boston: Little, Brown, 1973).

4. Theodor Adorno and Max Horkheimer, *Dialectic of Enlightenment*, trans. John Cumming (New York: The Seabury Press, 1972), 120.

5. Ibid., 121.

6. Theodor Adorno, "On the Fetish-Character in Music and the Regression of Listening," in *The Essential Frankfurt School Reader*, eds. Andrew Arato and Eike Gebhardt (New York: Continuum, 1988), 276.

7. See also Adorno, "On the Fetish-Character in Music," 278–79.

8. Theodor Adorno, "The Culture Industry Reconsidered," in *Critical Theory and Society: A Reader*, ed. Stephen Bronner and Douglas Kellner (New York: Routledge, 1989), 134–35.

9. Theodor Adorno, *Aesthetic Theory*, trans. C. Lenhardt (New York: Routledge, 1984), 4, 6, 7.

10. Adorno, *Aesthetic Theory*, 322.

11. See Lambert Zuidervaart, *Adorno's Aesthetic Theory: The Redemption of Illusion* (Cambridge, MA: MIT Press, 1991), 88.

12. Adorno, *Aesthetic Theory*, 323–24.

13. Ibid., 323.

14. Ibid., 196.

15. Ibid., 27–28.

16. Horkheimer and Adorno, *Dialectic of Enlightenment*, 139–40.

17. For a penetrating account of the self-understanding that fashioned Adorno's approach to musical analysis, see Lydia Goehr's "Dissonant Works and the Listening Public: Or 'How One Becomes Lonely' and the 'Solitary Theoretician,'" in *The Cambridge Companion to Adorno* (Cambridge: Cambridge University Press, forthcoming).

18. Theodor Adorno, "On Jazz," trans. Jamie Owen Daniel, *Discourse* 12, vol. 1 (1989–90): 45.

19. On the primitivist assumptions underlying the French reception of black culture, see, for example, Bernard Gendron, "Fetishes and Motorcars: Negrophilia in French Modernism," *Cultural Studies* 4 (1990): 141–55; and Henry Louis Gates Jr. and Karen C. C. Dalton, eds., *Josephine Baker and La Revue Nègre: Paul Colin's "Le Tumulte Noir"* (New York: Henry N. Abrams, 1998).

20. Adorno, "On Jazz," 47; emphasis added.

21. Ibid., 48.

22. Ibid., 53. It is perhaps worth noting here that his operative distinction between the immediacy of nature and the mediatization of the capitalist culture industry recalls Georg Lukàcs's distinction between the concrete content of the "given" on the one hand, and the laws of bourgeois society on the other. Both Adorno and Lukàcs extend Marx's theory of reification.

23. Ibid, 49.

24. Ibid., 54.

25. Ibid., 60.

26. Ibid., 60–61. In a later essay, Adorno concedes jazz's origins in the African-American folk tradition, but he holds that even that tradition was in some respects "always already commercialized." See Theodor Adorno, review of Wilder Hobson, *American Jazz Music*, and Winthrop Sargeant, *Jazz: Hot and Hybrid*, in *Studies in Philosophy and Social Science* 9, no. 1 (1941): 169.

27. Adorno, "On Jazz," 64. See also Theodor Adorno, *Philosophy of Modern Music*, trans. Anne Mitchell and Wesley Blomster (New York: Continuum, 1994), 145–48. In

general, it is interesting to note that Adorno levels at Stravinsky's work many of the criticisms that he levels at jazz. He reproaches the former for its rhythmic inflexibility, dominated as it is by a rigid beat (154–55) and its resultant static and timeless quality, which prevent it from exhibiting organic development and from having an inevitable "end" (187–201), all of which corresponds to a reified bourgeois consciousness. That he makes these charges against Stravinsky and, to some extent, against the impressionist school of Debussy et al. for its spatialization of time in its search for the sensory moment outside time, as well as against even Wagner, should mitigate somewhat the oft-repeated charge of Adorno's elitism. But the decisive difference remains that Adorno never reduced the works of these composers to their function within the culture industry, nor did he fail to treat them as worthy of serious aesthetic analysis, something he notoriously did with jazz.

28. Adorno, "On Jazz," 66.

29. Ibid. In fact, during the latter part of the nineteenth century, many of the dances performed by blacks were actually competently executed parodies of whites rather than manifestations of their own incompetence. For an interesting response to Adorno's "castration thesis," see Krin Gabbard, "Signifyin' the Phallus: Representations of the Jazz Trumpet," in his *Jammin' at the Margins: Jazz and the American Cinema* (Chicago: University of Chicago Press, 1996).

30. Adorno, "On Jazz," 67.

31. Ibid., 52–53.

32. Adorno, review of Hobson and Sargeant, 173.

33. See J. Bradford Robinson, "The Jazz Essays of Theodor Adorno: Some Thoughts on Jazz Reception in Weimar Germany," *Popular Music* 13, no. 1 (1994): 1–25.

34. Ibid., 6.

35. The recording is "No Foolin'" (Victor 20019). See Harry Cooper, "On Uber Jazz: Replaying Adorno with the Grain," *October* 75 (1996): 123–28.

36. See James A. Snead, "Repetition As a Figure of Black Culture," in *Black Literature and Literary Theory*, ed. Henry Louis Gates Jr. (New York: Methuen, 1984).

37. Søren Kierkegaard, *Either/Or*, vol. 1, trans. David F. Swenson and Lillian M. Swenson, rev. Howard A. Johnson (Princeton, NJ: Princeton University Press, 1959), 364.

38. See Paul Bowles, "Duke Ellington in Recital for Russian War Relief," in Mark Tucker, ed., *The Duke Ellington Reader* (Oxford: Oxford University Press, 1993), 166.

39. See Adorno, review of Hobson and Sargeant, 171.

40. Paul Berliner, *Thinking in Jazz: The Infinite Art of Improvisation* (Chicago: University of Chicago Press, 1994), 389, 399.

41. Ibid., 417; see also Tony Scherman's interview with Wynton Marsalis, *American Heritage*, October 1995, 66–85.

42. Paul Gilroy, *The Black Atlantic: Modernity and Double Consciousness* (Cambridge, MA: Harvard University Press, 1993), 200. Also not to be neglected here is the factious issue of the interplay between jazz and dance. On this, see Robert Crease, "Jazz and Dance," in the *Cambridge Companion to Jazz* (Cambridge: Cambridge University Press, forthcoming). These considerations suggest that, in addition to what I shall call his overly compositionalist bias, Adorno also evinces an overly "intellectualist" approach to understanding music, again neglecting Herder's warnings against the abstract segregation of the human faculties.

43. For another argument to the effect that Adorno flirts with offering musical unintelligibility as a critical counterpoint, see Lee B. Brown, "Adorno's Critique of Popular Culture: The Case of Jazz Music," *Journal of Aesthetic Education* 26 (1992): 28–29.
44. Berliner, *Thinking in Jazz*, 244–47.
45. Ibid., 806, n. 39.
46. Ibid., 246.
47. Ibid., 247–50.
48. Ibid., 250–52.
49. Ibid., 253–55.
50. Ibid., 255–59.
51. Ibid., 259–62.
52. Ibid., 262–67.
53. Ibid., 268–73.
54. Ibid., 410.
55. Ibid., 273–76.
56. See R. D. Darrell, "Duke Ellington," in Tucker, ed., *Ellington Reader*, 127.
57. See André Hodeir, "A Masterpiece: *Concerto for Cootie*," in Tucker, ed., *Ellington Reader*, 286.
58. See Gunther Schuller's evaluation, "Ellington in the Pantheon," 414–17 in Tucker, ed., *Ellington Reader*.
59. See Charles Taylor's discussion of such non-distortive comparisons in his *Philosophical Arguments* (Cambridge, MA: Harvard University Press, 1995), 146–64.
60. On the priority of composition over performance, see Adorno, *Aesthetic Theory*, 146–47. Of course, jazz practitioners too, most notably Ellington, Charles Mingus, and more recently the clarinetist Don Byron, take composition seriously, but do not make reifying distinctions between composition and performance.
61. On the very idea of a jazz tradition, see Scott DeVaux, "Constructing the Jazz Tradition: Jazz Historiography," *Black American Literature Forum*, 25, no. 3 (1991): 525–60.
62. On Adorno's ignoring of musical instrumentation see Zuidervaart, *Adorno's Aesthetic Theory*, 107.
63. See Andre Hodeir's "A Masterpiece: *Concerto for Cootie*," in Tucker, ed., *Ellington Reader*, 276–88; and Ken Rattenbury, *Duke Ellington: Jazz Composer* (New Haven, CT: Yale University Press, 1990), 199.
64. Berliner, *Thinking in Jazz*, 261.
65. Ibid., 108, 126–27.
66. Adorno, "On Jazz," 67.
67. Again, this is a distinction in degree rather than in kind. But it has been pointed out that at least since the time of J. S. Bach, European concert music has established rather strict tonal criteria for the instruments comprising a symphony orchestra, a practice that has led to a considerable standardization of tone production; see William P. Nye, "Theodor Adorno on Jazz: A Critique of Critical Theory," *Popular Music and Society* 12 (1988): 72. Jazz musicians often refer to this as a "legit" sound. Stories abound about musicians who aspire to positions in classical orchestras who have been turned away because their sound was thought too distinctive for a given orchestra; see, for example, Joseph Robinson, "What I Learned in the Lenoir High School Band," *The Wilson Quarterly*, 19 (1995): 106. In symphonic orchestras, a premium is placed on blending and, therefore, on standardization, within instrumental families. Further, for

most instruments there are sonic models which historically have set de facto tonal standards for the instrument—for example, the very dark sound of the Chicago Symphony Orchestra's principal oboist. Of course, such *orchestras* often have distinctive sounds (e.g., that of the Philadelphia Orchestra or the Chicago Symphony or the Vienna Philharmonic), and this is, in large measure, a result of conductors having at their disposal the spectrum of tonal variation allowable in a "legit" sound. To oversimplify somewhat, if the characteristic tonality of a particular symphonic orchestra is the result of a particular, vertically imposed tonal standardization, then the characteristic tone colors of, say, Ellington's orchestra were the result of a particular mixture of *instrumentalists*. I am grateful to my composer/colleague Alfred Cohen for a helpful conversation about some of these matters. The conclusion that I draw is, however, my own.

68. This has been a staple of attentive jazz analysis since at least 1936 (again the year in which Adorno's *Uber Jazz* appeared), when Alain Locke, in his *The Negro and His Music* (Washington, DC: The Associates in Negro Folk Education, 1936), emphasized the importance of performance and participation in this music. See also Ted Gioia, *The Imperfect Art: Reflections on Jazz and Modern Culture* (Oxford: Oxford University Press, 1988), 15–16.

69. Adorno, review of Wilder and Hobson, 168. The criticism implicit here ought not to be confused with what I take to be the misguided criticism of Adorno to the effect that his failure to do justice to jazz follows from the fact that jazz cannot be "written down." For it is clear that *every* musical performance, including those of the classical repertoire, goes beyond what is on the page, that every such performance involves processes of interpretation.

70. See Ingrid Monson's "Doubleness and Jazz Improvisation: Irony, Parody, and Ethnomusicology," *Critical Inquiry* 20 (1994): 283–13.

71. Albert Murray, *The Omni-Americans* (New York: Da Capo Press, 1970), 58–59.

72. Herbert Marcuse, *An Essay on Liberation* (Boston: Beacon Press, 1969), 36–38.

73. Theodor Adorno, "Perennial Fashion—Jazz," in *Prisms*, trans. Samuel and Shierry Weber (Cambridge, MA: MIT Press, 1981), 122; emphasis added.

74. Ralph Ellison, *Shadow and Act* (New York: Vintage Books, 1964), 254.

75. Ibid., 189–90.

76. Albert Murray, *The Blue Devils of Nada: A Contemporary American Approach to Aesthetic Statement* (New York: Pantheon Books, 1996), 7. This idea, about jazz's capacity to give form and meaningful structure to the flux, to the absurd forces of life, from within the flux itself, can perhaps be usefully compared to the philosopher of music Lydia Goehr's idea of progressive musical forms whose autonomy is manifested in their "freedom within" the ordinary world of social and political forces. The autonomy of such music would then be marked by its "patterning *within* social forces and not *by* them"; Lydia Goehr, "Political Music and the Politics of Music," *Journal of Aesthetics and Art Criticism* 52, no. 1 (1994): 108–10.

77. For Adorno's invidious treatment of sonority, see his *In Search of Wagner*, trans. Rodney Livingstone (London: Verso, 1981), 62–70.

CHAPTER 3

1. See my "On Habermas and Particularity: Is There Room for Race and Gender on the Glassy Plains of Ideal Discourse?" *Praxis International* 6 (1986): 328–40.

2. Jürgen Habermas, *Legitimation Crisis*, trans. Thomas McCarthy (Boston: Beacon Press, 1975), 108. If *all* interests were sheerly particular then we *would* have to

Notes

resign ourselves to what he would call "an impenetrable pluralism of apparently ultimate [and incommensurable] value orientations." However, as I shall suggest, reflection upon the hermeneutic dimension of social interaction from the standpoint of a possible fusion of horizons may help to soften conflict even at this more purely cultural level.

3. Jürgen Habermas, "A Postscript to *Knowledge and Human Interests*," *Philosophy of the Social Sciences* 3 (1973): 177.

4. See Habermas's discussion of John Rawls in *Justification and Application: Remarks on Discourse Ethics*, trans. C. Cronin (Cambridge, MA: MIT Press, 1993), 93–96.

5. See Georgia Warnke, *Justice and Interpretation* (Cambridge, MA: MIT Press, 1993), 108.

6. Jürgen Habermas, *Justification and Application*, 94, 181 (n. 58).

7. Ibid., 94.

8. Ibid., 100–1. See also my discussion of this issue in MacIntyre's work in my *Technology, Time and the Conversations of Modernity* (New York and London: Routledge, 1995), 130–31.

9. Habermas, *Justification and Application*, 103, 105.

10. Ibid., 69.

11. Ibid., 87. On the idea of an "identity related difference," see Avigail Eisenberg, "The Politics of Individual and Group Difference in Canadian Jurisprudence," *Canadian Journal of Political Science* 27, no. 1 (1994): 3–21.

12. Jürgen Habermas, *Moral Consciousness and Communicative Action*, trans. Christian Lenhardt and Sherry Weber Nicholsen (Cambridge, MA: MIT Press, 1990), 65; emphasis in the original.

13. Habermas, *Justification and Application*, 59–60.

14. Cf. ibid., 105–6.

15. Ibid., 12.

16. Cf. Jürgen Habermas, "Struggles for Recognition in the Democratic Constitutional State," in *Multiculturalism: Examining the Politics of Recognition*, ed. Amy Gutmann (Princeton, NJ: Princeton University Press, 1994), 132–33, 139.

17. Thomas McCarthy, "Practical Discourse: On the Relation of Morality to Politics," in *Ideals and Illusions: On Reconstruction and Deconstruction in Contemporary Critical Theory* (Cambridge, MA: MIT Press, 1991), 191f, cited in Habermas, *Justification and Application*, 90.

18. Habermas, *Justification and Application*, 90–91.

19. Ibid., 91.

20. Ibid., 13–14.

21. Habermas, "Struggles for Recognition," 113.

22. Ibid., 129.

23. Ibid., 112–13, 116.

24. Ibid., 129.

25. Ibid.

26. Ibid., 137.

27. Ibid., 139.

28. Ibid., 130.

29. I have argued that his rational reconstructive demonstrations are flawed by their unacknowledged hermeneutic moments in my *Technology, Time and the Conversations of Modernity*, 92–93.

30. Habermas, "Struggles for Recognition," 116.

31. Jürgen Habermas, *The Theory of Communicative Action* vol. 1, trans. Thomas McCarthy (Boston: Beacon Press, 1984), 113–15.
32. Iris Marion Young, "Communication and the Other: Beyond Deliberative Democracy," in *Democracy and Difference*, ed. Seyla Benhabib (Princeton, NJ: Princeton University Press, 1996), 123.
33. See James Tully, *Strange Multiplicity: Constitutionalism in an Age of Diversity* (Cambridge: Cambridge University Press, 1995).

CHAPTER 4

1. Cf. Iris Marion Young, "Communication and the Other: Beyond Deliberative Democracy," in *Democracy and Difference*, ed. Seyla Benhabib (Princeton, NJ: Princeton University Press, 1996), 131–32.
2. Iris Marion Young, *Justice and the Politics of Difference* (Princeton, NJ: Princeton University Press, 1990), 235.
3. Young, "Communication and the Other," 127.
4. See Hans-Georg Gadamer, *Truth and Method* (New York: Seabury Press, 1975), 331, 348; and Charles Taylor, "Understanding and Ethnocentricity," in *Philosophy and the Human Sciences* (Cambridge: Cambridge University Press, 1985), 125. Both Taylor's account and mine are inspired by Gadamer's conception of the "fusion of horizons."
5. Cf. also James Tully, *Strange Multiplicity: Constitutionalism in an Age of Diversity* (Cambridge: Cambridge University Press, 1995), 111, on intercultural dialogue.
6. See Charles Taylor, "Interpretation and the Science of Man," *Review of Metaphysics* 25 (1971): 27, 29–30. See also my discussion of what I refer to as the distinction between "meaning" and "value" in my *Technology, Time, and the Conversations of Modernity* (New York and London: Routledge, 1995).
7. Anna Lowenhaupt Tsing, *In the Realm of the Diamond Queen: Marginality in an Out-of-the-Way Place* (Princeton, NJ: Princeton University Press, 1993).
8. Ibid., 152.
9. See my *Technology, Time, and the Conversations of Modernity*, 106–7, 201, 202 (n. 21).
10. Charles Taylor, *Philosophical Arguments* (Cambridge, MA: Harvard University Press, 1995), 163. I have already alluded, in chapter 2, to Adorno's failure to seek such a nondistortive representation. Tsing also nicely illustrates a case where difference manifests itself in invidiously drawn cross-cultural representations of self and other (Tsing, *Diamond Queen*, 178–91). The higher-status Islamic Banjar of the region she focuses on view the lower-status, nomadic Meratus as primitive "others." Banjar representations of the Meratus are structured by a host of oppositions, articulated in a way that characterizes the Meratus as lacking a good that the Banjar possess: rational/irrational; cosmopolitan/local; lawful/lawless; civilized/wild; and what for the Banjar is the most basic, Muslim/not Muslim. Not surprisingly, Tsing points out that this representation does not command the resources to render an account of what the Meratus *are*, as opposed to what they fail to be. This is instructively displayed in a discussion of Banjar perceptions of Meratus shamans, who are both feared by the Banjar as the source of bodily dissolution and sought out by them as possessing the key to its cure. At issue for the Banjar are the implications of what they view as Meratus sorcery for the maintenance of the body's boundaries and sense of self. For the Banjar, illness is a matter of the body's dissolution, occasioned by its vulnerability to contamination

Notes

from external forces. Health, on the other hand, is equated with boundary protection. However, these are not the relevant categories for capturing the intention of the Meratus shaman, Tsing argues. For the latter, curing is effected through overcoming what they view as the *limitations* of localized boundaries, rather than by reinforcing them; "the spiritually empowered skin does not guard against disease, but instead opens up to admit the fullness of the whole world" (188). Banjar-Meratus intercultural dialogue is compromised by these mutually incompatible valuations. Stated most starkly, on the side of the Banjar, the boundary protects; on the side of the Meratus, the boundary impedes. On the Banjar side, separation, isolation, and boundary maintenance are invidiously compared with contamination and the dissolution of boundaries, and the latter characterize, for the Banjar, the Meratus. For the Meratus, we see connection and incorporation invidiously compared to isolation and the limitations imposed by boundaries, which, insofar as they care to think of it, are the terms that structure their view of the Banjar. The role of the shaman is to breach the body's boundary so that, at least metaphorically, a healing breath, animated by the spiritual power of the entire cosmos, can enter. The boundaries of the self, for the shaman, are blurred ideally, so that "there is no single line between . . . body and world" (190). The shaman's concern is to reanimate the health-promoting connections between individuals and social and cosmic matrices. I would argue that what the shaman is enacting—by implying that the healthy body is one that is defined by its incorporation of others—can be read as a critique, highlighting the limitations of the (Banjar?) ideal of self-sufficiency, of the dream of containing within one's own borders all of the resources necessary for one's flourishing. From this standpoint, what from the Banjar perspective could be viewed only privatively and as testifying to a lack could at the very least be seen as not unreasonable in context and, at best, perhaps as insightful. Tsing's commentary, insofar as it invokes Julia Kristeva's discussion of abjection, also suggests the role that fear, in particular fear of the dissolution of the boundary separating self and other, plays in generating and maintaining distortive representations of the other. I will not here speculate on the role that this mechanism may have played in Adorno's case.

11. See my *Technology, Time, and the Conversations*, 106–7.
12. Gadamer, *Truth and Method*, 261–62. I am grateful to Georgia Warnke's insightful commentary in her *Justice and Interpretation* (Cambridge, MA: MIT Press, 1993) for encouraging me to take a closer look at this idea of Gadamer's.
13. Gadamer, *Truth and Method*, 262.
14. See ibid., 331.
15. John Searle, *Speech Acts: An Essay in the Philosophy of Language* (Cambridge: Cambridge University Press, 1969), 19–20.
16. On the obstacles posed to intercultural translation by asymmetrical power relations, see Talal Asad, "The Concept of Cultural Translation in British Social Anthropology," in *Writing Culture: The Poetics and Politics of Ethnography*, ed. James Clifford and George E. Marcus (Berkeley and Los Angeles: University of California Press, 1986).
17. Georgia Warnke, *Gadamer: Hermeneutics, Tradition and Reason* (Stanford, CA: Stanford University Press, 1987), 104.
18. On the phenomenon of defamiliarization, see George E. Marcus and Michael M. J. Fischer, *Anthropology As Cultural Critique: An Experimental Moment in the Human Sciences* (Chicago: University of Chicago Press, 1986), 137–64.
19. Bernhard Waldenfels, "Der Andere und Der Dritte im interkultureller Sicht," in R. A. Mall and N. Schneider eds., *Ethik und Politik aus interkultureller Sicht* (Amsterdam: Rodopi, 1996).

20. Hans-Georg Gadamer, *Philosophical Hermeneutics*, trans. and ed. D. Linge (Berkeley and Los Angeles: University of California Press, 1988), 11.

21. There are two constraints on the metalinguistic predicates that are invoked in a situated metalanguage. On the one hand, we have to avoid vacuity; the predicates must have sharp enough boundaries to be meaningfully applied. On the other hand, we need capaciousness; the predicates must be flexible and expansive enough to subsume competing conceptions. So, the Sache, or topic, that we dialogically adduce in the analogical process I discuss here must be fashioned at a sufficiently "low altitude" to have adequately concrete criteria of application to *exclude* some candidates for inclusion. Yet such a topic must have purchase at a sufficiently high altitude or level of generality to embrace or fuse conceptions on both sides of an intercultural dialogue. There has been a great deal of discussion among cultural anthropologists, art historians, and philosophers of art regarding the transcultural status of aesthetic judgment, that usefully illuminates these issues. Participants in that discussion have demonstrated, for instance, that judgments of aesthetic merit have *meaning* on both sides of cultural divides. The social anthropologist Howard Morphy has argued, for example, that, when *aesthetic* is taken to name the dimension within which *formal* properties are apprehended independently of function, the "aesthetic" meets the criteria that I have adduced for a viable cross-cultural predicate. In this way he offers an illuminating account of the cross-cultural purchase of the concept of the aesthetic; see Howard Morphy et al., "Aesthetics is a Cross Cultural Category," in Tim Ingold, ed., *Key Debates in Anthropology* (London: Routledge, 1996), 258. And, to illustrate the point, many experts claim that, despite differences in what counts as aesthetically satisfying, many African societies, for example, seem to acknowledge a meaningful, if not absolute, distinction between aesthetic value and functional sufficiency; see Robert Ferris Thompson, "Esthetics in Traditional Africa," *Art News* 66 (1968): 44–45, 63–66; and the summary discussion in Frank Willett, *African Art* (New York: Thames and Hudson, 1971), 208–22. And, as H. Gene Blocker implies in his *The Aesthetics of Primitive Art* (Lanham, MD: University Press of America, 1994), 147–48, even if members of the culture in question do not have anything in their vocabulary corresponding to our word *art*, they may well have practices that overlap saliently with those that we associate with art. That is, they may treat a class of objects in their world in ways that are analogous to the ways we treat art objects.

22. Akeel Bilgrami, "What Is a Muslim? Fundamental Commitment and Cultural Identity," *Critical Inquiry* 18 (1992): 821–42.

23. Ibid., 823. When we think of a recent controversy, the so-called Rushdie affair, we should note that, given the highly charged and contested nature of intracultural struggles to articulate and systematize expressions of cultural identity, the Muslim reaction to Salman Rushdie's *The Satanic Verses*, and to the *fatwah* following its publication that called for his death, was hardly uniform; see Sadik J. al-Azm, "The Importance of Being Earnest about Salmon Rushdie," *Die Welt des Islams* 31 (1991): 1–49, esp. 34. An evaluation of the charges and countercharges made in the course of this episode would take me beyond the scope of this study, but a brief comment informed by the spirit of this essay would be in order. This affair amply illustrates, for me, the importance to intercultural understanding of attempting to strike a delicate balance between critical discrimination and hermeneutic modesty. On the side of hermeneutic modesty, we should acknowledge that the understandable "Western" defense of Rushdie was deployed in terms of sets of contrasts that may have little or no purchase in Islamic cultural contexts and in terms of liberal commitments with unacknowledged Christian roots—both historical and normative—that beg important

questions within Islamic traditions. Accordingly, as Charles Taylor wisely avers, "To live in this difficult world, the western liberal mind will have to learn to reach out more"; see Taylor, "The Rushdie Controversy," *Public Culture* 2 (1989): 118–22; L. A. Siedentop, "Liberalism: The Christian Connection," *The Times Literary Supplement*, March 24–30, 1989, 308; and, of course, Hegel's comments throughout the corpus of his writings claiming the Western conception of individualism to be a secularized version of the Christian notion of the equality of all before God. On the side of critical discrimination, we cannot avoid believing that critical pressure has to be brought to bear on a regime that believes itself entitled to sentence a person to death for exercising his creative freedom. And the point that a writer like Akeel Bilgrami would like to make here is that, given the spectrum of positions actually occupied by members of Muslim communities, such pressure need not necessarily be viewed as an ethnocentric, imperialistic imposition from the outside, but that rather it can be applied from the inside, where there are indigenous resources and aspirations that can fuel *internal* processes of critical response; see Bilgrami, "Rushdie, Islam, and Postcolonial Defensiveness," *The Yale Journal of Criticism* 4 (1990): 301–11.

24. Yael Tamir, " Liberal Nationalism," *Philosophy and Public Policy* (1993): 4.

25. See, for example, Georgia Warnke, "Communicative Rationality and Cultural Values," in *The Cambridge Companion to Habermas*, ed. Stephen K. White (Cambridge: Cambridge University Press, 1995), 139–40. Might it be the case, however, that some cultures survive only by being *insulated* from this particular sort of criticism? This question is ambiguous, however. It might be taken to mean, Can a culture maintain its identity in meeting such a critical response? To this we might reply, as I suggested above, that the elasticity of cultural identity prevents its being a foregone conclusion that accommodating criticism would be tantamount to the erasure of identity, for such identity is not an all-or-nothing affair. On the other hand, the question might be taken to mean, Might there be cultures that can be understood to have no *interest* in what they can learn about themselves from an "external" assessment? My discussion later of what I refer to as "second-order rationality" gives us reason to be skeptical here as well. Still, one might argue that a culture will understand itself *for itself*, i.e., explicitly, as in need of the self-assurance that depends upon testing its presuppositions against alternatives only insofar as it is *aware* of alternatives and of their possible value. This is an awareness, one might argue, that is all but unavoidable for the cosmopolitan West, despite its ethnocentrism, racism, sexism, and so on. Yet, I would suggest that, given the conditions of modernity and postmodernity, such an awareness is also increasingly unavoidable for the West's increasingly hyperreflexive others. In any event, cultures will, in fact, be more or less open to this type of critical self-distance.

26. Ronald Dworkin, *Taking Rights Seriously* (Cambridge, MA: Harvard University Press, 1978), 226–27. See also his more recent attempt to mediate the abortion controversy in *Life's Dominion* (New York: Knopf, 1993).

27. I discuss this at somewhat greater length in my *Technology, Time and the Conversations*, 117–19.

CHAPTER 5

1. See especially Iris Marion Young, "Asymmetrical Reciprocity: On Moral Respect, Wonder and Enlarged Thought," *Constellations: An International Journal of Critical and Democratic Theory* 3, no. 3 (1997): 340–63.

2. Iris Marion Young, *Justice and the Politics of Difference* (Princeton, NJ: Princeton University Press, 1990); "Communication and the Other: Beyond Deliberative Democracy," in *Democracy and Difference: Contesting the Boundaries of the Political*, ed. Seyla Benhabib (Princeton, NJ: Princeton University Press, 1996); and "Asymmetrical Reciprocity."
3. Young, "Communication and the Other," 122.
4. Ibid., 123.
5. Ibid., 128–32.
6. Ibid., 130.
7. Ibid., 126–27.
8. Jürgen Habermas, *Moral Consciousness and Communicative Action*, trans. Christian Lenhardt and Shierry Weber Nicholsen (Cambridge, MA: MIT Press, 1991), 65; emphasis in the original.
9. See Seyla Benhabib, *Situating the Self* (New York: Routledge, 1991), 8.
10. Young, "Asymmetrical Reciprocity," 346.
11. Cf. Ibid., 346.
12. Ibid., 347.
13. Ibid.; see also Laurence Thomas, "Moral Deference," *The Philosophical Forum*, 24, nos. 1–3 (1992–93): 235.
14. In another context I make this argument myself in my *Technology, Time, and the Conversations of Modernity* (New York: Routledge, 1995), 219 (n. 115).
15. Young, "Asymmetrical Reciprocity," 347.
16. Ibid., 351.
17. Ibid., 346–47.
18. See ibid., 348–49.
19. Ibid., 352.
20. Cf. Ibid., 352–55.
21. Ibid., 352.
22. See my response to Hannah Arendt's discussion of novelty in my *Technology, Time, and the Conversations of Modernity*, 57.
23. Cf. Young, "Asymmetrical Reciprocity," 354.
24. Cf. Ibid.
25. One of the deepest flaws of neoconservatism is what might be called the fallacy of inferring values from behavior. Contrary to what many of these analysts seem to believe, values are not observable in any straightforward way, and certainly not in the way in which behavior is. Values are held within some conceptual scheme or other and emerge in behavior in a mediated way. Rather than viewing behavior as an immediate reflection of values, it can be more adequately understood as a manifestation of valuation within the context of a particular conception of social life. In order, therefore, to understand what sort of valuing is going on, one must gain access to the view of the social world held by the agents in question. In other words, one must seek an answer to the hermeneutic question, What do they take themselves to be doing? See my "Values, Respect and Recognition: On Race and Culture in the Neoconservative Debate," *Praxis International* 7 (1987): 164–73.
26. See, for example, Young, *Justice and the Politics of Difference*, 231, 233–34.
27. Ibid., 234–36.
28. Robert Bernasconi, "'You Don't Know What I'm Talking About': Alterity and the Hermeneutical Ideal," in *The Specter of Relativism: Truth, Dialogue, and Phronesis in Philosophical Hermeneutics*, ed. Lawrence K. Schmidt (Evanston, IL: Northwestern University Press, 1995), 178–79.

Notes

29. Ibid., 180.
30. Ibid., 182, 184–85.
31. Ibid., 190–91, 193.
32. Hans-Georg Gadamer, *Truth and Method*, cited in Bernasconi, "'You Don't Know,'" 186. The distinguished German philosopher, Bernhard Waldenfels, also writing from a perspective that is sympathetic to Levinas, defends a position similar to Bernasconi's. In Waldenfels's view, thinkers who tout the virtues of mutual understanding presuppose a viewpoint that he denominates "the third," a standpoint that, in allowing for comparability, is a moment of convergence, stability, and universality that effaces difference, a moment that necessarily obscures the singularity of the other; see Waldenfels, "Responding to the Other," unpublished manuscript presented at The Humanities Institute at the State University of New York at Stony Brook on November 2, 1999; and his "Der Andere und Der Dritte im interkultureller Sicht," in R. A. Mall and N. Schneider, eds., *Ethik und Politik aus interkultureller Sicht* (Amsterdam: Rodopi, 1996), 71–83. Again, by arguing that we should view the "third" along the lines suggested by my account of a situated metalanguage—where it is understood to be reflexively and indexically coconstituted by self and other—I would contest this view that the other can be rendered intelligible only by reducing it to the same.
33. Bernasconi, "'You Don't Know,'" 184.
34. Ibid., 190.
35. See John R. Searle, *Speech Acts: An Essay in the Philosophy of Language* (Cambridge: Cambridge University Press, 1969), 64; and Bernasconi, "'You Don't Know,'" 190.
36. Searle, *Speech Acts*, 67; and John R. Searle, *Expression and Meaning* (Cambridge: Cambridge University Press, 1979), 15.
37. Bernasconi, "'You Don't Know,'" 192.
38. It has been argued, for example, that the Greeks did not take their mythical discourse to be making truth claims, at least not in any ordinary sense. As *muthos*, or likely stories, mythical stories were among those narratives that were understood to be neither true nor false. For a general discussion of this matter, see Paul Veyne, *Did the Greeks Believe in Their Myths?* trans. Paula Wissing (Chicago: University of Chicago Press, 1988). See also Alasdair MacIntyre, *After Virtue* (Notre Dame, IN: University of Notre Dame Press, 1981), 201, on the role of mythology as a dramatic resource of the construction of social identity. Further, as Sabina Lovibond has reminded me, one might also see Wittgenstein's *Remarks on Frazer's "The Golden Bough"* for comments on the scientistic misunderstanding of mythical narrative.
39. Peter Winch, "Understanding a Primitive Society," *American Philosophical Quarterly* 1 (1964): 307–24.
40. See the qualifications of this discussed in chapter 4, note 21.
41. See, for example, Sandra Harding, *Is Science Multicultural? Postcolonialisms, Feminisms, and Epistemologies* (Bloomington: Indiana University Press, 1998). Though some of the work produced by scholars in this area is insightful in the challenge it offers to the hubris of modern science in the West, I must confess to considerable skepticism about *some* claims made on behalf of the multicultural status of science in that they sometimes uncritically conflate a number of important and related distinctions: the context of generation with the context of testing; cultural neutrality with universal validity; science itself with technology; causal implications with conceptual implications; problem selection and identification with methods of problem solution; the natural with the social sciences; and so on. Not that these distinctions are unassailable, but the science and multiculturalism debate would benefit from a more dialectical discussion.

42. Bernasconi, "'You Don't Know,'" 192.
43. Ibid., 192–93.
44. See, for example, George E. Marcus and Michael M. J. Fischer, *Anthropology As Cultural Critique: An Experimental Moment in the Human Sciences* (Chicago: University of Chicago Press, 1986), 118, 127, though they do not put the point in this way.
45. See ibid., esp. 64, 66. On the sort of critique of postmodernism that I have in mind here, see my *Technology, Time, and the Conversations of Modernity*, 108–9.
46. Stephen A. Tyler, "Post-modern Ethnography: From Document of the Occult to Occult Document," in *Writing Culture: The Poetics and Politics of Ethnography*, eds. James Clifford and George E. Marcus (Berkeley and Los Angeles: University of California Press, 1986), 123.
47. Ibid., 128–29.
48. Ibid., 130.
49. Ibid., 138.
50. See Ibid., 137–38.
51. Actually, given the postmodernist critique of the idea of the fictional—such an idea presupposes the existence of the real—it would be more accurate to view a postmodernist ethnography as an instance of what Baudrillard would call a simulacrum, as an item of the hyperreal, a realm of copies that stand in no relation to an original.
52. On "dialogical anthropology," see D. Tedlock, "The Analogical Tradition and the Emergence of a Dialogical Anthropology," *Journal of Anthropological Research* 35 (1979): 387–400.
53. On this conception of "objectification," see Dale F. Eickelman and James Piscatori, *Muslim Politics* (Princeton, NJ: Princeton University Press, 1996), 38.
54. See, for example, Jocelyn Linnekin, "On the Theory and Politics of Cultural Construction in the Pacific," *Oceania* 62 (1992): 249–63. I am grateful to Anne Feldhaus, a colleague at the Woodrow Wilson International Center for Scholars, for bringing this essay to my attention and for many engaging conversations about these matters.
55. See Gadamer, *Truth and Method* (New York: Seabury Press, 1975), 330–31, 347–50.
56. See Eickelman and Piscatori, *Muslim Politics*, 44, and Akeel Bilgrami, "What Is a Muslim? Fundamental Commitment and Cultural Identity," *Critical Inquiry* 18 (1992): 821–42.
57. On the occasion of a seminar that he offered at the Humanities Institute at the State University of New York at Stony Brook on September 9, 1999, I understood Renato Rosaldo to offer the following methodological advice in response to a question that I put to him concerning strategic representation: One should in the first instance take what is said at face value, but be prepared to question it when, for instance, conversations with others seem to contradict it or when the respondent's own behavior seems to belie what s/he has said. Then go on to hazard interpretive projections of the form, "What would be the case if what the 'informant' has said is true, or false?" Then, making the process recursive, return to engage the interlocutor in a confirmatory or disconfirmatory dialogue informed by what one has learned.
58. See my "On Habermas and Particularity: Is There Room for Race and Gender on the Glassy Plains of Ideal Discourse?" *Praxis International* 6, no. 3 (1986): 328–40.
59. See Lionel Trilling's classic *Sincerity and Authenticity* (New York: Norton, 1969) on the relationship between sincerity and situations of perceived power asymmetry.

Notes

60. George E. Marcus and Michael M. J. Fischer, *Anthropology*, 159–60.
61. Ibid., 157–77.
62. Ibid., 167.

EPILOGUE

1. Charles Taylor, *Multiculturalism and "The Politics of Recognition"* (Princeton, NJ: Princeton University Press, 1992; reissued in expanded paperback edition as *Multiculturalism: Examining the Politics of Recognition*, ed. Amy Gutmann (Princeton, NJ: Princeton University Press, 1994), 68–70.
2. Linda Nicholson, "To Be or Not to Be: Charles Taylor and the Politics of Recognition," *Constellations* 3 (1996): 14–15.
3. Taylor, *Multiculturalism*, 70.
4. See my discussion of second-order rationality in chapter 4; and see my *Technology, Time, and the Conversations of Modernity* (New York: Routledge, 1995), 104, for further discussion of this point.
5. See Hilary Putnam, "Why Epistemology Can't Be Naturalized," in *After Philosophy: End or Transformation?* ed. Kenneth Baynes, James Bohman, and Thomas McCarthy (Cambridge, MA: MIT Press, 1987), 232–35. Some of the conclusions I have reached in this book regarding the plausibility of horizontal fusion are supported also, though in a quite different idiom from the one through which I pursue it here, by considerations drawn from the philosophy of language, particularly from the reflections of the later Wittgenstein. In principle, our use of words and understanding of concepts is always essentially and dialogically contestable, for there will always be the possibility of new applications of a term, with each such application *extending* its meaning, since *ex hypothesi* for Wittgenstein such applications cannot be construed as simple instances or applications of an already-at-hand set of necessary and sufficient conditions or rules for the application of a term. Discovering new metaphorical relations of similarity, or new relations of analogy, or extending a network of "family resemblance" will thus extend the meaning of the term. In his *Strange Multiplicity: Constitutionalism in an Age of Diversity* (Cambridge: Cambridge University Press, 1995), 110–11, James Tully draws our attention to the important paragraph 122 of Wittgenstein's *Philosophical Investigations* (trans. G. E. M. Anscombe [Oxford: Basil Blackwell, 1958], 49). There Wittgenstein speaks of the importance of finding examples that mediate between two competing usages of terms. Competing sets of illustrative examples—that is, competing accounts of the correct application or meaning of terms—can be mediated, Wittgenstein implies, by finding *intermediate* cases. Adducing such intermediate cases—for example, recognizing that, say, Duke Ellington's use of timbral harmonics or tone colors stands in an analogical relationship to the impressionists' use of harmonics of pitch—would be tantamount to demonstrating that the interlocutors were playing the same general language game (say, ethical, political, religious, or aesthetic), that they are addressing the same Sache, albeit in different ways. And at the same time, the production of the analogical framework that allows the intermediate cases to be appreciated *as* intermediate cases, mediating between one's own position and that of the other, is ipso facto an expansion of both horizons, for it renders intelligible to both sides an intelligible application of their term that they were not in a position to entertain prior to their collaborative work.
6. Thomas McCarthy and David Couzens Hoy, *Critical Theory* (Oxford: Blackwell, 1994), 86–93; Homi K. Bhabha, *The Location of Culture* (London: Routledge,

1994), 223–33; Paul Gilroy, *Against Race: Imagining Political Culture Beyond the Color Line* (Cambridge, MA: Harvard University Press, 2000).

7. Charles Verharen of Howard University, whose philosophy department Locke cofounded and chaired for almost four decades, pointed out to me the affinities between some of the ideas I was developing and Locke's.

8. Alain Locke, *The Negro and His Music* (Washington, DC: The Associates in Negro Folk Education, 1936), 72. See also Leonard Harris, ed., *The Philosophy of Alain Locke: Harlem Renaissance and Beyond* (Philadelphia: Temple University Press, 1989), 90–92.

9. Harris, *The Philosophy of Alain Locke*, 92.

10. See Susan Wolf, "Comment," in *Multiculturalism and "The Politics of Recognition."*

11. Further, Robert Gooding-Williams has suggested that it is an implication of my discussion that procedural or deliberative democracy should be understood to be not only the preferred context within which promising programs are chosen, but also, arguably, a criterion of program choice. It is certainly likely that insofar as a program itself promotes discursive democracy, its choice will, reflexively, help to realize the ideal context for program choice.

12. See W. E. B. Du Bois, *The Souls of Black Folk*, ed. David W. Blight and Robert Gooding-Williams (Boston: Bedford Books, 1997); and Robert Gooding-Williams, "Between the Masses and the Folk: Du Bois, Culture and Political Leadership," in his *Du Bois and the Politics of Double Consciousness* (Cambridge, MA: Harvard University Press, forthcoming).

13. Martha Nussbaum, "Patriotism and Cosmopolitanism," in *For Love of Country: Debating the Limits of Patriotism*, ed. Joshua Cohen (Boston: Beacon Press, 1996).

14. In "'Stuck Inside of Mobile with the Memphis Blues Again': Interculturalism and the Conversation of Races" (in Cynthia Willett, ed., *Theorizing Multiculturalism* [Oxford: Blackwell, 1998], 289–90), Robert Bernasconi helpfully suggests we adopt the term *interculturalism* as a corrective to the Herderian-inspired strands of multiculturalism that suggest that cultures are discrete, autonomous, and relatively static. For a sustained, trenchant response to race-based cultural discourse, see Gilroy, *Against Race*.

15. These comments are drawn from my reply to Philip Kitcher's paper "Biology, Race, Ethnicity and Culture," presented at a conference on "Race: Its Meaning and Significance," sponsored by the Department of Philosophy, Rutgers University, in November 1994. Kitcher's paper was subsequently published as "Race, Ethnicity, Biology, Culture," in *Racism*, ed., Leonard Harris (Amherst, NY: Humanity Books, 1999).

16. For an illuminating discussion of the distinction between culture and ethnoracial classification in American society, see David A. Hollinger, *Post-Ethnic America: Beyond Multiculturalism* (New York: Basic Books, 1995).

17. See Gary Giddins, *Visions of Jazz: The First Century* (New York: Oxford University Press, 1998), 646–50.

18. Given the disanalogies between cultural transmission and genetic transmission—salient among them being the fact that there are creative discontinuities in the transmission of ethnicity (even from one's biological parents) because of ineluctable acts of reinterpretation and reinvention as ethnicity is passed down from generation to generation—ethnic transmission is even more vulnerable to contestation; see James

Notes

Clifford, *The Predicament of Culture: Twentieth-Century Ethnography, Literature, and Art* (Cambridge, MA: Harvard University Press, 1988), 341.

19. I explore this phenomenon within the context of a discussion of postmodernism in my *Technology, Time, and the Conversations of Modernity*, 164–65.

20. For an examination of the connection between racialized discourse and the idea of cultural pluralism, see Walter Benn Michaels, "Race into Culture: A Critical Genealogy of Cultural Identity," in *Identities*, ed. Kwame Anthony Appiah and Henry Louis Gates Jr. (Chicago: University of Chicago Press, 1995).

21. Alasdair MacIntyre, in his *Whose Justice? Which Rationality?* (Notre Dame, IN: University of Notre Dame Press, 1988), 354 ff, makes a similar point in his discussion of the rationality of tradition-constituted inquiry.

22. Ernesto Grassi, *Heidegger and the Question of Renaissance Humanism* (Binghamton, NY: Center for Medieval and Renaissance Studies, 1983), 20.

23. Ibid., 70–71.

24. Quentin Skinner, *Reason and Rhetoric in the Philosophy of Hobbes* (Cambridge: Cambridge University Press, 1995), 9, 10, 15–16.

25. Sabina Lovibond, "Plato's Theory of Mind," in Stephen Everson, ed., *Companions to Ancient Thought 2: Psychology* (Cambridge: Cambridge University Press, 1991), 55.

Bibliography

Adorno, Theodor. *Aesthetic Theory*. Trans. C. Lenhardt. New York: Routledge, 1984.
———. "The Culture Industry Reconsidered." In *Critical Theory and Society: A Reader*, ed. Stephen Bronner and Douglas Kellner. New York: Routledge, 1989.
———. *The Culture Industry: Selected Essays on Mass Culture*. Ed. with intro. by J. M. Bernstein. London: Routledge, 1991.
———. *In Search of Wagner*. Trans. Rodney Livingstone. London: Verso, 1981.
———. "On the Fetish-Character in Music and the Regression of Listening." In *The Essential Frankfurt School Reader*. Eds. Andrew Arato and Eike Gebhardt. New York: Continuum, 1988.
———. "On Jazz." Trans. Jamie Owen Daniel. *Discourse* 12, no. 1 (1989–90).
———. "On Some Relations between Music and Painting." *The Musical Quarterly* 79, no. 1, (1995).
———. *Philosophy of Modern Music*. Trans. Anne Mitchell and Wesley Blomster. New York: Continuum, 1994.
———. *Prisms*. Trans. Samuel and Shierry Weber. Cambridge, MA: MIT Press, 1981.
———. Review of Wilder Hobson, *American Jazz Music* and Winthrop Sargeant, *Jazz: Hot and Hybrid*, Studies in Philosophy and Social Science 9, no. 1 (1941).
———. "A Social Critique of Radio Music and Theses upon Art and Religion Today. *Kenyon Review* 18, nos. 3–4 (1996).
Adorno, Theodor, and Max Horkheimer. *Dialectic of Enlightenment*. Trans. John Cumming. New York: Seabury Press, 1972.
al-Azm, Sadiq J. "The Importance of Being Earnest about Salman Rushdie." In *Die Welt des Islams* 31 (1991).
———. "Islamic Fundamentalism Reconsidered: A Critical Outline of Problems, Ideas, and Approaches, Part I." In *South Asian Bulletin* 13, no. 1 (1993).
———. "Islamic Fundamentalism Reconsidered: A Critical Outline of Problems, Ideas, and Approaches, Part II." In *South Asian Bulletin* 13, no. 2 (1993).
Appiah, Kwame Anthony. *In My Father's House: Africa in the Philosophy of Culture*. Oxford: Oxford University Press, 1992.
Arnold, Matthew. *Culture and Anarchy: An Essay in Political and Social Criticism*, 1869. New York: Macmillan, 1919.
———. "Dover Beach." In *New Poems*. London: Macmillan, 1867.
Asad, Talal. "The Concept of Cultural Translation in British Social Anthropology." In *Writing Culture: The Poetics and Politics of Ethnography*, ed. James Clifford

and George E. Marcus. Berkeley and Los Angeles: University of California Press, 1986.

Baker, G. P., and P. M. S. Hacker. *An Analytical Commentary on the "Philosophical Investigations,"* vols. 1–3. Oxford: Basil Blackwell, 1980–1990.

Bakhtin, Mikhail. *The Dialogic Imagination.* Ed. M. Holquist, trans. C. Emerson and M. Holquist. Austin: University of Texas Press, 1981.

Barnard, F. M., ed. *Herder on Social and Political Culture.* Cambridge: Cambridge University Press, 1969.

———. "National Culture and Political Legitimacy: Herder and Rousseau." *Journal of the History of Ideas* 44 (1983).

Bayles, Martha. *Hole in Our Soul: The Loss of Beauty and Meaning in American Popular Music.* New York: The Free Press, 1994.

Bell, Bernard W. *The Folk Roots of Contemporary Afro-American Poetry.* Detroit: Broadside Press, 1974.

Benhabib, Seyla. *Situating the Self: Gender, Community and Postmodernism in Contemporary Ethics.* New York: Routledge, 1992.

———, ed. *Democracy and Difference: Contesting the Boundaries of the Political.* Princeton, NJ: Princeton University Press, 1996.

Berlin, Isaiah. *Four Essays on Liberty.* Oxford: Oxford University Press, 1969.

———. *Vico and Herder: Two Studies in the History of Ideas.* New York: Viking Press, 1976.

Berliner, Paul. *Thinking in Jazz: The Infinite Art of Improvisation.* Chicago: University of Chicago Press, 1994.

Bernasconi, Robert. "'Stuck Inside of Mobile with the Memphis Blues Again': Interculturalism and the Conversation of Races." In *Theorizing Multiculturalism,* ed. Cynthia Willett. Oxford: Blackwell, 1998.

———. "'You Don't Know What I'm Talking About': Alterity and the Hermeneutical Ideal." In *The Specter of Relativism: Truth, Dialogue and Phronesis in Philosophical Hermeneutics,* ed. Lawrence K. Schmidt. Evanston, IL: Northwestern University Press, 1995.

Bernotas, Robert. "Critical Theory, Jazz, and Politics: A Critique of the Frankfurt School." Ph.d. Dissertation, Johns Hopkins University, Baltimore, 1987.

Berreby, David. "The Unabsolute Truths of Clifford Geertz," *New York Times Magazine,* April 9, 1995.

Bhabha, Homi K. *The Location of Culture.* London: Routledge, 1994.

Bilgrami, Akeel. "Rushdie, Islam, and Postcolonial Defensiveness." *The Yale Journal of Criticism* 4 (1990).

———. "What Is a Muslim? Fundamental Commitment and Cultural Identity." *Critical Inquiry* 18 (1992).

Blocker, H. Gene. *The Aesthetics of Primitive Art.* Lanham, MD: University Press of America, 1994.

Brown, Lee B. "Adorno's Critique of Popular Culture: The Case of Jazz Music." *Journal of Aesthetic Education* 26 (1992).

Burton, Steven J. *An Introduction to Law and Legal Reasoning.* Boston: Little, Brown, 1985.

Carrithers, Michael. *Why Humans Have Cultures: Examining Anthropology and Social History.* Oxford: Oxford University Press, 1992.

Clifford, James. *The Predicament of Culture: Twentieth-Century Ethnography, Literature, and Art.* Cambridge, MA: Harvard University Press, 1988.

Clifford, James, and George E. Marcus, eds. *Writing Culture: The Poetics and Politics of Ethnography.* Berkeley and Los Angeles: University of California Press, 1986.

Cooper, Harry. "On *Uber Jazz*: Replaying Adorno with the Grain," *October* 75 (1996).

Cousineau, Robert Henri. *Humanism and Ethics: An Introduction to Heidegger's Letter on Humanism.* Paris: Beatrice-Nauwelaerts, 1972.

Crease, Robert, "Jazz and Dance." In the *Cambridge Companion to Jazz.* Cambridge: Cambridge University Press, forthcoming.

Davidson, Donald. *Inquiries into Truth and Interpretation.* Oxford: Oxford University Press, 1984.

Derrida, Jacques. "Heidegger, l'enfer des philosophes." In *Le Nouvel Observateur*, November 6, 1987.

———. *Margins of Philosophy.* Trans. A. Bass. Chicago: University of Chicago Press, 1982.

———. *Of Spirit: Heidegger and the Question.* Trans. G. Bennington and R. Bowlby. Chicago: University of Chicago Press, 1989.

DeVaux, Scott. "Constructing the Jazz Tradition: Jazz Historiography." *Black American Literature Forum* 25, no. 3 (1991).

Du Bois, W. E. B. *The Souls of Black Folk.* Ed. David W. Blight and Robert Gooding-Williams. Boston: Bedford Books, 1997.

Dworkin, Ronald. *Life's Dominion.* New York: Knopf, 1993.

———. *Taking Rights Seriously.* Cambridge, MA: Harvard University Press, 1978.

Eickelman, Dale F., and James Piscatori. *Muslim Politics.* Princeton, NJ: Princeton University Press, 1996.

Eisenberg, Avigail. "The Politics of Individual and Group Difference in Canadian Jurisprudence." *Canadian Journal of Political Science* 27, no. 1 (1994).

Ellison, Ralph. *Shadow and Act.* New York: Vintage Books, 1964.

Epstein, Joseph. "Matthew Arnold and the Resistance." *Commentary* 73, no. 4 (1982).

Ferry, Luc. *Political Philosophy 2: The System of Philosophies of History.* Trans. Franklin Philip. Chicago: University of Chicago Press, 1992.

Ferry, Luc, and Alain Renaut. *French Philosophy of the Sixties: An Essay on Antihumanism.* Trans. M. Cattani. Amherst: University of Massachusetts Press, 1990.

———. *Heidegger and Modernity.* Trans. Franklin Philip. Chicago: University of Chicago Press, 1990.

Fideler, Paul. "Toward a 'Curriculum of Hope.'" In *Teaching the Humanities.* American Council of Learned Societies Occasional Paper no. 23 (1994).

Foucault, Michel. *The Foucault Reader.* Ed. P. Rabinow. New York: Pantheon Books, 1984.

———. *The Order of Things.* New York: Vintage Books, 1973.
Gabbard, Krin. "Signifyin' the Phallus: Representations of the Jazz Trumpet." In *Jammin' at the Margins: Jazz and the American Cinema.* Chicago: University of Chicago Press, 1996.
Gadamer, Hans-Georg. "Herder und die Geschichtliche Welt." In *Kleine Schriften III.* Tübingen: J.C.B. Mohr, 1972.
———. *Philosophical Hermeneutics.* Trans. and ed. D. Linge. Berkeley and Los Angeles: University of California Press, 1988.
———. *Truth and Method.* 2d English ed. London: Sheed and Ward, 1979.
Gates, Henry Louis Jr. *The Signifying Monkey: A Theory of Afro-American Literary Criticism.* New York: Oxford University Press, 1988.
Gates, Henry Louis Jr., and Karen C. C. Dalton, eds. *Josephine Baker and La Revue Nègre: Paul Colin's "Le Tumulte Noir."* New York: Henry N. Abrams, 1998.
Gendron, Bernard. "Fetishes and Motorcars: Negrophilia in French Modernism." *Cultural Studies* 4 (1990).
Giddins, Gary. *Visions of Jazz: The First Century.* New York: Oxford University Press, 1998.
Gilbert, Paul. *The Philosophy of Nationalism.* Boulder, CO: Westview Press, 1998.
Gilroy, Paul. *Against Race: Imagining Political Culture Beyond the Color Line.* Cambridge, MA: Harvard University Press, 2000.
———. *The Black Atlantic: Modernity and Double Consciousness.* Cambridge, MA: Harvard University Press, 1993.
Gioia, Ted. *The Imperfect Art: Reflections on Jazz and Modern Culture.* Oxford: Oxford University Press, 1988.
Giustiniani, Vito R. "Homo, Humanus, and the Meanings of 'Humanism.'" *Journal of the History of Ideas* 46 (1985).
Goehr, Lydia. "Dissonant Works and the Listening Public: Or 'How One Becomes Lonely' and the 'Solitary Theoretician.'" In *The Cambridge Companion to Adorno.* Cambridge: Cambridge University Press, forthcoming.
———. "Political Music and the Politics of Music." *Journal of Aesthetics and Art Criticism* 52, no. 1 (1994).
Goldberg, David T., ed. *Multiculturalism: A Critical Reader.* Oxford: Basil Blackwell, 1994.
Goodheart, Eugene. "Arnold: Critic of Ideology." *New Literary History,* 25 (1994).
Gooding-Williams, Robert. *Du Bois and the Politics of Double Consciousness.* Cambridge, MA: Harvard University Press, forthcoming.
Gracyk, Theodore A. "Adorno, Jazz, and the Aesthetics of Popular Music." *Musical Quarterly* 76, no. 4 (1992).
Grassi, Ernesto. *Heidegger and the Question of Renaissance Humanism.* Binghamton, NY: Center for Medieval and Renaissance Studies, 1983.
Guillory, John. *Cultural Capital.* Chicago: University of Chicago Press, 1993.
Habermas, Jürgen. *Justification and Application: Remarks on Discourse Ethics.* Trans. Ciaran P. Cronin. Cambridge, MA: MIT Press, 1993.

———. *Legitimation Crisis*. Trans. Thomas McCarthy. Boston: Beacon Press, 1975.
———. *Moral Consciousness and Communicative Action*. Trans. C. Lenhardt and S. Nicholsen. Cambridge, MA: MIT Press, 1990.
———. *Postmetaphysical Thinking: Philosophical Essays*. Trans. W. Hohengarten. Cambridge, MA: MIT Press, 1992.
———. "A Postscript to *Knowledge and Human Interests*." *Philosophy of the Social Sciences* 3 (1973).
———. "Struggles for Recognition in the Democratic Constitutional State." In *Multiculturalism: Examining the Politics of Recognition*, ed. Amy Gutmann. Princeton, NJ: Princeton University Press, 1994.
———. *The Theory of Communicative Action*, vol. 1. Trans. Thomas McCarthy. Boston: Beacon Press, 1984.
Hall, Stuart. "What Is This 'Black' in Black Popular Culture?" In *Black Popular Culture*, ed. Gina Dent. Seattle: Bay Press, 1992.
Harding, Sandra. *Is Science Multicultural? Postcolonialisms, Feminisms, and Epistemologies*. Bloomington: Indiana University Press, 1998.
Harris, Leonard, ed. *The Philosophy of Alain Locke: Harlem Renaissance and Beyond*. Philadelphia: Temple University Press, 1989.
Heidegger, Martin. *Basic Writings*. Ed. D. Krell. New York: Harper and Row, 1977.
Herder, Johann Gottfried von. *Reflections on the Philosophy of the History of Mankind*. Ed. F. Manuel. Chicago: University of Chicago Press, 1968.
———. *Sämtliche Werke*. Ed. B. Suphan. Berlin: Georg Olms Verlagsbuchhandlung, 1887–1913.
Hollinger, David. *Post-ethnic America: Beyond Multiculturalism*. New York: Basic Books, 1995.
Husserl, Edmund. *The Crisis of European Sciences and Transcendental Phenomenology*. Trans. David Carr. Evanston, IL: Northwestern University Press, 1970.
Ingold, Tim, ed. *Key Debates in Anthropology*. London: Routledge, 1996.
Jameson, Fredric. *Postmodernism, or the Cultural Logic of Late Capitalism*. Durham, NC: Duke University Press, 1991.
Jay, Martin. *The Dialectical Imagination: A History of the Frankfurt School and the Institute of Social Research, 1923–1950*. Boston: Little, Brown, 1973.
Kierkegaard, Søren. *Either/Or*, vol. I. Trans. David F. Swenson and Lillian M. Swenson, rev. Howard A. Johnson. Princeton, NJ: Princeton University Press, 1959.
Kitcher, Philip. "Race, Ethnicity, Biology, Culture." In *Racism*. Ed. Leonard Harris. Amherst, NY: Humanity Books, 1999.
Kohn, Hans. *The Idea of Nationalism*. New York: Collier Books, 1967.
Krausz, Michael, ed. *Relativism: Interpretation and Confrontation*. Notre Dame, IN: University of Notre Dame Press, 1989.
Kristeller, Paul O. *Renaissance Thought: The Classic, Scholastic, and Humanist Strains*. New York: Harper Torchbooks, 1955.
Kuhn, Thomas. S. *The Essential Tension*. Chicago: University of Chicago Press, 1977.

Latour, Bruno. *We Have Never Been Modern.* Cambridge, MA: Harvard University Press, 1993.
Lewandowski, Joseph D. "Adorno on Jazz and Society." *Philosophy and Social Criticism* 22 (1996).
Linnekin, Jocelyn. "On the Theory and Politics of Cultural Construction in the Pacific." *Oceania* 62 (1992).
Lloyd, David. "Arnold, Ferguson, Schiller: Aesthetic Culture and the Politics of Aesthetics." *Cultural Critique* 1, no. 2 (1989).
Locke, Alain. *The Negro and His Music.* Washington, DC: The Associates in Negro Folk Education, 1936.
Lovibond, Sabina. "Plato's Theory of Mind." In *Companions to Ancient Thought 2: Psychology,* ed. Stephen Everson. Cambridge: Cambridge University Press, 1991.
Lowith, Karl. *Martin Heidegger and European Nihilism.* Ed. Richard Wolin, trans. Gary Steiner. New York: Columbia University Press, 1995.
MacIntyre, Alasdair. *After Virtue.* Notre Dame, IN: University of Notre Dame Press, 1981.

———. *Whose Justice? Which Rationality?* Notre Dame, IN: University of Notre Dame Press, 1988.
Marcus, George E., and Michael M. J. Fischer. *Anthropology As Cultural Critique: An Experimental Moment in the Human Sciences.* Chicago: University of Chicago Press, 1986.
Marcuse, Herbert. *An Essay on Liberation.* Boston: Beacon Press, 1969.
McCarthy, Thomas, *Ideals and Illusions: On Reconstruction and Deconstruction in Contemporary Critical Theory.* Cambridge, MA: MIT Press, 1991.
McCarthy, Thomas, and David Couzens Hoy. *Critical Theory.* Oxford: Blackwell, 1994.
McDowell, J. "Aesthetic Value, Objectivity, and the Fabric of the World." In *Pleasure, Performance, and Value,* ed. Eva Schaper. Cambridge: Cambridge University Press, 1983.
Michaels, Walter Benn. "Race into Culture: A Critical Genealogy of Cultural Identity." In *Identities,* ed. Kwame Anthony Appiah and Henry Louis Gates Jr. Chicago: University of Chicago Press, 1995.
Mohanty, S. P. "Us and Them: On the Philosophical Bases of Political Criticism." *Yale Journal of Criticism* 2 (1989).
Monson, Ingrid. "Doubleness and Jazz Improvisation: Irony, Parody, and Ethnomusicology." *Critical Inquiry* 20 (1994).
Morphy, Howard. "From Dull to Brilliant: The Aesthetics of Spiritual Power among Yolngu." In *Anthropology, Art, and Aesthetics,* ed. Coote and Schelton. Oxford, 1992.

———. "The Interpretation of Ritual: Reflections from Film on Anthropological Practice." *Man* 29 (1994).
Morphy, Howard, Joanna Overing, Jeremy Coote, and Peter Gow. "Aesthetics Is a Cross Cultural Category." In *Key Debates in Anthropology,* ed. Tim Ingold. London: Routledge, 1996.

Bibliography

Moses, Wilson. *The Golden Age of Black Nationalism 1850–1925.* Oxford: Oxford University Press, 1988.

Munson, Henry Jr. *Religion and Power in Morocco.* New Haven, CT: Yale University Press, 1993.

Murray, Albert. *The Blue Devils of Nada: A Contemporary American Approach to Aesthetic Statement.* New York: Pantheon Books, 1996.

———. *The Omni-Americans.* New York: Da Capo Press, 1970.

Nicholson, Linda. "To Be or Not to Be: Charles Taylor and the Politics of Recognition." *Constellations* 3 (1996).

Nussbaum, Martha. "Patriotism and Cosmopolitanism." In *For Love of Country: Debating the Limits of Patriotism,* ed. Joshua Cohen. Boston: Beacon Press, 1996.

Nye, William P. "Theodor Adorno on Jazz: A Critique of Critical Theory." *Popular Music and Society* 12 (1988).

Putnam, Hilary. "Why Epistemology Can't Be Naturalized." In *After Philosophy: End or Transformation?* ed. Kenneth Baynes, James Bohman, and Thomas McCarthy. Cambridge, MA: MIT Press.

Ragussis, Michael. *Figures of Conversion: "The Jewish Question" and English National Identity.* Durham, NC: Duke University Press, 1995.

Rattenbury, Ken. *Duke Ellington: Jazz Composer.* New Haven, CT: Yale University Press, 1990.

Robbins, Bruce. "Comparative Cosmopolitanism." *Social Text* 10 (1992).

———. "Other in the Academy: Professionalism and Multiculturalism." *Social Research* 58 (1991).

Robinson, J. Bradford. "The Jazz Essays of Theodor Adorno: Some Thoughts on Jazz Reception in Weimar Germany." *Popular Music* 13, no. 1 (1994).

Robinson, Joseph. "What I Learned in the Lenoir High School Band." *Wilson Quarterly* 19 (1995).

Roblin, Ronald, ed. *The Aesthetics of the Critical Theorists: Studies on Benjamin, Adorno, Marcuse, and Habermas.* Lewiston, NY: Edwin Mellen Press, 1990.

Rockmore, Tom. *Heidegger and French Philosophy: Humanism, Antihumanism and Being.* London: Routledge, 1995.

Rorty, Richard. *Contingency, Irony, and Solidarity.* Cambridge: Cambridge University Press, 1989.

———. "Postmodernist Bourgeois Liberalism." *Journal of Philosophy* 80 (1983).

Said, Edward W. "Representing the Colonized: Anthropology's Interlocutors." *Critical Inquiry* 15, no. 2 (1989).

———. *The World, the Text, and the Critic.* Cambridge, MA: Harvard University Press, 1983.

Schatzki, Theodore. *Social Practices: A Wittgenstein Approach to Human Activity and the Social.* Cambridge: Cambridge University Press, 1996.

Scherman, Tony. Interview with Wynton Marsalis. *American Heritage,* October 1995.

Searle, John R. *Expression and Meaning.* Cambridge: Cambridge University Press, 1979.

Searle, John R. *Speech Acts: An Essay in the Philosophy of Language.* Cambridge: Cambridge University Press, 1969.
Sidentop, L. A. "Liberalism: The Christian Connection." *The Times Literary Supplement*, March 24–30, 1989.
Siebers, Tobin. "The Ethics of Anti-ethnocentrism." *Michigan Quarterly Review* 32 (1993).
Sikka, Sonya. "Heidegger's Conception of *Volk.*" *Philosophical Forum* 26 (1994).
Simpson, Lorenzo C. "On Habermas and Particularity: Is There Room for Race and Gender on the Glassy Plains of Ideal Discourse?" *Praxis International* 6 (1986).
———. *Technology, Time, and the Conversations of Modernity.* New York: Routledge, 1995.
———. "Values, Respect and Recognition: On Race and Culture in the Neoconservative Debate." *Praxis International* 7 (1987).
Skinner, Quentin. *Reason and Rhetoric in the Philosophy of Hobbes.* Cambridge: Cambridge University Press, 1995.
Snead, James H. "Repetition As a Figure of Black Culture." In *Black Literature and Literary Theory*, ed. Henry Louis Gates, Jr. New York: Methuen, 1984.
Southern, Eileen. *The Music of Black Americans: A History.* New York: W. W. Norton, 1971.
Sperber, Dan. *On Anthropological Knowledge.* Cambridge: Cambridge University Press, 1985.
Swoyer, Chris. "True For." In *Relativism: Cognitive and Moral*, ed. Michael Krausz and Jack Meiland. Notre Dame, IN: University of Notre Dame Press, 1982.
Tamir, Yael. "Liberal Nationalism." *Philosophy and Public Policy* 4 (1993).
Taylor, Charles. "Interpretation and the Science of Man." In *Review of Metaphysics* 25 (1971).
———. *Multiculturalism and "The Politics of Recognition."* Princeton, NJ: Princeton University Press, 1992; reissued in expanded paperback edition as *Multiculturalism: Examining the Politics of Recognition*, ed. Amy Gutmann. Princeton, NJ: Princeton University Press, 1994.
———. *Philosophical Arguments.* Cambridge, MA: Harvard University Press, 1995.
———. *Philosophy and the Human Sciences: Philosophical Papers.* Cambridge: Cambridge University Press, 1985.
———. "The Rushdie Controversy." *Public Culture* 2 (1989).
Tedlock, D. "The Analogical Tradition and the Emergence of a Dialogical Anthropology." *Journal of Anthropological Research* 35 (1979).
Thomas, Laurence. "Moral Deference." *Philosophical Forum* 24, nos. 1–3 (1992–93).
Thompson, Robert Ferris. "Esthetics in Traditional Africa." *Art News* 66 (1968).
Todorov, Tzvetan. *The Conquest of America: The Question of the Other.* Trans. Richard Howard. Norman: University of Oklahoma Press, 1984.
Trilling, Lionel. *Sincerity and Authenticity.* New York: Norton, 1969.

Tsing, Anna Lowenhaupt. *In the Realm of the Diamond Queen: Marginality in an Out-of-the-Way Place*. Princeton, NJ: Princeton University Press, 1993.

Tucker, Mark, ed. *The Duke Ellington Reader*. Oxford: Oxford University Press, 1993.

Tully, James. *Strange Multiplicity: Constitutionalism in an Age of Diversity*. Cambridge: Cambridge University Press, 1995.

Tyler, Stephen A. "Post-modern Ethnography: From Document of the Occult to Occult Document." In *Writing Culture: The Poetics and Politics of Ethnography*, ed. James Clifford and George E. Marcus. Berkeley and Los Angeles: University of California Press, 1986.

Veyne, Paul. *Did the Greeks Believe Their Myths?* Trans. Paula Wissing. Chicago: University of Chicago Press, 1988.

Volkan, Vamik. *The Psychodynamics of International Relationships*. Lexington, MA: Lexington Books, 1990–91.

Waldenfels, Bernhard. "Der Andere und Der Dritte im interkultureller Sicht," in R.A. Mall and N. Schneider, eds., *Ethik und Politik aus interkultureller Sicht*. Amsterdam: Rodopi, 1996.

Walzer, Michael. "What Does It Mean to Be an 'American'?" *Social Research* 57 (1990).

Warnke, Georgia. "Communicative Rationality and Cultural Values." In *The Cambridge Companion to Habermas*, ed. Stephen K. White. Cambridge: Cambridge University Press, 1995.

———. *Gadamer: Hermeneutics, Tradition and Reason*. Stanford, CA: Stanford University Press, 1987.

———. *Justice and Interpretation*. Cambridge, MA: MIT Press, 1993.

West, Hugh. *From Tahiti to the Terror*. Chapel Hill: University of North Carolina Press, forthcoming.

———. Review of Johann Gottfried von Herder's *Selected Early Works, 1764–67*. *Central European History* 25 (1992).

Whitebook, Joel. "Perversion and Utopia: A Study in Psychological and Critical Theory." *American Journal of Sociology* 102, no. 1 (1996).

———. "Reflections on the Autonomous Individual and the Decentered Subject." *American Imago* 49, no. 1 (1992).

Willett, Frank. *African Art*. New York: Thames and Hudson, 1971.

Winch, Peter. "Understanding a Primitive Society." *American Philosophical Quarterly* 1 (1964).

Wittgenstein, Ludwig. *Philosophical Investigations*. Trans. G. E. M. Anscombe. Oxford: Basil Blackwell, 1967.

Young, Iris Marion. "Asymmetrical Reciprocity: On Moral Respect, Wonder, and Enlarged Thought." *Constellations: An International Journal of Critical and Democratic Theory* 3, no. 3 (1997).

———. "Communication and the Other: Beyond Deliberative Democracy." In *Democracy and Difference: Contesting the Boundaries of the Political*, ed. Seyla Benhabib. Princeton, NJ: Princeton University Press, 1996.

———. *Justice and the Politics of Difference.* Princeton, NJ: Princeton University Press, 1990.

Young, Robert J. C. *Colonial Desire: Hybridity in Theory, Culture and Race.* London: Routledge, 1995.

Zuidervaart, Lambert. *Adorno's Aesthetic Theory: The Redemption of Illusion.* Cambridge, MA: MIT Press, 1991.

Index

Adderly, Julian (Cannonball), 56
Adorno, Theodor W., 11, 12, 13, 27, 42–59 *passim*, 63, 108, 128, 131, 133, 145n.13, 149n.22, 149n.26, 150n.27, 150n.29, 150–51n.42, 152n.69, 154n.10
aesthetics, 25, 28, 43, 44–46, 47, 48, 55, 57–59, 115, 133, 156n.21
aesthetic judgement, 156n.21
aesthetic theory, 59
African-American culture. *See* culture, African-American
Afrocentrism, 15, 25, 41, 123, 127, 134. *See also* nationalism, black
Agrippa, Menenius, 141
alterity, 6, 8, 14, 22, 30, 34, 38, 39, 68, 79, 80–81, 84, 85, 86, 87, 88, 89, 91, 92, 93, 94, 95, 97, 99, 101, 102, 104, 105–109, 110, 111–119 *passim*, 121, 122, 126, 128, 130, 131, 134, 137, 138, 140, 141, 145n.11, 154–55n.10, 159n.32. *See also* difference
Althusser, Louis, 8
analogy, 90, 156n.21, 161–62n.5
anthropology, 14, 36, 119–122, 125, 160n.51
  postmodern 14, 36, 119–122, 160n.51
Arendt, Hannah, 38, 145n.11
Aristotle, 30, 134
Armstrong, Louis, 48, 53, 54
Arnold, Matthew, 3, 12, 13, 19–26 *passim*, 27, 31, 42, 63, 128, 132, 133, 144n.1, 144–45n.10, 145n.11, 145n.13, 145, n.21, 145n.22, 146n.26
art, 42, 44–49, 51, 57, 81, 90, 92, 133, 156n.21. *See also* music
  autonomous, 45–46
  heteronomous. *See* Culture Industry
  high vs. low, 44–45

authenticity, 30–31, 69, 119, 124, 125
autonomy 6, 24, 45, 47, 73–74, 129, 145n.13, 147n.42, 152n.76. *See also* freedom
autonomous art. *See* art, autonomous

Bach, Johann S., 151n.67
Bakhtin, Mikhail M., 37, 78, 82
Baldwin, James, 136
Balliet, Whitney, 51
Banjar (Indonesian ethnic group), 115, 154–55n.10
Basie, William (Count), 50
Baudrillard, Jean, 160n.51
Beaufret, Jean, 4
Benhabib, Seyla, 145n.11
Benjamin, Walter, 48, 49
Berlin, Isaiah, 27, 28, 33, 35, 38
Berliner, Paul, 52, 53, 54
Bernasconi, Robert, 14, 99, 111–119 *passim*, 162n.14
Bhabha, Homi K., 131
Bilgrami, Akeel, 91, 157n.23
Blocker, H. Gene, 156n.21
blues. *See* music, blues
Blyden, Edward, 146n.26
Borgmann, Albert, 13
Bourdieu, Pierre, 44
Byron, Don, 136, 151n.60

Chicago Symphony, 152n.67
classical music. *See* music, classical
Clifford, James, 35
Coleman, Ornette, 54
Collingwood, Robin G., 90
Coltrane, John, 54, 56, 108
commercial art. *See* Culture Industry
commodity, 44, 45, 48, 49
  fetish, 45, 48
communitarianism, 11, 14, 30, 31, 35, 39, 73, 89, 110, 132
community, 10–11, 13, 14, 15, 28, 46, 52, 54, 65, 74, 75, 79, 81, 89,

175

92, 95, 97, 108, 109,110, 111,
132, 145n.11
composition, musical 55, 56, 57, 59,
151n.60
compositionalist bias of Adorno, 55–56,
59, 150n.42, 151n.60
cosmopolitanism, 14, 30, 41, 92, 131,
134, 138
situated, 14, 41, 92, 131, 134,
138, 159n.32
Critical Theory, 42–43, 63, 111. *See also*
Frankfurt School; Adorno; Habermas
cross-cultural understanding. *See* understanding, cross-cultural
Crummell, Alexander, 146n.26
Culture Industry, 43–46, 47, 149n.22,
150n.27
and jazz, 47, 54
culture, 6, 11, 12, 19, 21–37, 39–45,
50, 57–58, 72, 74, 75, 79, 80,
81, 82, 83, 88, 91, 92, 93, 94,
95, 96, 108, 111, 115, 117, 119,
121–124, 125, 126, 128,
131–132, 134, 136, 138, 139,
144n.1, 145n.21, 145n.22,
146n.26, 147n.55, 148n.66,
149n.26
African-American, 36, 43, 56, 57,
117, 133, 146n.26, 149n.26,
150n.29
Arnold on, 12, 19, 21, 22–27
passim, 144n.1, 144–45n.10,
145n.21, 145n.22
Herder on, 12, 27–41 *passim*, 134,
147n.55, 148n.66
high vs. low, 132
popular, 36, 43
Culture and Anarchy
(Matthew Arnold), 21–22, 26
cultural criticism, 43
cultural holism, 29, 36–40
cultural studies, 37

Davidson, Donald, 34
Davis, Miles, 54, 56
Debussy, Claude, 48, 55, 150n.27
Delius, Frederick, 55
Derrida, Jacques, 8, 113
Descartes, René, 5
detachability thesis, 49, 55
dialogue, 12, 13, 14, 64, 65, 78, 85,
88–89, 91, 93, 100, 101,
105–106, 112, 122, 123, 141.
See also hermeneutics
cross-cultural, 13, 78, 88–89, 91,
112
hermeneutic, 12, 13, 14, 76, 105.
See also fusion of horizons
Dialectic of Enlightenment (Horkheimer
and Adorno), 44, 46
dialectic of Enlightenment, 48
Diderot, Denis, 4
difference, 1–2, 6, 9–14, 23, 26–27, 31,
33, 35, 36, 42, 43, 44, 63–64,
69, 74, 76–77, 78–81, 85, 89,
97, 100–103, 105–107, 109,
111–112, 126, 137–138,
159n.32. *See also* alterity
Dilthey, Wilhelm, 28, 105, 106
discourse, 5, 15, 19, 64, 65, 66, 69, 70,
71, 72, 75, 76, 79, 80, 91, 101,
110, 120, 121, 133, 137. *See also*
dialogue
ideal, 65, 81, 100
practical, 64–66, 69, 71, 72, 79,
80, 91
theoretical, 64
discursive democracy, 13, 14, 63–64, 78,
133
Du Bois, W. E. B., 59, 133, 146n.26
Dworkin, Ronald, 93

Ellington, Edward Kennedy (Duke),
47, 51, 53, 54, 56, 151n.60,
152n.67
Ellison, Ralph, 57, 58, 117
Enlightenment, the, 4, 10, 15, 27, 31,
40, 45, 97, 127
equality, 15, 25, 73–74, 93, 100, 105,
126–127, 157n.23
essentialism, 14, 35, 138
ethics (Habermas), 68–71, 77, 79.
See also morality
ethnicity, 123, 134–136, 163n.18
ethnocentrism, 2, 8, 10, 80, 90–92, 108,
132
transcendental versus empirical,
91, 92
Evans-Prichard, Sir Edward, 84

female circumcision, 124, 126
Ferry, Luc, 11, 63
Fischer, Michael M. J., 125

Index

Foucault, Michel, 8, 11, 129
Frankfurt school, 43, 57. *See also* Critical Theory; Adorno
Frazer, Sir James, 85
freedom, 2, 3, 5, 9, 11, 24, 31, 37, 48, 50, 57, 65, 73, 140. *See also* autonomy
Freud, Sigmund, 44, 94
fusion of horizons, 23, 59, 68, 80, 93, 109, 130, 153n.2, 154n.4, 161–62n.5. *See also* dialogue, hermeneutic

Gadamer, Hans-Georg, 14, 79, 81, 87, 88, 90, 93, 105, 106, 111, 112, 114, 116, 120, 129, 154n.4
Geertz, Clifford, 1, 6
gender, 123
generalizable interest, 64–65, 111, 124, 140
Gillespie, John Birks (Dizzy), 56
Gilligan, Carol, 93
Gilroy, Paul, 131
Goehr, Lydia, 152n.76
Goethe, Johann W. von, 3
good, the, 29, 55, 67, 68, 69, 71–72, 75, 96, 97, 131, 139, 140. *See also* right, the
Gorelick, Kenny (Kenny G), 54
Grassi, Ernesto, 140

Habermas, Jürgen, 11, 13, 31, 43, 63–77 *passim*, 78–79, 81, 84–86, 100, 102, 105, 114, 116, 122, 124, 140, 147n.50. *See also* rationality, communicative
Hall, Stuart, 36
Hawkins, Coleman, 53, 54
Hegel, Georg W. F., 6, 13, 24, 44, 107, 110, 118, 128, 140, 157n.23
Heidegger, Martin, 4, 5, 6, 8, 9, 11, 12, 66, 104, 140, 143n.16
Herder, Johann Gottfried von, 3, 11, 12, 19, 20, 26–41 *passim*, 42, 50, 63, 73, 79, 87, 133, 134, 145–46n.26, 147n.42, 147n.46, 147n.55, 148n.66, 151n.42, 162n.14
hermeneutic charity. *See* principle of charity, hermeneutic
hermeneutic circle, 28, 36

hermeneutic dialogue. *See* dialogue, hermeneutic
hermeneutics, 8, 14, 33, 76, 106, 109, 111–112, 115, 116. *See also* dialogue; Gadamer
hermeneutics of suspicion, 49, 122–124
heteroglossia, 37, 82–83, 113, 138. *See also* Bakhtin
Hirsh, E. D., 21
historicism, 44, 96, 133
Hobbes, Thomas, 141
Hodeir, André, 54
Hodges, Johnny, 56
Horkheimer, Max, 43, 44
humanism, 2–6, 8, 10–12, 15, 19–20, 43, 63–64, 81, 97, 131, 138–141
and Foucault, 8,
and Heidegger, 4, 5–6, 8, 140
New Humanism, 3
postmetaphysical, 78. *See also* humanity as an unfinished project
Renaissance, 3, 5, 140–141
and Rorty, 4
humanity, 2–5, 9–15, 21, 27–28, 31–33, 37, 49, 58, 89, 97, 109, 111, 119, 138–141, 146n.26
and Herder, 31–32, 37
humanity as an unfinished project, 11, 12, 13–14, 15, 88, 96–97, 109, 113, 127–128
Husserl, Edmund, 8

ideal speech situation, 65, 81, 100
identity, 15, 22, 24, 27, 68–70, 71, 73, 74, 79, 84, 89, 91–92, 93, 94, 97, 98, 100, 113, 134, 137, 147n.42, 156–57n.23, 157n.25
identity politics, 74
ideology critique, 122, 145n.21
impressionism, 48, 150n.27. *See also* Debussy; Ravel
improvisation, 48, 50–51, 53–54, 56–57. *See also* music, jazz
individuality, 2, 30, 41, 44, 46, 48–50, 52, 57, 58, 59, 73, 74, 75, 81, 92, 94, 138, 140, 157n. 23
and collective in jazz, 47, 48, 49, 52, 57, 58
and community, 46, 75, 81, 92
and dignity, 2, 138, 140
interpretive conflict, 83–84, 123

intersubjective meanings, 29, 83, 146n.35
irony, 7
Islam, 91, 123, 148n.63, 154n.10, 156–57n.23

jazz. *See* music, jazz
Jordan, Mike [Michael], 137

Kant, Immanuel, 12, 31, 38, 45, 74, 105, 113, 137, 138, 145n.13, 147n.42
Kierkegaard, Søren, 51
Kitcher, Philip, 134–137
Kramer, Hilton, 132
Kristeva, Julia, 155n.10
Kuhn, Thomas S., 5, 36, 136

language, 6, 8–9, 12, 28–29, 34, 37, 39, 46, 52, 53, 54, 58, 63, 65, 68–69, 80–81, 84, 89, 95, 97, 103, 105–108, 120–121, 134, 139, 140, 161–62n.5. *See also* situated metalanguage
"Letter on Humanism" (Heidegger), 4, 8
learning process, 15, 23, 27, 37–38, 67, 68, 73, 74–75, 77, 85, 116, 138
Levinas, Emmanuel, 111, 118, 159n.32
liberalism, 11, 13, 25, 69, 79, 132
life programs, 15, 127, 130–132, 133, 136, 162n.11
Locke, Alain, 131, 152n.68
Lovibond, Sabina, 141, 159n.38
Luckàcs, Georg, 149n.22
Lyotard, Jean-François, 31

MacIntyre, Alasdair, 32, 68, 148n.69, 163n.21
MacLean, Jackie, 56
Marcus, George E., 125
Marcuse, Herbert, 43, 44, 48, 57
Marsalis, Wynton, 52
Marx, Karl, 4, 8, 44, 49, 132, 149n.22
McCarthy, Thomas, 72, 131
metaphysics, 4–6, 9, 12, 66, 140
  Habermas on, 66
  Heidegger on, 4–5, 6, 9, 66, 140
"metaphysics of subjectivity" (Heidegger), 6, 9, 12
Meratus Dayaks (people of Indonesian rainforest), 83, 115, 154–55n.10
  adat of, 83

Mingus, Charles, 151n.60
Mirandola, Giovanni Pico della, 3
modernity, 6, 11, 44, 46, 66
  aesthetic modernity, 48
morality (Habermas), 68–71, 74–75, 79, 81. *See also* ethics
Morant Bay Rebellion, 21
Morphy, Howard, 156n.21
Morrison, Toni, 136
multiculturalism, 10, 15, 27, 41, 64, 68, 72–73, 116, 127–138, 159–60n.41, 162n.14
Murray, Albert, 57–58, 117, 133
music, 13, 36, 42–43, 46–59, 108, 128, 131, 133, 135, 136, 137, 150n.42, 152n.76
  blues, 56, 58, 136
  classical 54, 55, 56, 59, 151–52n.67
  impressionism, 48, 150n.27
  jazz, 13, 42–43, 46–59, 108, 128, 131, 133, 135, 136, 150n.42, 152n.76. *See also* performance, musical
  spirituals, 57, 133
  Tanzjazz, 50
mythical narratives, 84–85, 115, 159n.38

nationalism, 27, 41, 134, 145–46n.26
  black, 134, 146n.26. *See also* Afrocentrism
neoconservativism, 144n.1, 158n.25
New Humanism movement. *See* humanism
Nicholson, Linda, 128–130
Nietzsche, Friedrich, 4
Nussbaum, Martha, 134

objectification, 122–124
other. *See* alterity
overlapping consensus, 11, 13, 67, 68, 70, 79
Parker, Charlie, 53, 54
pedagogical representations. *See* representation, pedagogical
performance, musical, 49, 51, 52–54, 56, 151n.60, 152n.68, 152n.69. *See also* music, jazz
Philadelphia Orchestra, 152n.67
Picasso, Pablo, 47
Plato, 4, 23, 46, 95, 141

Index

politics of recognition. *See* recognition, politics of
Popper, Karl 140
popular culture. *See* culture, popular
postmetaphysical humanism. *See* humanism, postmetaphysical
postmetaphysical worldviews, 66, 92, 116
postmodern anthropology. *See* anthropology, postmodern
postmodern ethnography. *See* anthropology, postmodern
postmodernism, 4, 6–9, 10–12, 15, 24, 27, 45, 64, 79, 89, 90, 91, 97, 109, 120, 121. *See also* poststructuralism; postmodern anthropology; Bernasconi; Young
and death of man, 8
poststructuralism, 4. *See also* postmodernism
power, 3, 6, 12, 22, 24, 33, 35, 46, 49, 81, 90, 100, 104, 117, 119, 123, 125, 128–130
practical discourse. *See* discourse, practical
pragmatist tradition, 4
primitivism, 47
principle of charity, 58, 87, 94, 123
  hermeneutic, 58, 94
  second-order, 87

race, 108, 111, 134–136, 144–45n.10, 146n.26, 162n.14
racism, 2, 9, 32, 117, 134, 136, 137, 157n..25
rationality 7, 14, 32, 68, 85, 91, 94, 95, 96, 130, 157n.25
  second-order, 14, 94, 96, 157n.25
Ravel, Maurice, 48, 55
Rawls, John, 67
recognition, 1–2, 15, 30, 57, 64, 73–75, 77, 80–81, 86, 88, 95, 100, 102–104, 109, 118, 128, 130, 134, 140
  politics of, 73
  social, 30, 75, 100, 134
  semantic, 103
Reflections on the Philosophy of the History of Mankind (J. G. von Herder), 28, 38
reification, 45
relativism, 10, 11, 14, 95–96, 132, 138.
  See also historicism
  critique of, 95-96
Renaissance Humanism. *See* humanism, Renaissance
Renaut, Alain, 11, 63
representation, 8, 13, 14, 31, 36, 43, 68, 71, 80–81, 85–88, 95, 96, 97, 99, 104, 106, 108, 117, 119–126
  crisis of, 14, 99, 119–120
  critical, 95, 96
  pedagogical, 71, 85–86, 87, 94, 95, 117, 122
  politics of, 37
  strategic, 122–125, 160–61n.57
repressive desublimation, 46, 48
reversibility of perspectives, 79, 102–103
rhetoric, 3, 100, 101
right, the, 67, 69, 71, 72, 75. *See also* good, the
rights, 21, 73, 76, 93, 139
Rite of Spring (Igor Stravinsky), 47, 49, 50
Roach, Max, 52
Rorty, Richard, 4, 7, 14, 67, 95, 147n.42
Rosaldo, Renato, 123, 160–61n.57
Rushdie, Salman, 156–57n.23

Sache (topic of concern, subject matter). *See* subject matter
Said, Edward W., 21, 25, 26
Sartre, Jean-Paul, 3, 5, 9, 12, 22, 105–106
Schiller, Friedrich, 3, 145n.13
Schleiermacher, Friedrich, 105, 106
Schoenberg, Arnold, 46, 57
science, 4, 15, 22, 70, 75, 81, 89, 92, 96, 116, 120–121, 127, 130, 139, 159–60n.41
Searle, John R., 88, 114, 116
second-order rationality. *See* rationality, second-order
second-order principle of charity. *See* principle of charity, second-order
semantic authority, 103, 110–111, 114
situated cosmopolitanism. *See* cosmopolitanism, situated
situated metalanguage, 13, 68, 81, 108, 156n.21, 159n.32
Skinner, Quentin, 141
spirituals. *See* music, spirituals

Stein, Gertrude, 47
strategic representation. *See*
 representation, strategic
Stravinsky, Igor, 47, 49–50, 150n.27
subject, 5–6, 9, 47–49, 58, 92, 104–5, 108, 123, 135
 jazz, 47, 48, 49, 58
subject matter (*Sache*), 81–88, 91, 93–94, 112, 114–115, 156n.21
syncopation, 46, 48, 49, 50–51, 53. *See also* music, jazz

Tamir, Yael, 91–92
Tanzjazz. *See* music, *Tanzjazz*
Taylor, Charles, 15, 29, 73, 74, 75, 76, 83, 86, 128–130, 132, 147n.46, 154n.4, 157n.23
Thomas, Laurence, 104
Trilling, Lionel, 161n.59
Tsing, Anna Lowenhaupt, 83, 115, 154–55n.10
Tyler, Stephen A., 121

understanding, 10, 12, 14, 23, 28, 34, 66, 76, 79–80, 85–90, 93–97, 99–100, 102, 104–113, 116–120, 122, 125, 134, 138, 141, 156–57n.23, 159n.32

cross-cultural, 34, 83, 111, 119, 138, 156–57n. 23
 mutual, 10, 12, 14, 23, 34, 66, 79, 88, 89, 93, 102, 104, 110, 118, 159n.32
unfinished project. *See* humanity as an unfinished project

Venturi, Robert, 55
Vienna Philharmonic, 152n.67

Wagner, Richard, 150n.27
Waldenfels, Bernhard, 89, 159n.32
Warnke, Georgia, 88
Weber, Max, 24, 44
Webster, Ben, 56
Weimar Republic, 50
Whiteman, Paul, 50
Williams, Charles (Cootie), 56
Winch, Peter, 84, 115
Winkelmann, J.J., 3
Wittgenstein, Ludwig, 4, 6, 37, 140, 161–62n.5
Wolf, Susan, 15, 132

Young, Iris Marion, 10, 14, 76, 79, 91, 99–111 *passim*, 118, 122, 128